O9-BRZ-862

Enlarging the Temple

Enlarging the Temple

New Directions in American Poetry during the 1960s

Charles Altieri

MIDDLEBURY COLLEGE LIBRARY

Lewisburg
Bucknell University Press
London: Associated University Presses

7/1980
am. Lit.

PS
325
A37

© 1979 by Associated University Presses, Inc.

Associated University Presses, Inc.
Cranbury, New Jersey 08512

Associated University Presses
Magdalen House
136–148 Tooley Street
London SE1 2TT, England

Library of Congress Cataloging in Publication Data

Altieri, Charles, 1942–
    Enlarging the temple.

    Bibliography: p.
    Includes index.
    1. American poetry—20th century—History and criticism.
2. Poetics. I. Title.
PS325.A37   811'.5'209   77-89773
ISBN 0-8387-2127-3
ISBN 0-8387-5012-5 (Paperback)

Reprinted 1980

First paperback edition 1980

PRINTED IN THE UNITED STATES OF AMERICA

Contents

If you find you no longer believe enlarge the temple
—W. S. Merwin, "A Scale in May"

Preface

My aims in this book are to explain the logic and implications of the aesthetic of presence that dominates much of the self-consciously postmodern poetry written in the 1960s and to describe some poetic careers I think representative of styles, values, problems, and achievements basic to the decade. I feel that critics have not yet fully appreciated the craft and intelligence of the poets studied herein, and I am convinced that general treatments of the period's literary climate have not paid sufficient attention to its poetry. A brief glance at studies of the sixties like Ronald Berman's or Morris Dickstein's, at anthologies like *The Discontinuous Universe* claiming to represent the period, or even at scholarly bibliographies, will show a disproportionate emphasis on metafiction, on theoretical movements stressing the problematic status of literary language, and on avant-garde experiments in music and the visual arts. The poets share the decade's general distrust of the values of Western humanism, but the alternatives they imagine are in my view more interesting as explorations of new sources of value and new definitions of the relationship between mind and world and clearly more typical of the ways of thinking that produced the decade's political turmoil and pursuit of alternative life-styles. In dealing with the sixties, we trivialize the life-choices of numerous serious and intelligent people if we too readily define the literary climate in the oversimplified terms propounded by the most radical avant-garde artists. And unless we try to understand the characteristic styles and visions of this formative period in American poetry, I suspect that we will not fully appreciate the best work being written in the present

Although presence is a basic theme of this study, it is difficult in writing this preface not to be uncomfortably aware of the way concerns for the present soon breed a sense of ironic absence. I began serious work on these poets in 1969 when I felt the need to understand the omnipresent challenges to my liberal humanism. As I began seriously reading contemporary poetry, I felt that I had discovered new ways of appreciating how poems can disclose a world. Now this completed study has all too many likenesses to a mausoleum—a monument to poets, questions and methods whose vitality is past and absent. Still, distance has its compensations: if I no longer feel passionately involved in these materials, I do think I understand their general conceptual and imaginative strategies, and if my critical language is somewhat outmoded, I feel that the work I have done has saved me from the excesses of ironic structuralist reductions of imaginative worlds to textual operations.

Most important, distance enables me to appreciate more fully the vitality and intelligence of those colleagues and students at SUNY/Buffalo who at once convinced me by their personal example that this poetry was worth taking seriously and gave me concepts and questions with which to pursue my study. I would like here to offer specific thanks to John Logan, Robert Creeley, Irving Feldman, Al Cook, Bob Hass, Jerome Mazzaro, Joe Riddel, and Dave Tarbet. Carl Gay and the staff of the Poetry Collection of SUNY's Lockwood Memorial Library should also be mentioned for their unfailing kindness and helpfulness. I would also like to thank the editors of the following journals, who gave me permission to reprint parts of my essays and, before that, gave me the time and the advice necessary to get the essays in shape for publication: *Boundary 2, Contemporary Literature, The Far Point, Iowa Review, Modern Poetry Studies,* and *Sun and Moon.* To my thanks for intellectual support, I must add my gratitude for the financial support provided by a summer grant from the Research Foundation of SUNY, and by a grant from the Julian Park Foundation to pay some of the expenses for typing and permissions.

Finally, I would like to express my deepest gratitude to two people whose presence remains for me a continual source of joy and intellectual stimulation. Carl Dennis read every chapter carefully, gave invaluable stylistic and conceptual advice, and with a charming stubbornness shamed me into one final revision. My wife, Joanne, did all that Carl did, even though she had to live daily with the consequences, and convinced me that, whatever the metaphysicians declare, there are indubitable modes of loving presence that provide numinous values centering our wandering minds and establishing homes for even the most solipsistic and self-reflexive literary sensibilities. I dedicate this book to her.

Acknowledgments

I wish to thank the following for having given me permission to quote from published works:

Ann Charters, for permission to quote from Charles Olson, *A Special View of History*, 1970.

Athenuem Publishers, for permission to quote from *The First Four Books of Poems* by W. S. Merwin, copyright © 1965, 1966, 1975 by W.S. Merwin. "The Annunciation" appeared originally in the book *Green With Beasts* by W. S. Merwin. Reprinted by permission of Atheneum Publishers.

Robert Bly, for permission to quote from his introduction to *Neruda and Vallejo: Selected Poems*, ed. Bly, 1971.

City Lights Books, for permission to quote from *Lunch Poems*, copyright © 1964 by Frank O'Hara. Reprinted by permission of City Lights Books.

Faber and Faber Ltd, for permission to quote from Robert Lowell, *Poems 1938–1949, Life Studies, For the Union Dead*, and *Notebook*. Reprinted by permission of Faber and Faber Ltd.

Farrar, Straus & Giroux, Inc., for permission to quote from *Life Studies* by Robert Lowell, copyright © 1956, 1959 by Robert Lowell; from *For the Union Dead* by Robert Lowell, copyright © 1956, 1960, 1961, 1962, 1963, 1964 by Robert Lowell; from *Notebook* by Robert Lowell, copyright © 1967, 1968, 1969, 1970 by Robert Lowell.

Four Seasons Foundation, for permission to quote from Charles Olson, *Poetry and Truth*, copyright © 1971 by the Estate of Charles Olson. Reprinted by permission of Four Seasons Foundation.

Grove Press, Inc., for permission to quote from Charles Olson, *Human Universe and Other Essays*, 1967, and *The Distances*, 1961.

Harcourt Brace Jovanovich, Inc., for permission to quote from Lord *Weary's Castle*, copyright, 1946, 1974, by Robert Lowell. Reprinted by permission of Harcourt Brace Jovanovich, Inc. And from *Ceremony and Other Poems*, © 1948, 1949, 1950, by Richard Wilbur. Reprinted by permission of Harcourt Brace Jovanovich, Inc.

Harold Ober Associates, Inc., for permission to quote from W. S. Merwin, *The First Four Books of Poems*. Reprinted by permission of

Harold Ober Associates Incorporated. Copyright © 1955, 1956 by W. S. Merwin.

Harper & Row, Publishers, Inc., for permission to quote from *The Light Around the Body* (1967) by Robert Bly: "Counting the Small-Boned Bodies," copyright © 1967 by Robert Bly; "Looking into a Face," copyright © 1965 by Robert Bly; "A Home in Dark Grass," copyright © 1964 by Robert Bly. By permission of Harper & Row, Publishers, Inc.

Alfred A. Knopf, Inc., for permission to quote from *The Collected Poems of Frank O'Hara*, 1971.

Laurence Pollinger Limited, for permission to quote from Denise Levertov, *Relearning the Alphabet* (Jonathan Cape Ltd, 1970); and from Gary Snyder, *Earth House Hold* (New Directions, 1969), *The Back Country* (New Directions, 1968), and *Regarding Wave* (New Directions, 1970).

Michigan Quarterly Review, for permission to quote from Denise Levertov, *Origins of a Poem*. First published in the *Michigan Quarterly Review*, Vol. III, No. 4, Fall 1968.

New Directions Publishing Corporation, for permission to quote from Gary Snyder, *Earth House Hold*, copyright © 1967, 1969 by Gary Snyder, reprinted by permission of New Directions Publishing Corporation. From Gary Snyder, *The Back Country*, copyright © 1960, 1963, 1965, 1966, 1968 by Gary Snyder, reprinted by permission of New Directions Publishing Corporation. From Gary Snyder, *Regarding Wave*, copyright © 1968, 1970 by Gary Snyder; "Wave" and "KyotoBorn in Spring Song" were first published in *Poetry*; reprinted by permission of New Directions Publishing Corporation. From Robert Duncan, *Bending the Bow*, copyright © 1968 by Robert Duncan, reprinted by permission of New Directions Publishing Corporation. From Robert Duncan, *Roots and Branches*, copyright © 1964 by Robert Duncan, reprinted by permission of New Directions Publishing Corporation. From Robert Duncan, *The Opening of the Field*, copyright © 1960 by Robert Duncan, reprinted by permission of New Directions Publishing Corporation. From Denise Levertov, *With Eyes at the Back of Our Heads*, copyright © 1959 by Denise Levertov Goodman, reprinted by permission of New Directions Publishing Corporation. From Denise Levertov, *Relearning the Alphabet*, copyright © 1966, 1968, 1970 by Denise Levertov Goodman, reprinted by permission of New Directions Publishing Corporation. From Denise Levertov, *The Poet in the World*, copyright © 1968 by Denise Levertov Goodman, reprinted by permission of New Directions Publishing Corporation.

W. W. Norton & Company, for permission to quote from A. R. Ammons, *Corson's Inlet*, 1965.

Rapp and Whiting Limited, for permission to quote from Robert Bly, *The Light Around the Body*, 1967.

Charles Scribner's Sons, for permission to quote from Robert Creeley, *For Love* (1962), *Words* (1963), and *Pieces* (1969).

Gary Snyder, for permission to quote from his *Myths and Texts*, 1960, and *Riprap*, in *Collected Poems of Gary Snyder*, ed. Stuart Montgomery, 1966.

Introduction

It seems difficult now to recover the excitement and the attendant controversy experienced by young poets in the early 1960s. Donald Hall's Introduction to his anthology *Contemporary American Poetry* at once summarizes the general feeling of the poets and indicates the distance our culture has since traveled:

> For thirty years an orthodoxy ruled American poetry. It derived from the authority of T. S. Eliot and the new critics; it exerted itself through the literary quarterlies and the universities. It asked for a poetry of symmetry, intellect, irony and wit. The last few years have broken the control of this orthodoxy. . . . Yet we must not regret the dissolution of the old government. In modern art anarchy has proved preferable to the restrictions of a benevolent tyranny.[1]

Now what seemed anarchy appears to have become another orthodoxy: despite the considerable differences among the poets who have since found their distinctive voices as self-proclaimed postmodern poets, one finds it all too easy to recognize and respond to general assumptions and stylistic modes that were once seen as radical innovations. In 1962 it seemed tremendously important to rebel against an aesthetic of impersonality that required poets to use overtly mythical or meditative themes and subjects and to develop these themes in complex linguistic and formal patterns. Then it was revolutionary to present an intensely personal voice dealing with topical and topological materials in forms that approximated direct statement before exploding into moderately surreal images. Then originality consisted in refusing the demands for poems that had to be given elaborate interpretations, in fostering poems based on the direct voices of oral readings, and above all in denying the authority of tradition and the balancing meditative mind while exploring directly religious sacramental aspects of secular experience. Now all these traits are both critical and poetic clichés, dominating the work in most poetry journals.[2]

There are some respects, however, in which critics treat the poetry of the sixties too lightly if they so quickly rest content with recognizing the styles it developed and conceive it as already an orthodoxy. It is true that now poems from the sixties are known primarily as anthology pieces, in much the same way as those poets read modern works. And

younger poets today, reveling in a comfortable freedom from any powerful authority figures, feel released to conceive the styles developed in
the sixties as merely alternatives, like more traditional models, to be
adapted and modified according to the needs of specific subjects and
ideas. In a sense, contemporary poets can now develop a genuine postmodernism because they no longer need to justify themselves by opposing
and subverting modernist values. But the price of this freedom is a
loss of philosophical depth and resonance. Precisely because the poets
of the sixties felt the need to destroy their poetic fathers, they had to
confront them on their terms. They had to make their poetry take
account of the underlying philosophical assumptions of high modernism
and had to develop their own alternative philosophical poetics. Under
the pressure of the past and aware of the cultural consequences of a
particular model of poetry, postmodern poets of the sixties found themselves repeating the Romantic experience. One could not simply write
in new ways; one had to understand his or her experiments as ex-
ploring/new ways of imagining relationships between mind and world,
and hence the poet was compelled to conceive his or her work as
ultimately proposing new models of value and of the meaning of culture.
Thus, fully to understand the stylistic experiments now taken for granted,
one must begin to appreciate the kind and quality of thought involved
in creating and testing them.

The basic subject of my book, then, is the project of postmodern
poets to invent a coherent philosophical poetics able to stand as an
alternative to the high modernism of Yeats and Eliot. Clarifying this
project entails defining the basic postmodern interpretations of their
predecessors' philosophical commitments. From these interpretations it is
possible to derive what I call a logical geography mapping the internal
relationships among various postmodern positions on the nature of the
poetic imagination, the relationship between the mind and nature or
objects, and the ways poetry can deal with mythic, historical, and
social themes in order to dramatize the importance of values radically
different from the essential conservatism of the modernists. Second, my
study entails demonstrating how specific poems, volumes of poetry, and
poetic careers can carry this philosophical burden—not as arguments but
as dramatic embodiments of ways in which the imagination can open
itself to possible experiences of value by asking its audience to reflect
upon certain epistemological aspects of style. The characteristic postmodern poem does not proceed by abstract meditation but seeks to
create a specific attitude or model for imaginatively perceiving relationships in a given situation, which—as attitude, not as symbol or statement—defines and gives value to a more general perspective on
experience.

In order to fulfill these purposes I begin by setting the opposition between modern and postmodern poetry in the larger context of English Romanticism. Here one finds the general assumptions about the nature of poetry and of the poets' social role, which establish the common ground on which postmodern and modern poetics can be opposed. Romanticism, in fact, in the very different variations on common themes expressed by early Wordsworth and by Coleridge, provides logical models for the conflict I wish to map. Coleridge's meditations on poetic structure and on the mind's dialectical pursuit of an ideal unity represent an essentially symbolist model that reaches its fruition in Eliot, Yeats, and some Stevens and then narrows into the academic criticism of second-generation New Critics and the attenuated verbal artifice characteristic of poetry in the 1950s. The central commitment of this tradition is to the creative, form-giving imagination and its power to affect society, or at least personal needs for meaning, by constructing coherent, fully human forms out of the flux of experience. Here the ultimate value of poetry is to re-create a believable image of ideal human order contained variously in tradition, in Yeats's daimonic self, or in glimpses the poet can offer of a heroic self figured in the angel or the man of ~Stevens~ capable imagination. I call the alternative logical model represented by early Wordsworth an essentially *immanentist* vision of the role of poetry.[3] Here poetic creation is conceived more as the discovery and the (disclosure of numinous relationships within nature than as the creation of containing and structuring forms.) Hence its basic commitment is to recovering familiar realities in such a way that they appear dynamically present and invigorate the mind with a sense of powers and objective values available to it. Where the symbolist poet seeks to transform nature into satisfying human structures, the immanentist poet stresses the ways an imagination attentive to common and casual experience can transform the mind and provide satisfying resting places in an otherwise endless dialectical pursuit by the mind of its own essences) and of Transcendental realities. |

These romantic models enable me to define both the specific positions and the internal logic informing the positions on which postmodern poetics rebels against modernism. The next chapter then tries to set a more specific historical context by articulating the basic New Critical assumptions that shaped the far less ambitious, more academic formal poetry that dominated poetry in the 1950s. Here Robert Lowell is my central figure, for his development of a confessional style is at once the best comment on the limits of fifties' formalism and, to younger poets assessing his work, the fullest example of the despair attendant upon not finding full philosophical alternatives to a symbolist faith gone dead. In my view, confessional poetry is essentially a transition between two faiths—one dead, the other desperately trying to be born.

The faith trying to be born takes three basic forms in the self-consciously postmodern poetry of the sixties. This at least is the claim of my third chapter. I begin there with Robert Bly's poetics of the deep image, which modifies and gives different psychological and ontological dimensions to surrealism. For Bly explicitly contrasts his imaginative pursuits of numinous moments, where the energies of psyche and of nature meet, to the nervous, pretentious, and despairing aspects of confessional *crie de coeur*. Bly's central enterprise is the articulation of new ways by which to ground one's sense of the personal so that the desire for authenticity does not drive one to the easy intensity of extreme psychological experiences, to life along what Lowell calls "the razor's edge." Here, despite his many differences from Bly, Charles Olson's poetic also begins. For Olson recognizes that there can be no escape from the neurotic displaced ego until the imagination learns to dwell on and to dwell in what he calls "the other side of despair."[4] In order to redefine the ego, the poet must return to imagining the ways in which the self participates in orders more encompassing than the fictions and personal preferences at the disposal of the individual will. The poet must return to the energies manifest in acts of intense perception and must locate the sources of personal value and dignity in the field of energies where subject and object can be seen as interpenetrating one another. The strident tones of so much of Olson's and Bly's poetics, however, betray the uneasiness inherent in seeking abstract epistemological and metaphysical resolutions to cultural problems, and they thus require as a complement the witty and utterly secular and empirical versions of objectivist poetics offered by Frank O'Hara. For O'Hara an aesthetics of presence needs neither a philosophy of a deep real self participating through metaphor in Bly's image of "Gott Natur" nor Olson's meditations on the balancing of subjective and objective energies. Presence in his poetic is simply the recovery of familiar aspects of urban contemporary life, aspects whose value resides not in the deeper forces they reveal but rather in the qualities of emotional expression or of wit they elicit.

One could, then, complete a study of postmodern poetry by showing how other poets combine and modify these three fundamental positions. But this strategy seems to me too programmatic and, more important, runs the risks of not recognizing the complex emotional and philosophical problems created by an aesthetics of presence. It threatens to simplify the depth of some of the poets of the sixties by conceiving them primarily as technicians. So I have posed two different goals for the rest of my study. First I try to dwell upon the internal dialectics in the careers of some of the age's best poets by concentrating on the ways they keep reflecting on and modifying or extending the basic images of immanent values they initially articulate. And second I organize my analyses to constitute a series of reflections on the problems raised by an aesthetics of presence and the various ways poets come to terms with them. Thus my fourth chapter is devoted to the careers of Gary Snyder and Robert Duncan as exemplars of what might be called the religious conscience of the poetry of the sixties. Both poets exhibit few doubts or reservations about their particular versions of natural supernaturalism but concern themselves instead with testing and expanding poetic stances and attitudes by which they can testify to the powers of the mind to connect phenomena in ways revealing possible forms of demystified religious awareness. These poets can be seen as architects of a new mental space whereby the imagination can image earth as a temple and poetic activity as a means of dwelling in what Heidegger calls "the house of being."

If Snyder and Duncan represent the Edenic possibilities of the post-modern imagination, Robert Creeley and W. S. Merwin, the poets studied in my next chapter, can be seen as their fallen counterparts—continually feeling themselves banished from that Eden and seeking to recover new forms of it. These poets reject even the naturalized restatements of religious mythologies in Snyder and Duncan and try to articulate purely secular states of mind where analogues to the religious vision are possible. Creeley and Merwin work from opposite poles: where the former is intensely personal, the latter explores radically abstract impersonal and surreal states of mind. But both share a sense that at the very moment of intense awareness of presence there is produced a terrifying self-consciousness of all that cannot be made present or numinously "here." And both seek to make their very sense of empti-ness or absence the source of more complex and satisfying modes of inhabiting the other side of despair, however bleak that territory might be. Consequently, both poets have more dialectical careers than the directly religious poets, and Merwin, in particular, recovers for Anglo-American poetry the mental landscape explored by the best Continental poets. Merwin makes loss itself the ground for numinous awareness that might suffice for the attentive imagination.

What becomes an essentially epistemological inquiry into the dia-lectic of presence and absence in Merwin and Creeley takes ethical and social form in my final chapter on the work of Denise Levertov. Levertov's work before the Vietnam war can serve as a kind of primer of the aesthetics of presence: her themes and formal strategies are the most direct and obvious examples of the postmodern recovery of the tradition going from Wordsworth to William Carlos Williams. But with the war, she encounters a problem that calls the entire aesthetics of presence into question, or at least circumscribes its limits. The central imperative of the aesthetics of presence is "be here intensely" and concentrate one's attention on the emergence of energies in the now, where "every step is an arrival." Yet when the "now" continually reminds her of the suffering created by an unjust war and focuses her awareness on the fact that she inhabits a society she is alienated from, the sense of "now" becomes psychologically and morally disturbing. Psychologically the "now" is certainly intense, but the intensity is extremely painful. And morally an aesthetics of presence cannot suffice, however one manipulates it, because one needs abstract intellectual and imaginative structures by which to judge the present and to pose alternatives to it. Levertov makes of these dilemmas one magnificent poem, "Relearning the Alphabet," which finds its moral ground in the implicit common moral vocabulary revealed in basic nonmythic and prereflexive cultural forms. This poem, I shall argue, is a poetic realization of the moral implications in the work of the later Wittgenstein. But Levertov's poetry during the years of the war becomes for the most part increasingly strident, abstract, and verbally dead as she grapples with reconciling essentially personal modes of poetic awareness with her need for public moral structures. Her work brings readers around to a point where they can recognize the achievement in high modernism's attempt to provide just these public structures. Here the need for some form of traditional humanism appears inescapable, although possibly based on prereflexive, common moral codes instead of the total imaginative mythologies envisioned by modernism. For no matter how acute one's sensibility, no matter how attentive one is to numinous energies, it is impossible to write public poetry or make poetry speak meaningfully about pressing social concerns without a return to some notion of cultural models preserving ethical ideals or images of best selves.[5] Whatever creative ground the poet cultivates, it must eventually produce images of a creative self in public ethical terms as well as in poetic ontological ones. Denise Levertov's work defines both the values and the limits of the Heraclitean desire to recover the familiar, and in so doing it makes the reader feel once again the need to reinvent Plato. Making this clear will be the burden of my closing remarks, as learning to live with the contradictory claims of Heraclitus and Plato has become the burden of poetry in the seventies.

Establishing the context I feel necessary for a full appreciation of postmodern poetry requires me to make generalizations I cannot sufficiently qualify. This said, I must go on to assert that I prefer inadequate generalizations to a scrupulous attention to particulars that ignores larger contexts. I take seriously my metaphor of charting a map for contemporary poetics, and I ask the reader to remember that maps can at times be most useful when they ignore endless byways. Moreover, I consider Alfred North Whitehead's formula that thought is primarily a lure for feeling, a formula influential on many postmodern poets, a suggestive model for criticism. Sloppy thoughts, of course, can only produce sloppy feelings, but Whitehead's notion need not lead to this reduction. His point is that only particular events are ultimately real (or, less contentiously, only poems finally matter for the critic), but the qualities one perceives in the particular depend on the depth and variety of provisional contexts he brings to bear on it.

It is not only in self-defense or justification for omitting so many accomplished poets that I invoke Whitehead here. I want to conclude this introduction by taking advantage of what might be called "Introducer's License" in order to assert two general claims that are enormously difficult to prove—one relating the poets' work to philosophy and the other relating the poets' work to the theory of criticism. I want first to suggest that one can see how central a place postmodern poetry might play in one's understanding of the spiritual history of the age if one recognizes its affinities with changes in the philosophical climate taking place during the fifties and the sixties. In the process of rejecting modernist emphases on the mind reflecting on its own structures, postmodern poets take attitudes toward immanence that parallel the work of Heidegger and the later Wittgenstein, the two most influential philosophers (on the Continent and in England and America, respectively) in the years from World War II to 1970.[6] The most striking feature of both men's work is the intensity with which they attack the entire tradition of Western philosophy. One sees in their work, as one sees in a different way in postmodern poets' attacking Western cultural tradition, no Kantian desire to reappropriate and synthesize competing philosophical traditions from the immediate past. Instead both men call the authority of the entire post-Platonic philosophical tradition into question. One important feature of this form of questioning is a resultant insistence on recovering parallels between poetic and philosophical thought, or, more precisely, acts of thinking. But the crucial fact is the way both men challenge the validity of conceiving philosophy as primarily an analytic discipline seeking to disclose the underlying logical structures of thought or to test them against some independent empirical order. Both seek to redefine philosophy as an essentially descriptive rather than an analytic activity, for they see that any attempt in philosophy to produce by logic the grounds for its own valid statements leads either to idealist metaphysics or to an infinite regressive defense of one's fundamental terms. As Wittgenstein put it, philosophers must recognize that the grounds for true statements, and hence the beginning for philosophy, are themselves neither true nor false, but simply there,

circle

like our lives. Hence one cannot justify truths: one can only describe) familiar realities and their contexts in such a way as to elicit the agreement of others. In a similar way, postmodern poets will argue that the poet can never reach a satisfactory relationship with his world, or even with his mind's relationship to the world, if he continually reflects on the acts of imagination as themselves constitutive of value. The philosopher's distinction between logical analyses or abstract metaphysics and descriptive method parallels the poet's insistence that the proper mode of activity for the creative self is not the creation or interpretation of values but the labor of disclosure, not the minds' attempt to understand its own acts of imaginative creation nor the pursuit of some principle of incarnation reconciling word and world but the discipline of attending carefully to the mind's concrete place in immediate existential contexts. The fundamental goals of both men's philosophizing (not "philosophies") is aptly summed up in the following statement of Maurice Merleau-Ponty, which might also have served as an epigraph to this study:

> Reflection does not withdraw from the world towards the unity of consciousness as the world's basis; it steps back to watch the forms of transcendence fly up like sparks from a fire; it slackens the intentional threads which attach us to the world and thus brings them to our notice; it alone is consciousness of the world because it reveals that world as strange and paradoxical.[7]

Given this goal of disclosure through description, it is evident that one cannot directly apply typical New Critical strategies to postmodern poetry. Indeed the poetry is explicitly written to counter tastes fostered by academic, pedagogical versions of the New Criticism, which stressed emphasizing the way formal structures, image patterns, and complex linguistic ironies allow one to conceive the poem as a polyvalent thematic interpretation of experience. The poets of the sixties tried to present their work as direct psychological or meditative experiences, not highly wrought linguistic artifacts, and direct experience is notoriously difficult for criticism to come to terms with. Yet the kind of criticism fostered by postmodern poetry in the sixties is no more helpful, for the poetry journals devoted to postmodern work offered only loose impressionistic essays or vacuous celebrations of a poet's sensitivity. And the most fashionable contemporary modes of criticism can only help one to deconstruct an aesthetics of presence, not to understand it or its possibilities for informing critical methodologies that need not purchase sophistication by irony. The result is that readers and critics have yet to arrive at a full appreciation of what these poets wrought, even if more recent criticism of their work has to a large extent surpassed the impressionistic mode of the poets' own critical comments.

It seems to me necessary then, before proceeding with my study, to offer a brief description of the assumptions I shall be making about the act and art of criticism. I find the basic precepts of the New Criticism about close reading inescapable tools for analyzing and appreciating poetry. Indeed one irony involved in my study is that reading postmodern poetry requires refining rather than rejecting these precepts. This should not be difficult to see—first because both movements derive from Romantic ideas about the logic of poetry, and second because the Romantic Tradition in poetic theory involves a continual need to keep balancing the competing concepts of the poem as rhetorical artifact and the poem as somehow containing experience within itself rather than pointing to or assessing some experience outside itself. The founders of the New Criticism reconciled these concepts through the notion of irony. For them only a complex paradoxical rhetorical structure could make the poem sufficiently nondiscursive to render experiences (usually tragic ones) not reducible to modes of analysis dependent on traditional logic. Then, as the New Criticism became an academic methodology, there was a tendency to pay lip service to the concept of experience and to concentrate instead on demonstrating the way image patterns and the texture of connotative language sustained specific thematic interpretations of experience. A sense of mystery or miracle, founded on the metaphor of incarnation as the image of fusion between word and flesh or substance, gave way to dry abstract analyses of thematic form. Perhaps because critics were uneasy about the value of their enterprise, the ideal of rendering experience became the project of comprehending or judging experience, and qualities of tone and dramatic texture were subordinated to intricate analysis of how a poet's thought or vision shaped his formal model for interpreting his world. In this context it seemed a necessary revolutionary step to take the other extreme and to insist on the nondiscursive immediacy of one's encounter with the poem and of the poem's relationship to nonlinguistic experience.

The critic's task now is to recognize the falseness of the opposition between artifact and experience in terms more philosophically defensible than those proposed by the founders of New Criticism. Hence the very pressure put on academic criticism by the poets of the sixties and their explorations in essentially phenomenological forms of imaginative activity can help one define more secure and flexible models of close reading. The first step is to recognize that poetry is a form of activity and that there are no essential verbal properties (like paradox) that distinguish poetry from other modes of discourse. Poetry depends on one's taking a certain attitude toward discourse (elicited by a wide variety of conventions), not on specific properties of the discourse. And in the same fashion, concepts like organic unity do not refer primarily to objective features of a poem; for example, that all the elements be interpretable in terms of specific themes. Rather, organic unity refers to a way of reading that attends carefully to implicit relationships among the verbal elements that constitute the text so that they constitute a complex mode of awareness presenting a mind or an actor engaged in different types of situations. Organic unity is one metaphor for "the logic of poetry," and its importance is its reminder that one reads poems with a kind of care that seeks resonance by attending to and contemplating similarity amid differences.

If one grants these preliminary matters, it becomes possible to define the special properties of poetry in terms of the attitude taken toward embodied acts of mind that the reader at once sympathizes with and reflects upon. Then form becomes a part of content, not its container, because form can be seen as the result of the poet's particular way of imagining how his activity arranges and synthesizes the dramatic material. This in turn allows one to separate the critical model from both symbolist aesthetics and the aesthetics of presence. One can see both, with their different senses of how the mind organizes experience and imagines the sources of value, as grounds for distinctive modes of poetry. In the symbolist aesthetic, especially in the enervated forms of it practiced in the 1950s, the central focus is on the mind's powers to balance opposites and to take up a perspective from which the mind can judge and interpret what it presents. In the aesthetics of presence, on the other hand, poems do not present direct experience but the aesthetic illusion of direct experience that depends on style and form as means for seeing the world freshly. In the symbolist aesthetic, formal properties are primarily means for evaluating experience and re-creating it to serve as metaphor or symbol of the mind responding to general problems and testing its own capacity to provide stays against chaos. The prevailing assumption is that without the poet's creating or invoking an order of significance, the external and social worlds would seem mere demonic and nauseating parodies of a desired "human truth" or civilized order. The New Criticism defines the poetic act almost exclusively in these terms. But the logic of poetry need not depend on formal structures seen as interpretive patterns. When poets conceive their work as presenting the action of disclosure rather than of creating order, the formal elements work somewhat differently. In a poetic of immanence, aesthetic elements have primarily epistemological rather than interpretive functions. The reader sees style and structure not as imposing order but as articulating modes of thinking and projecting relationships through which latent values and orders can be perceived. In this mode, aesthetic form reflects qualities of the mind engaging the world rather than structuring it into created orders, and the critic's goal is to recover an attitude or stance and its implications, not to posit hypotheses about the author's interpretation of the dramatic situation. Readers need, in short, to temper New Criticism with phenomenological ways of conceiving aesthetic structures if they are to save its insights into the logic of poetry from its narrow fidelity to one particular model of that logic. It is no small achievement of postmodern poetry to have taught readers the need for these distinctions and to have rewarded their efforts to put them into practice.[8] Whether I can adequately represent the methods these poets require must be judged from what follows. Generalizations, however unstable, do serve the critic in at least one way by posing for him tasks of analysis requiring his utmost concentration and labor.

Notes to Introduction

1. Donald Hall, *Contemporary American Poetry* (Baltimore, Md.: Penguin, 1962), p. 17.

2. One sign that these traits now constitute an orthodoxy is the uncommon agreement among critics describing the poetry of the era. I list some of the best general works that have helped define that orthodoxy: A. Poulin, Jr., "Contemporary American Poetry: The Radical Tradition," in Poulin, ed., *Contemporary American Poetry* (Boston: Houghton Mifflin, 1971), pp. 387–400; Paul Carroll, *The Poem in Its Skin* (Chicago: Follet, 1968), pp. 203–59; Kenneth Rexroth, in *Assays* (Norfolk, Conn.: New Directions, 1961), passim; idem, *The Alternate Society* (New York: Herder and Herder, 1970); M. L. Rosenthal, *The New Poets* (New York: Oxford University Press, 1967); and idem, "Dynamics of Form and Motive in Some Representative Twentieth Century Lyric Poems," *English Literary History*, 37 (1970): 136–51. This last essay is the only decent generalized stylistic analysis of the poetry of the sixties. Ihab Hassan, "POSTmodernISM," *New Literary History* 3 (1971): 5–31 presents a good survey of critical opinions and themes relevant to the discussion of the relationship between modernism and postmodernism. On this theme see also Monroe Spears, *Dionysus and the City: Modernism in Twentieth-Century Poetry* (New York: Oxford University Press, 1970), pp. 229–60; Frank Kermode, *Continuities* (New York: Random House, 1968), pp. 1–32; R. K. Meiners, *Everything to be Endured: An Essay on Robert Lowell and Modern Poetry* (Columbia, Mo.: University of Missouri Press, 1970); and Herbert Schneidau, "The Age of Interpretation and the Moment of Immediacy: Contemporary Art vs History," *English Literary History* 37 (1970): 287–313. For specific discussion of the poems, Rosenthal, Carroll, and Richard Howard, *Alone With America: Essays on the Art of Poetry in the United States since 1950* (New York: Atheneum, 1971) are basic. Howard in particular is a very suggestive, though idiosyncratic, critic. And for philosophical backgrounds of postmodern poetics, see Nathan A. Scott, *The Wild Prayer of Longing: Poetry and the Sacred* (New Haven, Conn.: Yale University Press, 1971); Denis Donoghue, *The Ordinary*

Universe: Soundings in Modern Poetry (New York: Oxford University Press, 1968); and L. S. Dembo, *Conceptions of Reality in Modern American Poetry*, (Berkeley, Calif.: University of California Press, 1966). Scott and Donoghue are close to my basic position, though neither has influenced it because I distinguish my own perspective on immanence from their neo-Christian search for alternatives to views of reality as essentially a product of the mind. Those who have influenced me a good deal are J. Hillis Miller, *Poets of Reality* (Cambridge, Mass.: Harvard University Press, 1965) and John Pierre Richard, *Onze Etudes Sur La Poesie Moderne* (Paris: Editions Du Seuil, 1964*)*—Miller because of his general schema and his illustrations of the philosophical weight poetry can carry, and Richard because he is a genius whose method of reading images one can recommend as an example but not imitate without running the danger of making himself look foolish. I am not sure that any work done on contemporary poetry will not in essence be footnotes to the schemas provided by these critics. For further bibliography, see my *Goldentree Bibliography of Modern and Contemporary Anglo-American Poetry*, forthcoming from AHM Publishing Company. Finally, I should point out that I shall use the term *postmodernism* as a convenient phrase for summarizing the poetry I study, even though it leads to absurd consequences like the need to define a post-postmodernism. I do so because the term already has some critical weight and because the poets I study define their own enterprise as essentially the creation of an alternative to high modernism.

3. I have tried to give a full description of early Wordsworth in "Wordsworth's Wavering Balance: The Thematic Rhythm of the *Prelude*," *The Wordsworth Circle* 4 (1973): 226–40, and in "Wordsworth's 'Preface' as Literary Theory," *Criticism* 18 (1976): 122–46. I also give a fuller treatment of my claims about modernist poetics in "Objective Image and Act of Mind in Modern Poetry," *PMLA* 91 (1976): 101–14.

4. Charles Olson, *Human Universe and Other Essays*, ed. Donald Allen (New York: Grove, 1967), p. 114. See also p. 112 for the first reference I know by a poet of the sixties to the idea of the "post-modern."

5. For another attempt of mine to assess the problems of making public poetry within an aesthetics of immanence, see "Gary Snyder's *Turtle Island*: The Problem of Reconciling the Roles of Prophet and Seer," *Boundary 2* 4 (1976): 761–77.

6. I have given a fuller description of the parallels between postmodernism and these philosophers, with additional comments on Whitehead's relationship to the poets, in "From Symbolist Thought to Immanence: The Logic of Post-Modern Poetics," *Boundary 2* 1 (1973): 605–41.

7. Maurice Merleau-Ponty, *The Phenomenology of Perception*, trans. Colin Smith (London: Routledge and Kegan Paul, 1962), p. xiii.

8. I should like to cite here a few of my theoretical essays that have developed out of my study of postmodern poetics and that give a fuller theoretical context for my claims about Derrida and the New Criticism: "Wordsworth's Preface as Literary Theory"; "Wittgenstein on Consciousness and Language: A Challenge to Derridean Theory," *Modern Language Notes* 91 (1976); "The Poem as Act: A Way to Reconcile Presentational and Mimetic Theories," *Iowa Review* 6 (1975*)*: 103–24.

Enlarging the Temple

1

Modern and Post Modern: Symbolist and Immanentist Modes of Poetic Thought

i

I have suggested in my introduction that there are coherent philosophical assumptions that underly the stylistic experiments of the poets in the sixties self-consciously revolting against the poetics of high modernism. I shall eventually show how these assumptions lead to specific lyric forms and varieties of poetic experience, but it seems to me a wise strategy to begin with the writers' abstract philosophical and aesthetic statements. For these establish some general contexts for understanding the poems while reducing the temptation later to violate specific poems by seeking out the ideas they embody. Thus in this chapter I will try to construct a logical geography of postmodern practice by mapping the basic values shared by the poets and by tracing their logical connections. These poets, I hope to show, are not insignificant thinkers, despite their tendency to adopt anti-intellectual poses.

The task of defining postmodernism leads first to Romanticism, for that is where one can discover the assumptions and concerns that then generate the opposing poetics of modern and postmodern poets. I need first to establish how the Romantics created the very possibility of taking the idea of revolution in poetry seriously by making poetics inseparable from questions of epistemology and of value, and hence immeasurably raising the stakes in younger poets resisting the authority of established poetic modes. Then I will try to elaborate fully the two basic Romantic models (not "sources" in any strict sense of the term), which can be used to see how both modern and postmodern poetry share the same ancestry despite their differences. The problem here is to show how Romanticism made possible both an essentially symbolist poetry concerned with the creative mind as the source of value and a more immanentist poetic placing value in the forces the poet can reveal at work in ordinary experience. By rooting the poetics of immanence in Romanticism, I should also be able to explain the philosophical resonance of the idea of "presence" so central to several of the fundamental concepts that distinguish postmodern from modernist poetics.

I can begin by noting the obvious fact that Romanticism breeds such different philosophies of poetry because it changes the status of poetics. Before Wordsworth and Coleridge, poetics was primarily either a descriptive or normative procedure for dealing with practical aesthetic questions. They insisted, on the contrary, that poetics depends on philosophy: one's sense of the nature of poetry must be derived less from describing successful poems or invoking ideas of taste than from speculating on the nature of poetic imagination and the special nature and powers of the objects it produces. The fact of this shift is obvious, the sources for it far less so, even though there are several distinguished critical works describing the development of Romantic poetics from eighteenth-century thought. I do not, however, want here to quarrel with these critical works. Instead I shall simply presuppose them and try to describe briefly how Whitehead's vision of Romantic philosophy provides a set of concepts I think capable of explaining three basic features of the Romantic tradition—the changed status of poetic language, the changed image of the poet's social role, and what I shall call the general logical structure informing recurrent Romantic fears and the various epistemological and ontological solutions these fears generate.

Whitehead sees Romantic thought as a reaction to "the fallacy of misplaced concreteness," which vitiates both the major philosophical traditions it inherited, *rationalism* and *empiricism*.[1] These traditions misplace concreteness because they ignore the synthetic nature of the event of coming to know or "prehend" a distinct object of thought and locate the fundamental nature of reality exclusively in the mind's orders or in an empirical realm external to the mind. However imprecise Whitehead's own epistemology, his achievement is to locate the problem of subject-object so prevalent in Romantic thought in a historical context that leads easily into problems of the status of poetic language. For if the philosophical traditions Romanticism inherits so separate mind and world, they also exclude "value from the essence of matter of fact"— rationalism (as in Kant's ethic) by relegating value to abstract universality and empiricism by reducing value to subjective preferences or moments of emotional satisfaction. Then the further problem arises of finding or inventing a language that can reconcile value and fact by integrating abstract and empirical orders. But the received public language could not function this way: as soon as one conceived discourse as separate from concrete perception, as *about* rather than *in* the world, one found oneself trapped into locating values in abstraction or distrusting all discourse not directly mirroring a realm of facts. To be a poet, to feel that one's discourse was at once concrete and revealing values significant for a whole community, required that one separate poetic discourse from public language. This leads to the need for inventing special categories of the mind like imagination, which justify claiming special status for the modes of discourse they produce. Hence the imagination can be said to produce symbolic structures that reconcile fact and value because they are not primarily descriptions of the world but occupy a distinctive epistemological and ontological space. Coleridge developed the concept of a "logic of poetry" in order to mark out this mode of discourse, where the usual problems of reference, and hence of subject and object, do not apply. The concept of poetic logic tries to show how poetic discourse has the special status of being self-referential and, through its self-reference, affording a unique dramatic experience synthesizing concrete and abstract, world and words, dynamic nature and prehending mind.[2]

Two consequences follow from this image of poetry as a distinctive mode of knowing the world. First, it becomes extremely difficult for poets to accept traditional images of the poem as elegant lyric expression, comment on experience, or meditation on moral and religious attitudes. Rather, the Romantic poet must see his poem as embodying experience, as directly presenting the act of prehension, instead of commenting after the fact on the nature of his thoughts or of objects confronting them. Simply to discuss values in a poem was to find oneself trapped in the opposition between thoughts and the world, so the poet needed to imagine his work as directly embodying the experience of value. But how describe the special experience of value, to himself and to his audience, without supplementing the poem by various self-reflexive acts, by making poetry largely concerned about its own nature and by indulging in amateur philosophizing? These supplements, in turn, tend to envision the special cognitive status of the poem's synthesizing mind and object in terms of two logical models—*symbolism* and *immanence*. If the poet stresses the synthetic activity of prehension itself, he can take natural energies as essentially symbolizing deeper creative sources of value and see the synthetic act of the poem as bearing witness to transcendental powers in the mind. And if he stresses the revelatory power of the poem's distinctive properties, he can imagine the primary function of poetic imagination as disclosing aspects of numinous experience not available to discursive acts of mind, which are trapped in a logic unable to capture the act of perception and thus incapable of reconciling fact and value.

One could also use the value-fact dichotomy as articulated by Whitehead to define some of the pressures affecting the image of the poet's social role in the Romantic tradition. For despite the many differences I shall mark between modern and postmodern definitions of the relationship between poetry and social authority, these differences stem largely from a shared commitment to envisioning a society governed by organicist assumptions. Whether the poet's political stance be arch-conservatism or radical anarchy, he or she is likely to pose his or her political views in terms of an attack on the authority of the dominant liberal rationalist mode of thought deriving from the eighteenth century. From Coleridge to Yeats to Bly and Snyder, the poets declared war on what Charles Olson calls "Whiggery" (*Human Universe and Other Essays*, ed. Donald Allen [New York: Grove, 1967], p. 99), on the liberal rationalist assumptions of bourgeois individualism, its faith in empirical and pragmatic modes of analysis that ignore first principles or Coleridgean "ideas," its utilitarian ethics, and its technological disdain for even the suggestion that there might be orders in the universe that should control the human will rather than be subject to it.

I could develop these themes, but they are finally derivative from the basic epistemological and ontological concerns worked out by Romantic poetics. I prefer, then, to complete my general introduction to a specific comparison of modern and postmodern assumptions by offering four general terms through which one can trace the emotional and logical structure informing those differences. The first two terms, *nausea* and *narcissism*, can serve as metaphors for the most basic demonic or desperate experience created by various versions of the value-fact dichotomy, while the next two, *creative ground* and *creative self*, provide concepts abstract enough to capture the different intellectual strategies poets explore as possible reversals of these demonic experiences. *Nausea*, as Sartre has made clear, is a sense of the divorce between self-consciousness and objective world whereby a person experiences the natural world as too much there, as completely self-sufficient in its impersonality and hence as mocking the emptiness of man's need to project desires and meanings on to it.[3] *Narcissism*, in its conventional, nonpsychoanalytic meaning, is one common psychological correlate to a sense of nausea. For if the world of objects is too much there in its otherness for consciousness, then those creative energies which the mind utilizes to project meanings come to be seen as mere phantasies. Unable to connect with sources of meaning and value outside itself, the mind is tempted to view its own creative acts as mere projections of a tragically isolated self speaking only to itself and confirming its own prison.

Goldsmith's "Deserted Village" provides the historical context for later Romantic explorations of nausea that range from Coleridge's "Dejection: An Ode" to Robert Bly's "dead world." When urban values and the industrial revolution come to the landscape, Goldsmith warns us, they destroy our sense that human virtues are analogically or sacramentally linked with that landscape. Pastoral becomes elegy for lost origins:

> I see the rural Virtues leave the land.
> . . . .
> Downward they move, a melancholy band,
> Pass from the shore, and darken all the strand
> Contented Toil, and hospitable Care,
> And kind connubial Tenderness are there;
> And Piety with wishes placed above,
> And steady Loyalty, and faithful Love,
> And Thou, sweet Poetry, thou loveliest maid,
> Still first to fly where sensual joys invade.

And the corollary experience of a mind that "rather makes/than finds what he beholds" finds its most powerful expressions in Wordsworth's fear of apocalypse, his war on easy Gothic emotion, and his terrifying dreams of Don Quixote in a desert as the exemplar of cultural life.[4]

Writers can, of course, choose either of these poles as authentic grounds for creation—one thinks of Beckett and Wilde as almost pure examples of the contrasting possibilities. But the basic importance of this distinction is the access it gives to the kind of dialectic poets need if they are to imagine ways of resolving those oppositions. The antithesis to nausea is a sense of what might be called a *creative ground*, a source of energy and value in the objective order that otherwise mocks subjective consciousness. And once one can imagine a creative ground, he then can oppose to narcissism a sense of the *creative self* whose activity discloses or produces aspects of that ground which have potential communal significance. Art becomes a social and cultural force and not some form of individual therapy or self-regarding indulgence in the resources of the individual's imagination.

Terms as abstract as *creative self* and *creative ground* are required to understand how the Romantic tradition generates a wide variety of imaginative solutions to the problems of nausea and narcissism. The creative ground need not be a quasi-theological sense of nature, and the creative self need not be the Coleridgean ego seeking to approximate the divine "I am." Indeed, after so many histrionic and melancholy Victorian laments over the impossibility of recovering a Romantic sense of nature, modern poets had to construct the creative ground, the source of meaningful and potentially universal creative activity, as itself somehow embodied in human consciousness. The Victorian sense of a creative ground in ethics, in one's pursuit of a moral best self, becomes more abstracted and psychological in Eliot's sense of tradition or in the various versions mentioned above of an inner ideal self recoverable by the imagination reflecting on its own desires and creative acts. Culture must play the role of Wordsworthian nature and Coleridge's *natura naturans,* be it a historical construct or an image of an ideal creative body, a major man, shadowed forth by the artifacts it preserves.

If culture can replace creative nature, it can also nauseate as nature does. This indeed is what occurred in the sixties: creative culture became an abstract academic culture, the figure of capable imagination came to appear the Polonian fool, and the war in Vietnam eventually created concrete moral doubts about the Western heritage, which made our culture seem the antagonist to genuine creative activity. Hence the need to return to a Wordsworthian position if poets were still to conceive poems as speculative instruments for discovering values and articulating stances by which these values might become accessible to the mind. The creative ground would once more become a sense of the vitality in nature or in ordinary social life, albeit in terms less theological and conventionally pastoral than Wordsworth's. And the creative self would be imaged as the attentive mind opening itself to the life of these familiar objects or disciplining itself to meditate on aspects of psychic phenomena that could be seen as participating in fundamental natural energies. But without Wordsworth's theological context, however secularized, postmodern poets would have to create new imaginative hypotheses for dealing with the following problems. First, they must conceive some substitute for a theologically based sacramentalism that would explain how nature and human feelings can interpenetrate and complement one another. Consciousness must be in contact with things, capable of expressing their mystery, and required as a complementary creative force that can fulfill meanings potential in nature. Thus language, which is envisioned as the cutting edge where consciousness and world meet, must always be a primary topic for poetic theory. And myth must once more issue from dynamic encounters with natural energies; it can no longer present itself as simply a fictive construct about experience. Furthermore, the wedding of man and nature experienced through myth and authentic language must be shown capable of resolving three forms of alienation attendant upon the value-fact split— the alienation of man from his body and his unconscious, from others, and from his environment.[5] Finally, a redefined nature must once again sustain ideas of *discordia concors,* not as a static three-dimensional balance of elements but as a creative process generating and resolving differences within a larger principle of identity. Hegel restated the dream of *discordia concors* in his model of Reason working through process to realize itself, and less idealistically oriented poets must appropriate similar principles to describe the workings of natural or, as the contemporaries came more and more to assert, cosmic processes.

ii

In order to delineate the specific forms taken by postmodern responses to these problems and to appreciate the logical opposition between these solutions and those of high modernism, one must begin by working out the general logic of immanentist and symbolist poetics as articulated by Wordsworth and Coleridge. (Similar, though less precise or resonant, prototypes might be found in America by examining the poetic theories of Emerson and Poe.) I take early Wordsworth's exploration of values immanent in the experience of secular, familiar objects as a model for poetics committed to what might be called the "prose tradition" or the reliance on horizontal, rather than vertical, symbolic sources of value.[6] One might conceive the entire "Preface" as a rejection of the principles informing Johnson's parody of "poetry in which the language closely resembles that of life and nature." Johnson's parody was intended to mock the poverty of naturalistic style; for Wordsworth, though, all it demonstrates is a poverty of significant subject matter. If the poet really sees into experience, only the simplest, most direct language will not distort the actual significance of what he sees. And more important, an artificially created syntax denies the full implications of an experience, while fidelity to one's actual response enables the syntax of the poem to capture the "deep impression of certain inherent and indestructible qualities of the human mind, and likewise of certain powers in the great and permanent objects that act upon it which are equally inherent and indestructible" ("Preface," pp. 249–50). The values revealed by the poem are intuitions of a lawful interpenetration of consciousness and natural being, and their interactions create the intensity of the poem's particular syntactic relationships:

[The poet] considers man and the objects that surround him as acting and reacting upon each other, so as to produce an infinite complexity of pain and pleasure; he considers man in his own nature and in his ordinary life as contemplating this with a certain quality of immediate knowledge, with certain convictions, intuitions, and deductions which by habit become of the nature of intuitions; he considers him as looking upon this complex scene of ideas and sensations, and finding everywhere objects that immediately excite in him sympathies which, from the necessities of his nature, are accompanied by an overbalance of enjoyment. ["Preface," p. 258]

In elaborating the ways the poem captures laws informing mind and world, Wordsworth works out several points that recur in subsequent aesthetics of immanent presence: the idea that experience has value without the artist intervening to rearrange and structure it (memory in Wordsworth performs the artistic function of restructuring in a less artificial, more naturally responsive way, since what memory preserves is what lawfully matters to and blends with the concerns of consciousness); a naturalistic theory of language opposing directness to creative artificiality; emphasis on the innate harmony between nature and the mind open to and actively participating in it; a theory of rhythm stressing its absolute qualities as a dimension of the experience, not its artifical functions; a consequent distrust of sophisticated culture and its mediated ways; and, finally, a morality of attention locating both moral and poetic values in one's capacity to look steadily at his object and to recover qualities inherent in it or in the act of perception.

Coleridge, on the other hand, provides a model for subsequent "symbolist" theories of poetry. "Symbolisme" is one radical version of these theories, but one must see symbolism essentially in its more philosophical definitions by neo-Kantian philosophers like Ernst Cassirer if one is truly to measure Coleridge's impact. Symbolism in this sense is not the pursuit of spiritual correspondences or Platonic essences, but an attitude that emphasizes the creative role of human consciousness as a force that actively transforms the flux of human experiences into coherent perceptual and axiological structures. Symbolism, too, can be conceived as immanent in the sense that there need be no transcendental ground for the values it creates, but as a way of thinking it alters the idea of numinous presence. What matters is not what is there in immediate experience but what the mind can make of it. As Coleridge puts it, "poetry elevates the mind by making its feelings the object of its reflection," and it approaches "the possibility of climax up to the perfect form of a harmonized chaos" by realizing the implicit potential for that unity within nature:

> In the objects of nature are presented, as in a mirror, all the possible elements, steps and processes of intellect antecedent to consciousness, and therefore to the full development of the intellegential act; and man's mind is the very focus of all the rays of intellect which are scattered throughout the images of nature. Now so to place these images, totalized and fitted to the limits of the human mind, as to elicit from, and to superinduce upon, the forms themselves the moral reflexions to which they approximate, to make the external internal, the internal external, to make nature thought and thought nature: this is the mystery of genius in the fine arts. Dare I add that the genius must act on the feeling, that body is but a striving to become mind,—that it is mind in its essence.[7]

There are many diverse ways in which Coleridge comes down to the moderns, but one can see here a basic element in the model informing their tendencies toward idealist meditations on the creative imagination as locus and even source of the values and images we live by. Ontological- ly, Coleridge anticipates the modernist love of dialectic and its tendencies to image the ultimate forms of reality as essentially human (for ex- ample, in Yeats's Christ as perfect man and his theories of the daimonic, in Joyce's Finnegan, and in Steven's major man), while in matters of poetic theory he provides a model for later emphases on the form- creating imagination and the autotelic poetic syntax sustained by that imagination. What matters in a poem is its power to create and bring into the sphere of mind a complex fusion of disparate events. The poem is in no way imitative, rather it is, in Kant's terms, a "secondary crea- tion," taking its purposiveness from an act of mind and thus appealing primarily to the meditative faculties of the audience.

Both poets seek to reconcile subjective and objective, to find value within fact, but while Wordsworth emphasizes reorienting the subjective consciousness by teaching it ways of attending to its participation in objective laws, Coleridge tries to redeem the objective by pointing to the ways it is formed and structured in creative acts of consciousness. Their differences are matters of emphases within a shared goal, and though the goal remains essentially the same in the twentieth century, the two positions have grown further apart while retaining their essential logical structure. For as a result of Victorian attacks on attributing any moral or teleological functions to nature, poets found that they could in no way pose even an idealist nature as their creative ground. Still, Coleridge's poetic could survive this attack better than Wordsworth's, could in fact be a major force in responding to it, because so much attention is paid there to the mind's creative powers. If one turns for a moment to modern critical theories like those of I. A. Richards or Cleanth Brooks, which claim dependence on Coleridge, one can see the change in radical form. These critics retain Coleridge's definitions of the creative imagination and of the organic poem, but ignore completely his philosophy of nature and the driving force of *natura naturans*, which in his view animates the imagination. In the work of modern critics, the creative mind enters a dialogue with itself, and poetic ontology gives way to psychology.

The response of the modern poets is more complex, but the result is similar. They for the most part recognize that their creative activity is a response to some dynamic principle outside consciousness, but they do not look for that force in natural objects. Landscape is either ignored, aestheticized in imagist lyrics, or psychologized and made symbolic of mental rather than spiritual forces; it is rarely a source of wisdom or a goal consciousness tries to ally itself to. There remains a sense that natural energies are the source of poetic creation, but nature is only a dim source, not a ground for satisfying imaginative needs. These energies only drive the poet to reach beyond himself to higher levels of consciousness.[8] One sees then in Yeats, in Stevens, in Crane, in Pound, even in the background of Eliot's critiques of modern society the insistence that the poet or hero keep in touch with natural energy paralleled by a distrust of the sheerly natural as objectifying and limiting the creative imagination. Thus while the concern for a ground outside ordinary states of consciousness remains, modernism shifts the emphasis from the force of creative nature to the ideal of creative culture. Value and fact can only merge in the imagination's creative response to whatever energies awaken it to the human meanings and forms potential in the experience. The ultimate desire of the moderns—most pronounced in Yeats, Eliot, and the Pound of the early Cantos but present in Crane and Stevens as well—is to liberate those potential forces in the culture which might provide models and sustenance for the imagination as it seeks to bring individuals and the culture to more complete, more fully humane uses of human energy. The real weakness of the New Critics in their redactions of modernism was to confuse the creative imagination seeking to transform cultural vision with the ordering imagination content with complicated aesthetic constructs.

When one turns to the contexts informing postmodern poetry in the sixties, one finds that it has become almost impossible to believe that culture as we know it can be a creative force awakening humanity to its own possibilities. Most simply, modernism failed; there seemed little point in repeating its dreams. Also, as critiques of society became more general and more concerned with humanistic fallacies that seemed to be destroying "backward nations" and perhaps the planet itself, it became harder to separate creative from demonic possibilities in our cultural heritage. Finally, the philosophical and scientific attitude toward nature changed, so in the light of ecological visions of purposive elements in an environment, in the light of scientific models of creative nature, and in the light of nonrepresentational philosophies linking the creative imagination with the creative energy of events, it became possible once more to conceive of nature as a source of religious and, in a loose sense, moral wisdom. Robert Duncan provides a representative summary of the new ideal:

> Central to and defining the poetics I am trying to suggest here is the conviction that the order man may contrive or impose upon the things about him or upon his own language is trivial beside the divine

order or natural order he may discover in them. ["Towards an Open Universe," in *Poets on Poetry*, ed. Howard Nemerov (New York: Basic Books, 1966), p. 139]

Models stressing the creative mind give way to a Wordsworthian emphasis on natural laws, and, like Wordsworth, poets are forced outside the high culture to find their models for authentic experience.

If one accepts these two models as informing modern and postmodern American poetry, one can use their logical structures to understand the coherence underlying the different positions of the two poetics on several topics that involve important ontological and ethical implications. Considered thematically, a *poetic* is a logical system in which the desired relationship between mind and nature determines many of the particular recurrent emphases. I shall first illustrate this with topics where clearly marked differences in Wordsworth and Coleridge produce contrasting perspectives in twentieth-century poetics, and then I will show how a similar logic underlies differences that come to be stressed only in later meditations on Romantic themes.

Corollary to Wordsworth's and Coleridge's different ideas on the relationships between mind and nature are constrasting attitudes toward the poet's fundamental ontological role. In essence, Wordsworth's poetic ideal is a state of being, Coleridge's state of doing. Wordsworth, like those contemporaries who take to heart Roethke's "Being not doing is my first joy," often conceives as models for his desired way of uniting the mind with natural force the state of childhood or of primitive man. A typical Coleridge reflection on childhood takes a very different tack:

> To the idea of life victory or strife is necessary; as virtue consists not simply in the absence of vices, but in the overcoming of them. So it is in beauty. The sight of what is subordinated and conquered heightens the strength and the pleasure. . . . And with a view to this, remark the seeming identity of body and mind in infants, and thence the loveliness of the former; the commencing separation in boyhood and the struggle of equilibrium in youth: thence onward the body is first simply indifferent; then demanding the translucency of the mind not to be worse than indifferent; and finally all that presents the body as body becoming almost of an excremental nature.[9]

A nauseating sense of the excremental awaits the imagination that ceases to be actively creative and falls back on the harmonies glimpsed in earlier stages of the mind's dialectic with nature and above all with itself.

Coleridge's perspectives on associationism and on opposites stem from that same fear of nature not transformed by mind. In Wordsworth the goal is to enjoy the free play of the mind in nature and to find in the associations that recur in that play and in memory the security of universal laws informing the interplay of forces. The source of the law is both without and within.[10] In Coleridge, on the other hand, the energy is both without and within; but form and law depend on the creative act of mind he found described in Continental philosophies. Thus, when confronted by opposites, Coleridge requires an act of mind to unify and form them in accord with the mind's orders. After years of conceiving the poetic treatment of opposites along Coleridgean lines, readers are only now coming to see that Wordsworth too offers us a viable possibility. In his early work opposites need not be reconciled by the mind, because it is sufficient and exalting to recognize that their ultimate unity depends not on man but on natural orders that treat man's desires as one of the dynamic energy fields it holds in balance:

> Dust as we are, the immortal spirit grows
> Like harmony in music; there is a dark
> Inscrutable workmanship that reconciles
> Discordant elements, makes them cling together
> In one society. How strange that all
> The terrors, pains, and early miseries,
> Regrets, vexations, lassitudes interfused
> Within my mind, should e'er have borne a part,
> And that a needful part in making up
> The calm existence that is mine when I
> Am worthy of myself! Praise to the end!
> (*Prelude*, bk. 1, ll. 340–50)

These lines occur in the first book of the *Prelude*, and in addition to their general implications, they help explain why Wordsworth's great philosophical work is autobiographical. It is not the philosophic mind that reconciles opposites but life itself, and the experience of a boy coming to maturity dramatizes how it is natural for the self to discover through time that what appears diverse, contrary, and enervating, has really manifested an inherent unity and purposiveness. Personal growth entails not creating unity but discovering it: as Wordsworth matures he comes to recognize that the opposites tormenting him were necessary forces in his development, and he realizes that his own growth makes him gradually capable of recognizing the full *discordia concors* that *is* creative nature. I shall explore Wordsworthian attitudes toward being, association, and opposites in Olson, Bly, O'Hara, Duncan, and Snyder, but all are perhaps most clearly exemplified in a passage from A. R. Ammons meditating on the landscape and on the place of the mind's activity within it:

manifold events of sand
change the dunes shape that will not be the same shape
tomorrow

so I am willing to go along, to accept
the becoming
thought, to stake off no beginnings or ends, establish no walls . . .

the news to my left was over the dunes and
reeds and bayberry clumps was
fall: thousands of tree swallows
gathering for flight
an order held
in constant change: a congregation
                    rich with entropy: nevertheless, separable, noticeable
as one event . . .

the possibility of rule as the sum of rulelessness:
the 'field' of action
with moving, incalculable center.[11]

Other dimensions of the different models are more clearly manifest
when one concentrates on twentieth-century examples. Ammon's vision
of an "incalculable moving center" introduces what is probably the most
basic issue—conflicting perspectives on the relationship of concrete
particulars to universals, which create their significance. Coleridge's
poetic made central for the moderns, especially for modernist criticism,
the idea of concrete universal. In poetics this idea calls for the poet to
synthesize his particulars into a single organic emotional whole. And
it often projects the additional philosophical implication that the significant poem is "ideal," that it raise its particulars to "philosophical"
and "weighty significance" by relating them to "the indwelling law which
is the true being of things."[12] Criticism at its worst tears the universal
from its dialectical and ontological contexts and reduces it to mere
propositional statement. But at its best, criticism seeking to define
what the indwelling law is, and what it involves brings poetics into one
main stream in nineteenth-century thought. Hegel is, of course, the chief
figure in establishing the significance of the interplay between particulars
and indwelling universals,[13] but similar concerns for the whole informing
and structuring particular phenomena are common throughout the idealist
tradition (particularly in ethics). In poetry the same need to subsume
particulars into informing universals torments the typical Victorian with
the distance between his imaginative fancy and the categories of significance maintained by social institutions. Later the moderns will try to
integrate these oppositions by making the imagination itself responsible

for the creation and definition of social categories. The poet, then, is also mythmaker; his fancies are not artificial idols but the acts of an imagination seeking to possess its own powers for giving meaning to social actions. And the quest for myth itself gives way in the modernist writer's moments of greatest pride, and perhaps of deepest vision, to the image of a single human shape as the source and meaning of all desire. Even the Romantic Image, that basic and widely accepted goal of the modernist poem, is conceived as transcendent because within the confines of the poem it is the still point, the momentary unity, which defines and stabilizes the significance of the poem's diverse elements.

The effects of thinking in terms of particulars and informing universals go far beyond poetics. Indeed it seems to me that such a notion goes a long way toward explaining the political conservatism so common among modernist poets. For when the concrete universal is applied to social question, it places the burden on the individual to reconcile himself to collective myths and authorities, myths and authorities, one might add, which depend on the poet's custodial function and his powers to remake what was vital in the culture and has gone dead.[14]

For the postmoderns, on the other hand, meaning and significance tend to depend on the immanent qualities manifested in the particular. As Olson put it, meaning is "that which exists through itself," or in Roethke's terms, "intensely seen, image becomes symbol"[15]—a symbol is not a way of raising particulars to higher orders of significance (as it is most clearly in sacramental theology and in semiology) but a particular charged with numinous force. This does not mean there are no universals, only that the universals that matter are not conceptual structures but energies recurring in numinous moments. D. H. Lawrence's gods, for example, are universal forces; yet they do not descend bringing the Law of the Logos but emerge from the darkness of the soil. Where sacramentalism meant for New Critics like Allen Tate and John Crowe Ransom a miraculous union of local texture and logical structure, it means something quite different for Nathan Scott, a critic applying Heidegger's opposition between Being and mere universals about Being to postmodern poetry. He describes the sacramental experience as a moment when "certain objects or actions or words or places belonging to the ordinary spheres of life may convey to us a unique illumination of the whole mystery of our existence, because in these actions and realities . . . something numinous is resident, something holy and gracious."[16] In Scott's description of the numinous there is nothing conceptual, no idea that the sacrament is a sign completed by another symbolic order for interpreting experience. The idea of concrete universal gives way to an exploration of the ways that the universal—be it Being or energy or the collective unconscious—manifests itself in the concrete moment. The emphasis is on the universal concretized, on event rather than on structure—a reversal of priorities that Whitehead states was his basic goal as a philosopher. No wonder then that the dream of a Romantic Image, like Stevens's "jar in Tennessee," which transforms the place in the terms of a created order, gives way to the ideal of a Deep Image that abides in the place where psyche and world share a sense of "the interdependence of all things alive" (Robert Bly, "The Dead World and the Live World," *The Sixties* 8 [1966]: 3). No wonder, too, that poets in the sixties tend toward Protestant models of individual salvation and conceive society as a loose aggregation of individuals each obliged, in Gary Snyder's terms, to go beyond the society to find values that are to shape his individual being.[17]

While insisting on the necessity of each individual's finding his unique relationship to immanent being, the new poets try at the same time to redefine what the individual is. A major dimension of their attack on modernism takes up the two basic modernist visions of the ego—Eliot's doctrines of impersonality and what Olson calls Pound's "nineteenth century stance"—where social and mental order depend upon the heroic will of an individual character trying to make it all cohere (Robert Creeley, ed., *Charles Olson: Selected Writings* [New York: New Directions, 1966], pp. 82–84). Both those visions stem from the idea of concrete universal: Eliot requires personae and tradition because of his Bradleyan and later his Christian sense that the individual ego can at best capture only single perspectives on absolute reality and must be surrendered to a more inclusive creative Logos, while Pound and Yeats see the universal as viable only if the individual can so enlarge his or her imaginative capacities as to hold all abstractions or all history in a single image or related set of images. For the postmoderns, on the other hand, the ego is not a thing or a place for storing and ordering experiences; the ego is not a force transcending the flux of experience but an intense force deepening one's participation in experience. The ego is not a created identity but, in a phrase borrowed from the *Bhagavad Gita,* an "organ" responding and reacting to experience in ways best symbolized by the musical and sexual implications of the term. The ego as organ has particular functions in experience—but its responses depend on being flexible to the impulses that initiate and direct its activity. Thus, even with poets as deeply personal in their work as John Logan, the ego does not create order but allows the poet to capture intimate energies and qualities also operating in the experiences of others. Less subjective poets are likely to invoke Keats's doctrine of negative capability to exemplify ways in which the ego is not a way of controlling but of actively entering and registering "the condition of things" (see especially Charles Olson, *A Special View of History*, ed. Ann Charters [Berkeley, Calif.: Oyez, 1970], p. 46). John Ashbery summarizes the various positions in his image of the personality as no longer "bound to the permanent tug which used to be its notion of home" but free "to branch out in all directions," as "a centrality but not a centre."[18]

The poetry of the sixties treads a narrow borderline between the personal and the egoistic. Despite their distrust of the ego, poets like Logan, Creeley, Olson, and Snyder are more directly personal and autobiographical than most poets in the language. One reason for this is the distrust of ideas and personae—what else can a poet suspicious of symbolic orders rely upon except individual experience? If one follows Kierkegaard's reasoning, religious poetry must always be personal since religion is a matter of individual not collective experience. Moreover, when the poet resists the norms of popular culture and finds no alternatives in its traditions, he has no referent, no norm for the validity of his visions except their effects on his own life and on the relationships his poetry can establish to others and to Being. Autobiography, then, as Wordsworth was perhaps the first to demonstrate, is evidence of the valuable effects of poetic experience on the self's subsequent relationship to his world. Finally, autobiographical poetry prevents the poet from the easy irrelevant metaphysical speculations encouraged by academic easy chairs and a taste for witty reflective poetry. Poems about the self involve one in the consequences of his thoughts; contemplation is measured by actions, and the dramatized self exemplifies how the immanent forces released by the poem affect the prehending consciousness. Gary Snyder is the appropriate figure to cite here:

> Wisdom is intuitive knowledge of the mind of love and clarity that lies beneath one's ego-driven anxieties and aggressions. Meditation is going into the mind to see this for yourself—over and over again, until it becomes the mind you live in. Morality is bringing it back out in the way you live, through personal example and responsible action. [Gary Snyder, *Earth House Hold* (New York: New Directions, 1969), p. 92]

Like concepts of the ego, ideas about language depend in large part on more general attitudes toward the relationship between the mind and nature. In immanentist thinking, symbolist theories of language as the creation of forms for experience give way to doctrines stressing the way authentic language grows out of the world's vitality and gives expression to it. It is, in fact, a remarkable testimony to "logical geography" that so many postmodern thinkers have held to notions that language

is directly linked with the experience of things despite common agreement in linguistics that language is an arbitrary code imposed upon and
not growing out of experience. Still there remains an aesthetic if not an
ontological foundation for the tradition in Romantic poetics distinguishing sharply between an essentially casual, articifial, social language
and a language directly attuned to the dimensions of value emerging
in natural events. Wordsworth's distinctions between artificial and natural
speech begin a framework of oppositions adapted in various ways by
thinkers as diverse as Emerson, T. E. Hulme, Heidegger, and Merleau-
Ponty. (Even the New Critics' insistence on the radical differences
between poetic and scientific discourse is a variant of that tradition.)
Hulme makes the epistemological and social implications of these oppositions most clear. He distinguishes sharply between on the one hand
a "counter" language of everyday speech (or, in Heidegger's terms,
"idle talk") where a word's energy is not referential but is used up in
a pattern of action and response to action that never visualizes or contemplates the materials being manipulated and, on the other, the precise
language of art that captures the real being of things and thus serves
as a compromise for a language of intuition that would "hand over
sensations bodily." For Hulme, however, poetic language ultimately serves
to separate clearly rendered images from the confusions of the flux. He
borrows vitalist strategies in the service of a faith in static, transcendent
works of art. To come to the postmoderns, one needs to complement
Hulme's meditative sense of poetic language with Fenollosa's vitalism;
words must not freeze natural objects into nouns but capture their
essential verbal qualities as transferences of force. Language reveals as
an action within nature not an attack on it. One arrives then at Denise
Levertov's reformulation of the Bergsonian ground:

> The poet's task is to hold in trust the knowledge that language,
> as Robert Duncan has declared, is not a set of counters to be manip-
> ulated, but a Power. And only in this knowledge does he arrive at
> music, at that quality of song within speech which is not the result
> of manipulations of euphonious parts but of an attention, at once
> to the organic relationships of experienced phenomena, and to the
> latent harmony and counterpoint of language itself as it is identified
> with those phenomena. Writing poetry is a process of discovery, re-
> vealing inherent music, the music of correspondences, the music of
> inscape. ["The Origins of a Poem," *Michigan Quarterly Review* 7
> (1968): 238]

Language, like the lover's eye, is most true when most "transparent,"[19]
and the poem in turn reinforces through its revelations the sense that
consciousness is wedded to and fulfills natural being.

The necessity, in Charles Olson's terms, is to remain aware that "definition is as much a part of the act as sensation itself," that "we ourselves are both the instrument of discovery and the instrument of definition" (*Human Universe*, p. 3). Words, one might say, are as natural as any other elements in experience, and they are the way man becomes conscious of his participation in being. Consequently, the poets are drawn to philosophers like Heidegger and Wittgenstein who conceive "the use of words as definition of words" (Robert Creeley, *A Quick Graph* [San Francisco, Calif.: Four Seasons Foundation, 1970], p. 312) and seek meaning not in systems but in existential contexts or "situations." Thus there are very few contemporary meditations on the image of Logos, the transcendent Word informing all words, whose fascination the symbolists passed on to the moderns. There is instead a faith that the true words lead back to a source in the interchange of psychic and natural energies, not beyond to an ideal verbal universe. Robert Bly describes the contemporary ideal with his usual panache in his discussion of Neruda's poetry:

> His imagination sees the hidden connections between conscious and unconscious substances with such assurance that he hardly bothers with metaphors—he links them by tying their hidden tails. He is a new kind of creature moving about under the surface of everything. Moving under the earth, he knows everything from the bottom up (which is the right way to learn the nature of a thing) and therefore is never at a loss for its name.[20]

Bly's linking his naturalistic theory of language with the fact that Neruda "hardly bothers with metaphors" is important. To understand the comment, one must first distinguish two modes of metaphor—a mode exemplified in Wallace Stevens's later poetry where the grounded imagination multiplies relationships that then constitute the "real" and another, exemplified by Yeats, where metaphor becomes a dramatic sign of the mind's powers to idealize and structure natural flux. It is this second mode Bly attacks, for it derives from Coleridgean fears of a nauseating nature requiring the supplementing activity of the creative imagination. For the postmoderns, then, elaborately self-conscious or idealizing metaphors seem to be admissions that one must create rather than reveal the significance of his experience. Thus their poetry tends toward what William Dickey calls "a poetic language that is shared and general"— so general in fact that one often can find no trace of individual styles in the writings of many deep-image and objectivist poets. Such a language not only allows the experience its particular identity and preserves its concreteness, but also embodies a consciousness that is never "at a loss," never losing touch with the simple and easy harmony consciousness can maintain with nature when not subjected to an anxiety-ridden quest for the perfect word and the transcendent form.[21] The ideal is to refute Freud and have art without neurosis, to have an art, in fact, which can cure and not displace man's most basic alienations.

The contrasts between modernist and postmodern ideas of poetic language grow more pronounced when one turns to the topic of myth, for myth is essentially a collective form of poetic language defining the way a culture experiences and structures those interchanges between human and natural orders which it finds most important for maintaining its identity. If one accepts the received critical opinion and takes as central to modernist poetry T. S. Eliot's definition of myth in his essay "Ulysses, Order, and Myth," one can briefly locate the impulses behind the two basic modernist approaches to myth. Eliot's essay is intended to refute charges that Joyce was "a prophet of chaos"; on the contrary, he argues, Joyce's love for multiple details only intensifies his success at what every major artist must accomplish—he cannot be content to create orders by carefully selecting his details, but he must confront and compose the central contradictions and confusions of his time:

> In using the myth, in manipulating a continuous parallel between contemporaneity and antiquity, Mr. Joyce is pursuing a method which others must pursue after him. . . . It is simply a way of controlling, of ordering, of giving a shape and a significance to the immense panorama of futility and anarchy which is contemporary history. It is a method already adumbrated by Mr. Yeats, and of the need of which I believe Mr. Yeats to have been the first contemporary to be conscious. . . . Instead of a narrative method, we may now use the mythical method. It is, I seriously believe, a step toward making the modern world possible for art, toward that order and form which Mr. Aldington so earnestly desires.[22]

This need for complex principles of order informs both the modernist use of anthropologists like Frazer to find universal spiritual dramas underlying cultural multiplicity and its use of the Blakean Romantic model proposing individual imaginative systems capable of holding "reality and justice in a single thought."

For the postmoderns, on the other hand, myth is less a way of ordering and comprehending experience than a means for experiencing events and actions charged with religious force and endowed with the collective psychic energies of an entire community aware that it in turn shares the event with past generations. Myth is not a way of universalizing the concrete, but of finding universal natural and cultural forces active in a numinous present. As Robert Duncan tells us, "Only the mythopoeic" can "reach the heart of the matter" where the energies of man and world are intensely fused and the ground "charged" with "reverberations" of a "plot that had already begun before the first signs and signatures we have found worked upon the walls of Altamira or Pech-Merle" ("Two Chapters from HD," *Tri Quarterly*, no. 12 [Spring 1968], p. 67). Similar ideals are expressed by poets as diverse as James Dickey and Denise Levertov (whose essay "A Personal Approach" is devoted to the topic), but one quotation from Gary Snyder captures most of the ethical and ontological implications that make this theme central:

> To live in the "mythological present" in close relation to nature and in basic but disciplined body/mind states suggests a wider ranging imagination and a closer subjective knowledge of one's own physical properties than is usually available to men living (as they themselves describe it) impotently and inadequately in "history," their mind content programmed, and their caressing of nature complicated by the extensions and abstractions which elaborate tools are. A hand pushing a button may wield great power, but that hand will never learn what a hand can do. [*Earth House Hold*, pp. 117–18]

The idea of myth brings me at last to the ultimate difference between the two poetics: they base their imaginative enterprises on two very different and incompatible models of the culture they would like to bring about and of the locus for the energies making such a transformation possible. The differences are all the more striking because they depend on very similar goals, on the dream of a society where a unified sensibility is possible and where value and fact, individual and his society, are not separated from one another. But for the moderns this culture depends on a unified structure of images and ideas, derived primarily from the traditions of "civilized" reflective societies. To be preserved, culture requires men of sufficient learning and imagination to master the contradictions unearthed by the rationalist tradition and resolve them in postlogical poetic myths and images. The modernists' ideal society will preserve humane aristocratic values and allow political authority to those who understand and represent these values. The poet works to make viable for many what is now merely potential in the cultural traditions.

When the poets of the sixties imagine ideal societies, on the other hand, they tend to renounce the heroic humanist tradition. They do not envision the success of a culture in terms of its power to preserve complex intellectual and emotional structures of ordered energy, but concentrate almost exclusively on the harmony between mental energies and natural processes a culture provides. This need not mean primitivism, although it often does, but it does involve very different democratic and Protestant priorities. Those seeking "primitivist" alternatives to a technological society that seems by now irrevocably cut off from its earlier humanism share D. H. Lawrence's notion that "culture and civilization are tested by vital consciousness;" thus the success of a culture is measured not by its "inventions" but "is revealed rather in sensitive life." They note ironically that what possibilities there are for "sensitive life" in our culture tend to be negated by the old humanism looking always toward absolute images and complex meditative structures. Other poets, who sympathize with primitive cultures but find them impossible alternatives for those with our traditions, place their hopes for a redeemed society on an awakened sensitivity to and reverence for the simplest experiences. Kenneth Rexroth provides one model for this vision in a discussion distinguishing between the work of William Carlos Williams and that of more ambitious poets seeking heroic ideals and total images for the meaning of their experience: "Civilization in Williams' work has a terrific power and an almost inextinguishable life because it consists of things like your cats stepping over the window sill. . . . That's why you [Williams] always had so much to give, because you never wanted anything but what you knew you had already."[23] Heraclitus said that "Man is estranged from what is familiar," and in that epigraph he predicted what contemporary poets see as the course of Western history. The time has come, they feel, to restore the familiar in its many modes of emerging. This restoration might not redeem society, but it is the necessary beginning by reorienting modern consciousnesses to what men have rather than what men desire. There was a curious poetic truth, accompanied by a not-so-strange note of desperation, in George McGovern's campaign slogan, "Come home, America." However, America chose Richard Nixon again and effectively defined the perennial state of exile that is the plight of contemporary poets.

Notes to Chapter 1

1. Alfred North Whitehead, *Science and the Modern World* (New York: Macmillan Free Press, 1967), pp. 93–94. All of chap. 5 of this work is relevant to my discussion.

2. Earl Wasserman in *The Subtler Language* (Baltimore, Md.: Johns Hopkins University Press, 1954), pp. 3–12, 169–88, gives the best description I know of how the concept of poetic logic enables the Romantics to imagine supplementary systems or a second syntax for replacing the theocentric syntax of value relation-

ships providing resonance for earlier poetic modes and, in its demise, creating the lack of poetic tension in eighteenth-century associative poems like "The Task." Wasserman's descriptions coincide nicely with Northrop Frye's "Towards Defining an Age of Sensibility" in *Eighteenth Century English Literature: Modern Essays in Criticism,* ed. James Clifford (New York: Oxford University Press, 1959), pp. 311–18, with its distinction between a poetry of process and a poetry of product. Wasserman, however, betrays his New Critical ideology when he argues that the second syntax created by the Romantics is purely aesthetic and self-referential. But the Romantics did not object merely to the aesthetics of associationist poetry. They saw the philosophical and psychological problems in a poetic that often was accompanied by madness and gave no ontological role to the creative mind. So their task was to imagine the second syntax as at once aesthetic and epistemological, to treat aesthetic relationships as possible features of a meditative mind discovering its place in nature and in human relationships.

3. One can subsume under the metaphor of nausea a variety of Romantic and modern themes, ranging from the image of intellect divorced from feeling, to Eliot's dissociation of sensibility, to the many versions of alienation theory. The best general description of the mental landscape within which the poles of nausea and narcissism become crucial is Northrop Frye's *A Study of English Romanticism* (New York: Random House, 1968), pp. 3–49.

4. The attack on Gothic emotions is in "Preface to Lyrical Ballads" in *Lyrical Ballads,* ed. R. L. Brett and A. R. Jones (London: University Paperbacks, 1963), pp. 249–50. The quotation is from *The Prelude: A Parallel Text,* ed. J. C. Maxwell (Baltimore, Md.: Penguin, 1971), bk. 13, ll. 518–19. I shall refer to these works by abbreviations in the text, with all citations of the *Prelude* from the 1850 text.

5. Meyer Abrams, *Natural Supernaturalism* (New York: Norton, 1971), pp. 145 ff., discusses how the necessary "reconciliation with nature" sought by Wordsworth and Coleridge might resolve these three forms of alienation.

6. On Wordsworth and the "prose tradition" see Basil Willey, *The Seventeenth Century Background* (New York: Anchor, 1934), pp. 294–95, and for a treatment of modern poetry and the prose tradition see Herbert Schneidau, *Ezra Pound: The Image and the Real* (Baton Rouge, La.: Louisiana State University Press, 1969), pp. 3–37. On the difference between Wordsworth's early and later poetic, see James Heffernan, *Wordsworth's Theory of Poetry: The Transforming Imagination* (Ithaca, N.Y.: Cornell University Press, 1969). It is also interesting to note that Abrams in *The Mirror and the Lamp* (New York: Norton, 1958), 118 ff., takes account of differences between Wordsworth's fidelity to the prose tradition and Coleridge's idealism, which he (Abrams) later in *Natural Supernaturalism* collapses in order to read both against a background of idealist dialectics. Nonetheless, I find *Natural Supernaturalism* a stimulating book because it uses the idealists as a model for Romantic attempts to redefine nature. While Professor Abrams is not always clear on how different Wordsworth is from Hegelian idealism, his work seems to me more fruitful than Paul De Man's intelligent but, I think, misdirected use of a rationalist opposition between nature and language to criticize Romantic attempts to get beyond that opposition. See his "Intentional Structure of the Romantic Image" in *Romanticism and Consciousness,* ed. Harold Bloom (New York: Norton, 1970), pp. 65–76, and "The Rhetoric of Temporality" in *On Interpretation,* ed. Charles Singleton (Baltimore, Md.: Johns Hopkins University Press, 1968), pp. 173–209.

7. All the quotations are from "On Poesy or Art" in Samuel Taylor Coleridge,

Biographia Literaria, ed. J. Shawcross (London: Oxford University Press, 1907*)*, 2: 254, 262, 257–58. Coleridge's quarrels with Wordsworth's "Preface" in the *Biographia* and his description of their differing intentions in the *Lyrical Ballads* further clarify the different models I am developing.

8. I am approaching in another way the balance of Dionysiac and Apollonian praised in the modernists most recently by Monroe Spears. See also Richard Ellmann's interesting essay on the need for "life" and vitality as a theme in Edwardian literature, which I think was extended and made philosophical in the high moderns, "Two Faces of Edward," in *Backgrounds to Modern Literature*, ed. John Oliver Perry (San Francisco, Calif.: Chandler, 1968), pp. 19–37.

9. "On Poesy or Art" in Coleridge, *Biographia*, ed. Shawcross, 2: 262–63. For a good illustration of many of the contemporary myths in a very casual, unphilosophical meditation, see Galway Kinnell's essay "Poetry, Personality and Death," *Field*, no. 4 (Spring 1971), pp. 56–75. True to form, he uses infancy as "the standard of what it is to be alive" (p. 68).

10. Critics have overlooked the possible vitality in the Hartleyan tradition because they accept idealist arguments that all associationism is behavioristic and rationalistic on Hume's model. Hartley, however, presented a moralistic Christian view of associationism that, although simplistic, did provide viable ethical and ontological models for poets with post-Christian visions. Walter Jackson Bate, *From Classic to Romantic* (New York: Harper Torchbook, 1961*)*, pp. 116–17, 127–28, observes the fact of two eighteenth-century associationist traditions and shows how Hartley validates instinct and primary ways of knowing over reason.

11. A. R. Ammons, "Corsons Inlet," in *Corson's Inlet* (Ithaca, N.Y.: Cornell University Press, 1965), pp. 6–7.

12. The quotations are from Coleridge, *Biographia*, ed. Shawcross, 2: 33, 101, 39.

13. That Hegel means something very different by "concrete" from its meaning in modern discussions of poetry and philosophy does not alter the general truth that his philosophy, even if it links concrete with Absolute Reason, proceeds by elaborating the need for particulars to be grounded in ever larger wholes.

14. Northrop Frye's recent criticism in *The Stubborn Structure* (Ithaca, N.Y.: Cornell University Press, 1971) and "The Critical Path: An Essay on the Social Context of Literary Criticism," *Daedalus* 99 (1970): 268–342, makes articulate and practical the social thinking of high modernism and the symbolist tradition.

15. Theodore Roethke, *The Poet and His Craft*, ed. Ralph Mills (Seattle, Wash.: University of Washington Press, 1965), p. 122.

16. Nathan A. Scott, *Wild Prayer of Longing: Poetry and the Sacred* (New Haven, Conn.: Yale University Press, 1971), p. 49.

17. See Alfred North Whitehead, *Process and Reality* (New York: The Free Press, 1969), pp. 106, 180–83, and passim. Olson cites Whitehead in a similar denial of the priority of universals (*A Special View of History*, p. 27), and Duncan offers similar sentiments ("Notes on Grossinger's Solar Journal: Oecological Sections" [Los Angeles, Calif.: Black Sparrow Press broadside, 1970], p. ii). On the deep image, see in addition to Bly: Ronald Moran and George Lensing, The Emotive Imagination: A New Departure in American Poetry," *Southern Review*, n.s. 3 (1967): 51–67; Robert Kelley, "Notes on the Poetry of Deep Image," *Trobar* 2 (1961): 14–15; and Jerome Rothenberg's use of primitive poetry as an analogue to the quest for presence and for a sense of the interpenetration

of man and nature in contemporary poetics in *The Technicians of the Sacred* (Garden City, N.Y.: Anchor, 1969), passim. Finally, the reference to Snyder is to "Changes" in *Notes From the New Underground,* ed. Jesse Kornbluth (New York: Viking, 1968), pp. 162–64.

18. The phrase "ego as organ" is borrowed from Clayton Eshelman, "Translating Cesar Vallejo: an Evolution" in *The Tri-Quarterly Anthology of Contemporary Latin American Literature* (New York: Dutton, 1969), p. 41. Ashbery is quoted from "The Definition of Blue" in his *The Double Dream of Spring* (New York: Dutton, 1970), p. 53. For a lovely example of contemporary visions of the ego, see the hilarious sequence in the second book of Ed Dorn's *Gunslinger,* (Los Angeles, Calif.: Black Sparrow, 1968, 1969), where the character named I is killed and reborn with LSD provided by Cool Everything to a new vision of reality.

19. This phrase is taken from Ed Dorn, *What I See in the Maximus Poems* (Ventura, Calif.: A Migrant Press Pamphlet, 1966), p. 13.

20. Robert Bly, ed., *Neruda and Vallejo: Selected Poems* (Boston: Beacon, 1971), pp. 14–15. For support of their theory of language, see J. L. Austin, *Sense and Sensibilia* (New York: Oxford University Press, 1962) and Paul Goodman, *Speaking and Language* (New York: Random House, 1972). Also relevant is Stanley Burnshaw's thesis in *The Seamless Web* (New York: Braziller, 1970*),* especially part 2, that poetry is the language of nature and hence is universal and opposed to the multiplicity of cultural languages. Burnshaw's book is a theoretical attempt to blend poetry and ecology and is an important discursive statement of contemporary myths.

21. For William Dickey's statement see his "A Time of Common Speech," *Field,* no. 4 (Spring, 1971), p. 344. Roland Barthes offers an interesting sociological analysis of the reasons for this plain transparent style in *Writing Degree Zero,* trans. Annette Lavers and Colin Smith (London, Jonathan Cape, 1967), pp. 80–93.

22. Eliot's essay is reprinted in Richard Ellmann and Charles Feidelson, eds., *The Modern Tradition* (New York: Oxford University Press, 1965), pp. 679–81. For a contrast more extreme than mine between modern and postmodern treatments of myth, see Richard Wasson, "Notes on a New Sensibility," *Partisan Review* 36 (1969): 460–77.

23. For Lawrence see his *Apocalypse* (New York: Viking, 1966), p. 74, and for Rexroth see his *Assays* (Norfolk, Conn.: New Directions, 1961), p. 204.

24. I have summarized the relevance of these thinkers to contemporary poetry in the essay on which a good part of this chapter is based, "From Symbolist Thought to Immanence: The Logic of Post-Modernist Poetry," *Boundary 2* 1 (1973): 605–41.

2

Robert Lowell and the Difficulties of Escaping Modernism

Large traditions and abstract logical geographies can help clarify the basic projects of particular poets and schools of poetry, but they cannot recover the specific historical context giving power and often pathos to the poets' activities. This chapter will attempt to create a limited literary context for the poetry of the sixties in order to provide this historical perspective. I want first to develop the basic values of what Hall called the orthodoxy inspired by the New Criticism in the fifties. As it entered the academy, New Criticism domesticated the prophetic symbolist claims of high modernism into a poetic mode best represented by Richard Wilbur's elegant celebrations of the mind's capacity to revel in its aesthetic ordering of natural flux. Then, I want to show how Robert Lowell's *Life Studies* (1959) interprets his break with his earlier commitment to both the poetics and the theology fostered by the New Critical use of the incarnation metaphor and provides terms for understanding the confessional style. My aim in dealing with both poets shall be less to give an impartial analysis of their work than to recover the way many younger poets came to view them. Lowell is the age's greatest poet, and one basic measure of his greatness is the intense energies other poets put into creating alternatives to his imposing tragic egotism. What Lowell self-consciously images as the pathos of confessional poetry, and later of an ennervated humanism, his successors took as poetic weakness. Thus they understood confessional poetry as essentially a transitional mode, wandering between a dead modernism and a world they thought they were capable of begetting. Their dream was to counter Lowell's pathos by restoring in fresh terms the modernist confidence in social and epistemological powers of the imagination.

The quickest way I know to indicate the effects of New Critical principles on the poetry of the fifties is to show how Josephine Miles's descriptions of the dominant mode in the forties applies equally to Wilbur. The crucial concept is the role of pattern:

> The poetry is therefore a poetry of pattern. It is devoted to the

linear, tonal, and qualitative arrangement of things according to a perspective in a state of mind. Its truth and beauty are in arrangements . . . .

The poetry of the decade, is, in its whole makeup, opposed to direct apprehension or intuition through substance. It is made out of abstract consideration . . . .

The varying styles, while they shade from brief immediacy to ironic analysis and to splendid encompassment, persist always in their emphasis on the pattern of things, made and natural, in the presence of mind.[1]

Gone is the modernist passion to re-create society by articulating deeper, mythical powers of the creative imagination. Yet the emphasis on imaginative order remains, applied now to providing a meditative balance amid the flux of experience. Prophetic order gives way to reflective private acts of balancing; if we gain sanity and humility we lose the passionate excess and the quest for large imaginative syntheses that perhaps are necessary for great poetry.

This emphasis on pattern and balance, in turn, derives from the specific ways critics like John Crowe Ransom and Allan Tate defined the possibility of poetry serving cognitive functions not subject to the epistemological authority wielded by the powerful voice of positivist scientism. Both critics insisted that good poetry reconciles a sharp awareness of particulars with a method of achieving universality not dependent on discursive logic. Ransom, for example, defined the poem as a delicate union of local texture and logical structure and devoted a good part of his critical work to trying out a variety of schemes to explain how that synthesis comes about. While never achieving that goal, he successfully defined the two extremes where poetry failed— at one "sentimental" pole the poem failed because its particulars were too easily stereotyped and abstracted, while at the "Platonic" pole the poem failed because its universals never achieved full embodiment in the texture of reality. Allen Tate's similar explanation of poetic failure is more suggestive here because he links the poles with what I have defined as the problems of nausea and narcissism. His version of excessive particularity is a poetry unable to blend its denotative language with a complex texture of affective connotations. Readers are left merely with things or with the logical relationships between things; the will to rational truths prevents the poet from presenting the complex interrelationships among objects when *experienced* by men. Narcissism, on the other hand, arises when poets leave the objective world to science and devote themselves almost exclusively to the subjective emotional connotations that the objects elicit.[2]

True poetry, of course, resides somewhere in the middle, but the middle is a notoriously difficult area to define (indeed Tate, true to his humanist heritage, only offers a variety of touchstones as examples of this middle ground). And because this middle ground is so slippery, two dangerous tendencies develop in the New Criticism. The first is present even in Ransom and Tate: because this middle is defined primarily as the tension between the two poles, it is tempting to describe the poem as a sphere of irony where particularity and generalization pull against one another. Why is one so aware of these different pulls in poetic discourse if the poem itself does not emphasize their tension? Moreover, a sense of irony goes hand in hand with a tragic religious humanism because it continually reminds one of the instability and imprecision of human speech, while demanding that speech at its most precise can only be understood by those with a mature sense of man's complexity. Tate attacks the romantic irony of the solipsist poet torn by science from any communion with the objective world only to propose instead a kind of religious irony demanding that men huddle in humble communal enclaves, protecting themselves against the paradoxes imposed by an angry and demanding God.

The emphasis on irony, then, has two important effects on the poems written after World War II. First, it makes poets suspicious of prophetic roles and of the highly subjective blends of abstract and mythical thought sustaining symbolist visions of value as based on the mind reflecting on its creative acts. To defend any claims for the truth of poetry in an increasingly positivistic age, poets would have to renounce speculative ambition in favor of accuracy and forego the dream of reconciling reality and justice in a single thought. Not passionate self-creation but witty self-deprecation and carefully balanced assertions where mythic order is replaced by defensible aesthetic orders would rule the age.

Second, concentration on irony leaves poets and critics uncomfortably aware of the tension inherited from Kantian thought between a natural order or realm of particulars and the interpretive structures used to interpret and order them. Unable to resist a conceptual need for universals and unwilling to trust Romantic claims for symbolic natural objects as reconciling the two orders, the New Critics find themselves tempted to buttress ideas of poetic miraculism by returning to the doctrine of incarnation.[3] Poetics, one might say, seemed to make Anglicans of them all. For incarnation provides a doctrinal basis by which an essentially symbolist poetic can assert the value of the mind's orders while insisting that universals are not mere fictions but contain the actual structure and meaning of particular experiences.

The doctrine of incarnation has an inherent appeal to poetic thought because it promises to resolve the two basic forms of contradiction bred by a sense of the ironic distance between concepts and world. Incarnation is first of all the union of flesh and spirit, the coming of a principle of divine order in the otherwise chaotic war between the ungoverned flesh and the harsh letter of the old law. The incarnation informs the flesh with spiritual force and, by thus transforming existence, allows the law to become more flexible, more symbolic, and more intimately linked to the inner life. Second, it is the intersection of time and timelessness, a way of altering the arbitrary orders of human law and human words so that they become more suited to the divine Word or Order, which understands the complexities of the flesh and natural flux. Thus natural experiences are given meaning and purpose in the timeless scheme of creation.

If one stresses the secular implications of an incarnational model for poetics, one is led with Ransom to a concept of miraculism. In the good poem, language admits the complexity of natural experience, yet transcends those complexities in a created, nondiscursive order. The poem becomes a microcosm of the relationship of Logos, or the informing word, to the multiple words and contradictions of secular experience. Because words approach Logos, elements in the poem approach the unity of flesh, spirit, and pattern that is symbolized in the notions of form or of the image. Yet man is a fallen animal, so he can recognize but not fully articulate the nondiscursive unity of poem or cosmos. The unity promised by the incarnation is always a problematic one and requires continual discursive interpretation. Moreover, and this is a crucial point for contemporary rejections of incarnation, the order perceived is always outside of existential time. It can be known only in contemplation, not in action. There is a sense, then, in which allegory, that literary form which builds discursive interpretation into its pursuit of the ineffable Logos, is the central literary form of Christian poetics. (And thus one might argue that New Criticism is so interpretation-oriented because it seeks to keep distinct and yet to join both the ineffable Image and the discursive allegorization warranted by the dream of a Logos.)

Augustine's *Confessions* may be taken as the archetypal text interpreting the relationship between incarnation and allegorical interpretation of the patterns that the union of flesh and word guarantees. Augustine's conversion is a movement from the temporal flux of his pagan life to the atemporal meditations on truth occupying the last books of the *Confessions*. These meditations discover a ground of value available always to the highest mode of activity—the disengaged contemplative life—but more important from a modern perspective, they also allow Augustine to redeem his past by recognizing the divine purpose and patterning that informed it. Pattern then iluminates flux, but it also leads inexorably to the celebration of contemplative experience ultimately divorced from that flux.

Modern writers still desire to achieve a position where they can at once be true to the flux and stand above it, but Augustine's incarnational model has grown more enervated and more problematic. It grows more enervated when men find it difficult to accept the theological grounds on which the idea of Logos is based. Pattern then comes dangerously close to mere aesthetic or fictive order, and the contemplative life tends to merge with the aesthetic and ultimately with the decadent one. Then one finds oneself no longer with Christianity or a Romantic humanism but with versions of Symbolisme or modifications of aesthetic formalism. Moreover, the Logos becomes an abstract Platonic entity no longer able to unify pattern with creative energy. One or the other becomes absolute, and Dionysius and Apollo are once again at war. At the same time, the incarnational model becomes more problematic as nature itself loses all immanence and comes to depend entirely on fictions for its significance. Between Augustine, or even the Romantics, and the moderns lies Mill's definition of nature and Darwin's struggle for survival. Nature becomes radical indifference to consciousness and to human assumptions about value, and allegory then becomes a created rather than a discovered order.[4]

Yet while it was losing its theological ground, incarnation remained symbolically important because it provided one of the few models whereby the creative mind could retain its place at once within and dominating natural flux. Not only poetry, but value itself (conceived as a sense that the world is adequate to satisfy human desires) depended on rejecting naturalism and preserving some version of the "spiritual" realm —hence the recurrent modernist flirtations with theology, and especially with gnostic and idealist modes of thought based on theology. In the words of Eliot (whose desperation led him to take his theological model literally) :

> Man is man because he can recognize supernatural realities, not because he can invent them. Either everything in man can be traced as a development from below, or something must come from above. There is no avoiding that dilemma: you must be either a naturalist or a supernaturalist.[5]

For Yeats and Stevens as well, either one retains the incarnational model (albeit complexly and naturalistically) in order to emphasize the creative presence of the Imagination or Word or Daimon or Supreme Fiction or Major Man, or he surrenders to the "flux" in the form of "the pressure of reality."

Later phases in the history of modern poetry consist in the weakening and simplification of these incarnational models and the consequent attempt to articulate how spiritual qualities and values can emerge from "below," from the priority of naturalistic experience. Both stages are evident if one contrasts a poem of Richard Wilbur's on incarnation with Robert Lowell's reflections in *Life Studies* on his earlier religious faith and the kind of poetry it had inspired. *Life Studies* might be considered the breaking of the allegorical or incarnational circle, but it is at the same time the transition into specific postmodern modes of articulating new values and poetic methods capable of exploring and witnessing those values.

Richard Wilbur's poetry is based on the tension between the richness of sensory experience and the elaborate patterning of mind. But Wilbur has no metaphysical ground for the dynamic activities of mind exhibited in his poetry, so the poems have difficulty transcending their own elegance and becoming genuine spiritual experiences or witnesses of value. They remain primarily statements *about* experience. "A World Without Objects is a Sensible Emptiness" perfectly exemplifies both Wilbur's considerable talent and the way that talent remains content to present in elegant and undramatic terms the conflicting pulls between a naturalist sense of value and a style based on orthodox views of the poem as balanced artifact:

> The tall camels of the spirit
> Steer for their deserts, passing the last groves loud
> With the sawmill shrill of the locust, to the whole honey of
> the arid
> Sun. They are slow, proud.
>
> And move with a stilted stride
> To the land of sheer horizon, hunting Traherne's
> Sensible emptiness, there where the brain's lantern-slide
> Revels in vast returns.
>
> O connoisseurs of thirst,
> Beasts of my soul who long to learn to drink
> Of pure mirage, those prosperous islands are accurst
> That shimmer on the brink
>
> Of absence; auras, lustres,
> And all shinings need to be shaped and borne.
> Think of those painted saints, capped by the early masters
> With bright, jauntily-worn

> Aureate plates, or even
> Merry-go-round rings. Turn, O turn
> From the fine sleights of the sand, from the long empty oven
> Where flames in flamings burn
>
> Back to the trees arrayed
> In bursts of glare, to the halo-dialling run
> Of the country creeks, and the hills' bracken tiaras made
> Gold in the sunken sun,
>
> Wisely watch for the sight
> Of the supernova burgeoning over the barn,
> Lampshine blurred in the steam of beasts, the spirit's right
> Oasis, light incarnate.[6]

Thematically the poem seeks to reverse Christian notions of the incarnation: the sensible world is source of value and the true home of spirit, with light replacing the word as the principle by which natural process generates meaning and hence value. Yet the style and texture of the poem conflict sharply with the theme. The poem gets its value not from re-presenting the intensity of natural experience but from its qualities as verbal artifice. Its metaphors are neither dramatic nor perceptual, but meditative. The poet does not stand within the oasis of sharply realized particulars; instead his elaborate metaphors and ornate sound play insist on the poem as a space of discourse, a space outside in the desert where the speaker imagines the oasis, reflects on his act of imagination, and arranges it into a kind of verbal clearing—fertile with artificial plants.

Wilbur, of course, is no fool. He knows exactly what he is doing and makes the witty contradiction between verbal and natural vitality the point of the poem. Incarnation to Wilbur is a paradox, to be enjoyed as such and not to be forced to yield a reality outside the fictional worlds of discourse it makes possible. This is, in short, an example of New Critical doctrines of irony and paradox. Now, however, irony and paradox are no longer metaphors for an essentially tragic context in which man must play out his fate and learn humility and sympathy; rather, they are simply the conditions of human discourse to be accepted and enjoyed. Yet how can he simply accept the contradictions of flesh and spirit without seeking in his poetry some way of resolving them or at least of determining priorities and the implications of such a condition for ethical behavior? This, I think, is the question lying behind the frequent attacks on Wilbur for lacking conviction and for wasting his great talent on sheer elegance. Moreover, Wilbur's lack of conviction seems here linked to the poem's playful and perhaps cold impersonality. It did not matter much to his successors that this is not

Eliot's impersonality—for that concept was the stratagem of a man oppressed by his own personality and seeking a larger poetic field of experience in which to place and compose that personality. Instead of seeing impersonality as a desperate quest for fictive order, these poets will concentrate on what it becomes with Wilbur—a means for disengaged, fictive play.

One still, however, must take Wilbur's implied values seriously. They are the values of Western literate man conscious that he can no longer claim special privileges because of his heritage, but content nonetheless with that heritage as the necessary equipment for enjoying the sensible oases he finds or can create out of experience. What Wilbur does not do, though, is follow up the metaphysical implications of the priority he posits for the physical world and of the contradictions between fictive and physical orders with which he plays. In *Life Studies* Robert Lowell will face both those contradictions head on and make it a good deal more difficult for self-respecting poets to maintain a Wilbur-like position without themselves engaging poetically in a reexamination of their values.

Robert Lowell has never been a very playful man, at least in his poetry. In his earlier work he exemplified the more radical and philosophic New Critical style of his masters Tate and Ransom. Yet it is precisely because he took the incarnation so seriously, as the basis for both his religious and his poetic lives, that he could so thoroughly alter those lives when his faith was no longer adequate to sustain their demands. It is a testament to the seriousness with which he took both religion and poetry that his shift from the dense linguistic structures and typology of his earlier mode to the confessional style constitutes the single most important phenomenon in the movement from a modernist to a postmodernist sensibility in American poetry. But one must not misunderstand the revolution he was instrumental in creating by overlooking the essential transitional quality of the self-criticism in *Life Studies*. Many critics have claimed that the confessional style, with its radical emphasis on subjective, psychological experience, was the central style of postmodernism in the sixties.[7] It is difficult, of course, to imagine objective ways of determining the truth value in any claim for the centrality of a given style, but from the perspective of recent poetry and poetics it seems clear that, important as it was, confessional poetry is perhaps best seen as the necessary radical break with modernism that allowed other less extreme and self-destructive modes to develop. Confessional poetry broke with symbolism and popularized ideals of presence and immediacy, but, as I shall soon demonstrate, its particular version of these ideals seemed much too solipsistic and extreme to solve the poets' needs for new nonhumanist values.

Lowell's *Life Studies* provides the terms one needs to comprehend the historical genesis of confessional poetry. The volume, taken as a unified set of poems, both interprets Lowell's own break with his past and self-consciously reflects on the implications of the new mode he is creating. The volume's first poem, "Beyond the Alps," introduces the break with the past by returning with a fresh perspective to the oppositions between natural process and an incarnational structure of values. On the one side, the poem indicates, are Rome, altitude, secular and religious authorities, church dogma, traditional symbols, and the heroic classical world; on the other, Paris breaking up, earth, landscape, and "pure prose." The old values have become fictions that no longer meet the test of fact or keep off Stevens's "pressure of reality." Mussolini is not the reincarnation of an Imperial Rome but "one of us / only, pure prose"; the pope's devotional candles are offset by his purring electric razor. Even Paris, the city of art, which might restore a Hellas or a viable paganism to replace Rome's authority, cannot do so, for it is breaking up. Man's dream of conquering mountains has not prevailed, and the train must "come to earth" for Lowell to begin the search anew. These oppositions are summarized in the line "Life changed to landscape," which one critic rightly sees could "serve as an epigraph for the volume as a whole."[8] For this line dramatizes Lowell's sense of the only models of meaning left when an essentially vertical symbolic order grounded by the doctrine of incarnation gives way to a primarily horizontal secular one. Landscape is the perfect secular horizontal form of art, for it has no objective center of meaning and depends for its resonance entirely on details and implications created by the painter's stance in relation to his materials. Landscape reveals no hierarchy, nothing valuable in itself. Its horizontality opposes both the typologies of Christianity and the symbolism of Romanticism where specific objects and actions take on sacred or privileged existences.

To appreciate what is at stake in this shift to landscape, one needs to examine a typical early poem based both thematically and stylistically on the incarnation as the reconciliation of secular experience with a timeless vertical order giving events significance. The typological style of "Colloquy in Black Rock" depends on the poet's ability to find patterns and symbolic schema capable of investing a moment of intense vision with intellectual and ethical significance. And thematically the poem depends literally on the incarnation as the typological moment that transforms suffering into value:

> Here the jack-hammer jabs into the ocean;
> My heart, you race and stagger and demand
> More blood-gangs for your nigger-brass percussions,
> Till I, the stunned machine of your devotion,

Clanging upon this cymbal of a hand,
Am rattled screw and footloose. All discussions

End in the mud-flat detritus of death.
My heart, beat faster, faster. In Black Mud
Hungarian workmen give their blood
For the martyre Stephen, who was stoned to death.

Black Mud, a name to conjure with: O mud
For watermelons gutted to the crust,
Mud for the mole-tide harbor, mud for mouse,
Mud for the armored Diesel fishing tubs that thud
A year and a day to wind and tide; the dust
Is on this skipping heart that shakes my house,

House of our Savior who was hanged till death.
My heart, beat faster, faster. In Black Mud
Stephen the martyre was broken down to blood:
Our ransom is the rubble of his death.

Christ walks on the black water. In Black Mud
Darts the kingfisher. On Corpus Christi, heart,
Over the drum-beat of St. Stephen's choir
I hear him, *Stupor Mundi*, and the mud
Flies from his hunching wings and beak—my heart,
The blue kingfisher dives on you in fire.[9]

The poem's predominant motif is the horror of mud as a symbol for
the all-leveling naturalistic world whose final conquest is the "mud-flat
detritus of death." Emerging from the poem's intense rhetoric, however,
are a series of typological relationships between suffering, martyrdom,
and the act of building the church, which establishes the alternative
possibility of redemption from this natural death. The poem then asserts
the power of redemption by two figures who gather the preceding themes
into their symbolic presence. First the protomartyr Steven integrates
the different sufferings of Lowell and the laborers into an image of the
creative role of suffering. But while Steven dies into the mud so that
others might live, Christ comes to illustrate how dying can be the way
to victory over the mud in this life. Christ comes in the traditional
symbolic form of the kingfisher, a literal enactment of the descent of
the vertical order into time, so that the destructive images of mud and
blood can be transformed into purifying fire and life-giving blood sacrifice. The traditional quality of this closing image, then, itself contributes
to the redemptive act. First of all, the traditional image suggests an
order of significance free of time, where fire and blood are spiritual
principles, not empirical destructive forces. Also one is tempted to

reflect that images endure because they have been effective, and the endurance of the kingfisher image suggests that the redemption imaged here is not mere fantasy but a process recurrent in human history. It is perhaps because images endure that typology is possible, for beneath that endurance must be a single spiritual principle shared in by diverse temporal acts and circumstances.

How different it is when one crosses the Alps from Rome to Paris and must imagine landscape as his artistic model. Lowell's insistence on the oppressive reality of the "prose" world indicates the historical and philosophical implications of his journey. For where poetry once defined itself in allegorical and symbolic terms, it now must recognize that it must take what sustenance it can from the affinities it shares with the novel, with the view of literary art developed when men turned from God to the landscape. The novel is the literary form born from the death of the epic.[10]

In all great epics, a vertical force—fate or destiny or the gods— invests the actions with significance and creates the values defining noble conduct. In the novel, on the other hand, action and value tend to be defined horizontally—by the flux of history, by the sociological conditions of the novel world, and by the interactions of the characters. Lowell's task then is to accept the empirical reductions of the old values to mere fictions, but not to stop there. He must suffer the pains of a naturalistic world—hence the volume's pervasive animal images and Lowell's stress on the past as the field of quest; but he must, at the same time, transform the landscape by finding through his suffering a secular basis for value that will make endurance possible. Lowell expresses this manner of quest most succinctly in a review of Robert Penn Warren's *Brother to Dragons*, where he speculates on poetry's need to reabsorb the prose world: "Eternal providence has warned us that our world lies all before us and nowhere else. Only the fissured atoms which destroyed Hiroshima and Nagasaki can build our New Atlantis" (*PG*, p. 120). Lowell's "New Atlantis" (the image is Plato's) will retain most of the old humanistic values, but now the values will be secularly grounded. Lowell calls these poems in *Life Studies* that seek the New Atlantis "more religious than the early ones" (*PR*, p. 352), but religion now is immanent and not transcendental, more informed by the dynamic qualities of natural experience than informing that experience with meaningful patterns.[11]

For value to emerge in the prose world, the poet must develop a style that can convey its glimpses of meaning within contingency without the aid of allegorical or paradigmatic structures. Poems must appear to remain faithful to the casual flux of experience even while actions and qualities recur so that some kind of generalization, however problematic, can make its appearance. What the mind seeks to bring together seems to yield a little, but nonetheless remains essentially rooted in a horizontal world, asserting its own inviolable uniqueness. Lowell solves the problem of making his poems seem contingent and moments of direct experience while providing patterns allowing interpretive structures by appropriating techniques from the prose tradition. He makes the primary source of interpretive meaning the volume as a whole. Hence what appears casual and momentary in individual poems becomes resonant and yields general significance when the reader learns to relate the instance, expression, or image to similar ones in other poems and to seek out a dramatic structure for the entire volume. I have worked out these patterns and their structure at some length in an essay on *Life Studies*,[12] so here I shall content myself with summarizing those patterns and showing how they all contribute to the climactic poem "Skunk Hour." As these patterns culminate in that poem, one can see the poem itself as a final interpretation of the confessional process leading up to it.

Thematically, the dramatic movement of the volume develops the quest exemplified in "Beyond the Alps." First the volume explores the tragedy of decaying fictions—in the culture as a whole and then in Lowell's private life. Left without external models of authority and faced with his own breakdown, Lowell must come to some self-definition. Yet his only materials for that definition are the *disjecta membra* of his own past and those of fellow artists in the same situation. The confessional style, then, is inextricable from the cultural and personal breakdowns that make one's self-consciousness at once the only imaginative force and the only locus of materials one can employ to achieve some tentative balance with the prose world. Finally, after articulating that plight, Lowell manages to wrest from the flux some bases for value and a source of dignity.

Complementing the dramatic movement are three patterns of recurrent images and actions that allow the intellect to interpret and grasp the emotional resonance of the contingent events. The first two patterns balance one another. Recurrent animal images (for example, in "The Banker's Daughter," "Mad Negro Soldier Confined at Munich," and "My Last Afternoon with Uncle Devereux Winslow") evoke the metaphysical and psychological plight of men deprived of transcendence and condemned to an essentially biological frame of reference. Reinforcing this subhuman state are repeated images of failed authority figures—pope, president, father, and ancestors—who should mediate the child from natural existence into a meaningful social order and provide him with viable models of human conduct. No wonder that a child "quite without hero-worship for my father, who actually seemed so inferior to the photographs in uniform he once mailed to us" (*LS*, p. 13) should find himself in an asylum seeking to define his identity amid a society of men all imaged as animals:

> After a hearty New England breakfast,
> I weigh two hundred pounds
> this morning. Cock of the walk,
> I strut in my turtle-necked French sailor's jersey
> before the metal shaving mirrors,
> and see the shaky future grow familiar
> in the pinched, indigenous faces
> of these thoroughbred mental cases,
> twice my age and half my weight.
> We are all old-timers,
> each of us holds a locked razor.
>
> (*LS*, p. 76)

Even the domestic order of life, that simplest and perhaps most assuring form of culture, is now horribly reversed and offers only momentary terror and a sense of time as infinite repetition. No wonder also that Lowell's isolation leaves him only the mirror as means for self-definition and for reconciling inner and outer realities. Yet this mirror is no ordinary domestic mirror: to see oneself in a metal mirror is here not to be given back one's ordinary selfhood but to be reminded, in the very attempt to grasp the self, how close one is to self-destruction. Even the ordinary tools of cultural life, like the razor, now are potential elements for suicide.

The one way beyond the mirror for Lowell is to find some form of communication or communion. Indeed, the dominant quest in the first three sections of the volume is for some form of communication, some external source of consolation. But the closest Lowell comes to a feeling of communion is his sense of sharing Hart Crane's plight. This identification, however, only drives him back to the solipsism of confession, "Who asks for me, the Shelley of my age, / must lay his heart out for my bed and board" (*LS*, p. 53). Yet in the midst of these failures, Lowell establishes a set of recurrent images of eating, which allow him to deepen the symbolic implications of his final encounter with the skunk. The volume progresses from the demonic, subhuman "feeding" of the mad Negro soldier, through the more humane pathos of his drinking with Delmore Schwartz to his identification with the skunk's quest for sustenance, a quest John Berryman sees as culminating in a parody of the Eucharist (*O*, 99–104). The basic context for Lowell's gradual recovery of ritual possibilities is provided by "Home After

Three Months Away." For in this poem Lowell nicely returns to his
earlier references to shaving in order to mark a recognition that domestic
life need not repeat the farce played out by his parents. The domestic
context can, in fact, provide a secular approximation of the symbolic
order by making shaving a kind of ritual and creating a sense of
shared humanity that redeems animal references. The reference to himself as a polar bear becomes now a playful epithet and allows him to
play a role that creates a moment of tender love.

The possible redeeming qualities of domestic life enable the starker
context of "Skunk Hour" to provide a somewhat satisfactory conclusion
to the volume's spiritual journey. In the context of the entire volume,
"Skunk Hour" articulates a ground of values that make it possible to
endure, if not to overcome, the anxieties of contemporary life and the
loss of traditional grounds for value. The poem first of all embodies
the ultimate lucidity, the denial of all imaginative evasions, which Lowell
has been seeking. This then brings him to a dark night of the soul,
a traditional religious image he takes now as "secular, puritan and agnos-
tical" (O, p. 107). There he encounters the ultimate nothingness or
absence of meaning, which is perhaps the result of all pursuits of sheer
lucidity (I am thinking of the nineteenth-century novel, particularly of
Flaubert). For Lowell the absence is dual—an emptiness he witnesses
in the scene of perverted love among the love cars, mirrored by a horrifying sense of his own inner emptiness, "I myself am hell; / nobody's
here." Hell here is the ultimate prose—a profound sense of the absence
of all sources of meaning and value in the public world represented by
the landscape and in the private realm where one defines his personal
identity. Yet Lowell has not lost his imaginative sense of redemptive
archetypes; having fallen to the depths of despair where the ascent
beckons, Lowell turns to the skunk—the figure of whatever possibilities
Lowell can find for a secular redemption from his despair:

> A car radio bleats,
> "Love, O careless Love. . . ." I hear
> my ill-spirit sob in each blood cell,
> as if my hand were at its throat. . . .
> I myself am hell;
> nobody's here—
>
> only skunks, that search
> in the moonlight for a bite to eat.
> They march on their soles up Main Street:
> white stripes, moonstruck eyes' red fire
> under the chalk-dry and spar spire
> of the Trinitarian Church.

I stand on top
of our back steps and breathe the rich air—
a mother skunk with her column of kittens swills the garbage
    pail.
She jabs her wedge-head in a cup
of sour cream, drops her ostrich tail,
and will not scare.

Thematically the skunk resolves several problems in the volume. By returning to the prereflective natural order symbolized by the many animal images, Lowell makes the skunk embody the determination and self-concern of all living beings and beyond that, as mother, a willingness to face danger in order to accept the responsibility of her role. (Family existence once again has value independent of all fictive or interpretative frames.) Now one sees both a parody of the Eucharist and, on another level, a genuine moment of communion, for, as the skunk swills from the garbage pail, Lowell finds precisely the image of endurance and survival he had sought in vain in the rest of the volume. In fact, Lowell's evening service to some extent reverses one of the final images of his father's impotence. For Commander Lowell's lettering his garbage cans was a pathetic alternative to Sunday church service he saw as beneath the dignity of a naval man. Here the very order his father so stupidly rejected is recovered precisely through those images of modern emptiness.

As the skunk makes her way beneath the "chalk-dry church spire" reminding the reader of the dead vertical world, she embodies whatever possibilities Lowell can find for restoring a context of value within secular and biological necessity. These possibilities are not very encouraging; man may learn to endure, but it must be with a dogged single-minded concentration that omits much of the old humanist possibilities for human development and enjoyment of the world. And the poetic process itself calls one's attention to these reduced possibilities. The skunk here plays the resolving role performed by Christ in much of *Lord Weary's Castle*. Christ as a resolving figure functions "metaphorically"; he pulls into himself all the disparate strands and adds an element that completes them and develops their meaning. Thus Christ's suffering both gives Lowell a personal meaning and adds to it a value not evident within secular experience. Lowell imaginatively participates in the same metaphorical project as poet by having the details he uses in describing Christ, particularly the name kingfisher and the redeeming fire, both define and give value to Lowell's pulsing blood and his resistance to the mud. (Only because Christ evokes an entire mythic structure, a structure of metaphors, can such specific details do so much work.) The skunk, on the other hand, functions metonymically. The analogy between man and skunk now creates only a partial contiguous resolution, so that the summary remains incomplete and ambiguous in relation to the conditions being explained. The presence of the skunk, in other words, forces on the reader a solution to the poem's despair, but it is a solution that does not incorporate the human and religious terms in which the despair had been framed. The analogical link, then, between Lowell and the skunk's not-quite-human resolve to endure can only be known sympathetically. The relation is too complex and diffuse for analysis, and the identification of man and skunk too foreign to one's sensibilities for there to be a completely affirmative resolution.[13] Finally, Lowell's identification with the skunk provides an emblem for the confessional style in the volume. Lowell learned in "Words for Hart Crane" that self-analysis and debasement were the preconditions for salvation in the American Wasteland. Now the skunk summarizes what it means to search for value and self-definition when all the sustaining fictions have failed. One is left only with the garbage of one's own past, which he must have the determination to explore and the courage to endure: "With Berryman, too, I go on a strange journey! Thank God, we both came out clinging to spars, enough floating matter to save us, though faithless" (O, p. 110).

Lowell's secular salvation frees his later work from the need to continue the personal confessional mode, but that work bears sufficient traces of Life Studies to make other poets remain uneasy about Lowell's authority. Having found a provisional basis for overcoming despair, Lowell tries to get off the tightrope and to explore more ordinary kinds of experience in a less intense, more reflective manner.[14] But the very terms of those explorations continue to be shaped by the values defined in Life Studies. First of all, the central contrast between the naturalistic prose world and the fictions generated by consciousness to make sense of that world remains a basic theme. The tension tends to shift from psychological to ontological concerns, but poem after poem sets the self-possession and indifferent temporal processes of the natural order in mocking contrast to the weak human consciousness seeking to express its own values and to find meanings not subject either to temporal decay or to the ironic indifference of the landscape. Yet Lowell's concentration on these oppositions in effect creates a context in which self-pity can give way to cosmic pity (see NO, p. 24), self-absorption to the tentative construction of a human community based on a humble grasp of the shared human condition. Much of Notebook, as I shall demonstrate, seems devoted to articulating a contemporary version of tragic wisdom, and, at the thematic center of that volume, one finds

Lowell summarizing its basic sense of value, "We are all here for such a short time, / we might as well be good to one another" (*NB*, p. 136).

Lowell's developing tragic sense, however, cannot easily overcome the intense privacy he associates with the fall into prose. In *Life Studies* the decay of cultural fictions and the consequent naturalism required that the person's sense of his own meaning be based on immediate tangible experience that could not be universalized. At best one could trust as valuable and meaningful only one's own vitality and those sharing one's domestic existence. This creates a radical tension between public and private realms that Hannah Arendt claims, with good reason, to characterize the development of Western culture. Lowell's finest rendering of this dilemma occurs in the two concluding summary poems of *For the Union Dead*. "Night Sweat" focuses on the way domestic life can generate a limited sense of values within the flux, while "For the Union Dead" embodies the terrors facing one when he turns outward to the contemporary public scene.

"Night Sweat" confronts Lowell's deepest fears about the flux—that surrender to it is really submission to the death instinct:

> my life's fever is soaking in night sweat—
> one life, one writing! But the downward glide
> and bias of existing wrings us dry—
> always inside me is the child who died,
> always inside me is his will to die—
> one universe, one body . . . in this urn
> the animal night sweats of the spirit burn.

Set against his own materiality and involvement in the dark "troubled waters" (an image that, along with the sweat, ties this poem to the destructive waters in the rest of the volume), Lowell sees "the lightness" of his wife:

> my wife . . . your lightness alters everything,
> and tears the black web from the spider's sack,
> as your heart hops and flutters like a hare.
> Poor turtle, tortoise, if I cannot clear
> the surface of these troubled waters here,
> absolve me, help me, Dear Heart, as you bear
> this world's dead weight and cycle on your back.

These lines recall the redeeming domestic context of "Home After Three Months Away," but the tone is more meditative and the situation more complex. Now the domestic context is an adult one, and it demands a complexity of tone incompatible with the anguished voice of confession. Here Lowell at once plays with and takes absolutely seriously the situation and his own medium. How silly to image an aging wife resisting time by assuming absurd exercise postures that evoke mythic properties! Yet the poem's own thematic play between weight and lightness is echoed tonally through the fact that the speaker is oppressed by time and materiality and hence *is* "the world's dead weight" her presence sustains. The domestic situation and the power of love create a linguistic space where the common myth of the tortoise as supporter of the world can be entertained wittily (as Wilbur might) and at the same time made serious and momentarily apt. In a complex way, the very absurdity of domestic love restores to Lowell possibilities for mythic dimensions of experience lost in "Beyond the Alps," and it does so in a manner whereby the fictive quality of myths is no longer a problem. It is precisely by utilizing their fictiveness that one creates complex tones and understands how myths can tie into prosaic emotional experience.

Behind this successful domestication of myth, however, there lies a deeper tragedy. With myth so localized, a deeper gap opens between private and public realms of experience. In the public realm myths cannot be dependent on wry wit or effective only in specific contexts of experience. The eros Lowell sets against the death wish is most emphatically not an oceanic feeling, and the corollary of so localized a sense of value is a profound despair at the possibility of effective social action. Lowell's characteristic public poem moves from the rage of *Lord Weary's Castle* to the pathetic contrast one finds in *Notebook* between the weak individual and the oppressive weight of a blind, huge, impersonal, and destructive society.[15] "For the Union Dead" is Lowell's most profound and most frightening evocation of the contrast that will more and more permeate his work. In part, at least, "For the Union Dead" presents the conflict between fictive dream and prose realities, this time in the form of a confusion between cultural and natural orders. The second and third stanzas present Lowell's bleakly contemplating a city landscape reduced to almost sheer nature and tempting him to deny his own cultural self, to submit to the utter prose of "the dark, downward and vegetating kingdom." Again pure prose is linked with Freud's *thanatos*. To resist this atavistic urge, Lowell turns for support to culture, hoping that it can provide acceptable definitions of specifically human actions. But in this poem the cultural order is completely empty—reduced to the lowest, most vicious modes of natural behavior. Hence the "dinosaur steamshovels," the Yeatsean turn from loved buildings to the muddy ditch, and the savage concluding lines:

> The Aquarium is gone. Everywhere,
> giant finned cars nose forward like fish;
> a savage servility
> slides by on grease.

The despair can be measured by a contrast with "Skunk Hour." There the savagery of the skunk was part of an epiphany, reminding cultured man of natural principles of values. In "For the Union Dead" the reader first sees culture's destroying the natural garden and the Aquarium where culture and nature had reached a kind of balance, then in turn the ugly, mechanical aspects of that cultured order are reduced to the savage servility of the cars' becoming fish (with serpent-like qualities). "Savage servility" combines the worst aspects of uncontrolled nature and overcontrolled culture with its machines and propaganda. And without a viable culture, neither communication nor interpretation is possible. The conclusion leaves not even a metonymic trace of hope; only a bleak perversity occupies the public stage.

In *For the Union Dead* Lowell preserves the sense of survival he achieved in *Life Studies*, but the very reflective freedom this gives him only deepens his awareness of how limited is the realm of values he can trust. There can be little doubt that his critics were correct in seeing much of the volume as excessively passive and self-pitying.[16] Still there are many ways in which his fidelity to the quest defined in "Beyond the Alps" justifies these features of his work. Indeed *Notebook*, his last volume during the sixties, can be seen as a deliberate justification for and exploration of the condition of passive self-pity. Here Lowell envisions the prose world and the demonic, paralyzing social order as requiring an essentially passive vision, for that passivity is necessary in order to reach the only mode of freedom that history still grants —the freedom of tragic vision. Consider first the implications of the title *Notebook*. John Reed points out that Lowell shifts from life studies, an artistic form composing experience into tentative patterns, to notebooks, the raw materials of the artist's experience. To be true to his sense of flux and of the prose world, the poet more and more imagines himself a "vehicle for" rather than a composer of his experiences. But, as Robert Boyers argues, precisely by becoming a vehicle for experience, Lowell has articulated a poetic stance adequate for envisioning value in a demythified world. He presents himself as accepting all, and hence as capable of a complete lucidity free from the temptation to create myths or structures that soon appear to be mere escapist fiction.[17] In passive acceptance Lowell finds his muted version of meditative tragic joy: "The reader has a sense of the poet as somehow equal to everything he describes."

If one ignores for the moment the potentially ironic pun on "equal," one can see that Lowell has in this volume achieved the ontological, if not the ethical and communal, dimensions of the tragic vision. He has become a poet of the possible. His lucid cosmic scope makes quite clear the pathos of the human condition, and within that condition he can approve and wonder at the sympathies and mutual understanding realized by those who see their plight. At their best, the poems include the reader in Lowell's charmed circle of those who, because of their despair, have developed the power to appreciate the limited joys and moments of shared feeling or clear insight that are all one can have. Value exists within the prose world and within the domestic context of shared feelings because men can be conscious of their dilemmas, and they can articulate and share them. Compare with the violence at the end of "Beyond the Alps" the acceptance of falling in *Notebook*, presented in a cadence no other American poet of the age can equal:

> this not the greatest thing, though great; the hours
> of shivering, ache and burning, when we'd charged
> so far beyond our courage—altitudes,
> then the falling . . . falling back on honest speech:
> infirmity, a food the flesh must swallow,
> feeding our minds . . . the mind which is also flesh.
>
> (*NB*, pp. 105–6)

Acceptance as Lowell images it, however, makes for a tragic vision composed entirely of moments of intense awareness of man's position in history and in a natural order dominated by death and decay. There are not, as in Yeats or even in Stevens, possibilities of glimpsing through tragedy the hope of more capacious civilized orders, and there is no body of Pentheus the witnesses to fatality can hope to reassemble. The very passivity of Lowell's style leaves no room for the counterassertive will one desires in tragedy: for Lowell there is only prose lucidity, no dream of a lucidity beyond an essentially empirical consciousness that is content to mirror external conditions. We are "only in touch with what we touch" (*NB*, p. 259), and hence unable to trust any fictive orders invoking contexts that cannot be located in immediate reality. Tragic vision then entails not reconciling opposites but recognizing that "Some alternatives have no answer; Time must answer" (*NB*, p. 242), and the Coleridgean symbolist dream itself becomes doubly a victim of time. The poet can feel public problems, but he is untrue to his visions of authenticity when he poses solutions for those problems. Thus Lowell's poem on Che Guevara gradually surrenders its initial moral vision to the flux:

> Week of Che Guevara, hunted, hurt,
> held prisoner one lost day, then gangstered down
> for gold, for justice—violence cracking on violence,
> rock on rock the corpse of the last armed prophet
> laid out on a sink in a shed, revealed by flashlight—

as the leaves light up, still green, this afternoon,
and burn to frittered reds; as the oak, branch-lopped
to go on living, swells with goiters like a fruit-tree,
as the sides of the high white stone buildings over-
shadow the poor, too new in the new world,
Manhattan, where our clasped, illicit hands
pulse, stop the bloodstream as if it hit rock. . . .
Rest for the outlaw . . . kings once hid in oaks,
watch prices on their heads, and watched for game.

(*NB*, p. 53)

Instead of becoming a focus for some mode of analysis and interpretation, the vision of Che's body disintegrates into a series of vague associations expressing the pathos of Lowell's private response (associations, one might add, that bring images far less striking than the initial object). The only structure for experience for Lowell is the cyclic patterns of the seasons, within which opposites are not so much reconciled as placed in a perpetually destructive interchange.

Lowell's one attack on this process of enervation is his practice of cultivating moments of vision: "He is groping for trout in the private river, / wherever it opens, wherever it happens to come" (*NB*, p. 100). Unfortunately, the river always seems to open for incisive epigrams at the conclusion of the poem. This quest for the epigram and its use as the conclusion of so many poems brings a curious aestheticism back into a deliberately antiformalist style. The poem is no longer dramatic event or exploration but the vehicle for intense moments, and perhaps even more for incisive statements about those moments. One can suspect that the epigrams are cultivated not so much for their existential value but in order that Lowell, too, (like the poets and friends he so often quotes) can make clever contributions to those lightened moments of family love and good fellowship. Again truth's public dimension is subjugated to the private and limited. Truth becomes the property of individual consciousness seeking moments the flesh can cherish before it dies. The confessional style has surrendered its inwardness and its extreme tensions, but it retains its ontology and its tragic egoism.

Lowell was (until his death in 1977) without much question America's greatest active poet: his verse has an authority, cadence, and intelligence that approximates Yeats. But the very intensity and intelligence he offers create problems in understanding how to take his work. One can, for example, view his work in terms of his later self-image as a spiritual historian of his age. Then one can have little quarrel with him. Both the nervous egotism of *Life Studies* and the passive

lucidity of his more public poetry become images measuring the difficulties of imaginatively surviving what intellectual and social history
have made of modern American life. From this point of view one is
less concerned with Lowell's specific beliefs than with his skill in dramatizing the necessity for such desperate conceptual and poetic strategies,
and one can view even his passive tragic vision as a triumphant assertion of imaginative lucidity. But younger poets were not so prone to
grant the age's most authoritative poet such distance from his own
stated beliefs, nor were they so willing to accept the cure of a tragic
vision, particularly in times as rife with conflict, hope, and demands
for action as the sixties. Hence these poets took Lowell's desolate introspection as blind egotism, as an unwillingness to attend carefully to
possible sources of value outside the self. Similarly, what Lowell projects
as a passive lucidity required by history, they understood as a surrender
of the imagination to external social forces and an inability to transcend
history. From this perspective, the tragic vision seems a tragic loss of
vision, and Lowell's desperate attempts to recover traces of humanism
in terms of a sense of community dependent on that vision appear as a
clear index of how bankrupt the humanist tradition has become. Reading
Notebook one is tempted to ask, "Hast thou given all to 'culture' and
hast thou come to this?" The humanist might point out that it is not
the tradition that fails, but Lowell who fails it—precisely because he
accepts the contemporary trend to distrust universals and the myth-
making or myth-restoring imagination. It is indeed ironic that Lowell's
despair stems from the fact that his fidelity to the prose world has
brought him very close to positions shared by many of those poets
who disparage him: Lowell insists that experience must be conceived
as process and that value must emerge from "below" within that process;
he shares their disdain for mechanistic bourgeois culture; and, finally,
he has come to reject the fallacy of individualism and its poetics of the
psychological tightrope (see *NB*, pp. 147, 208).

But Lowell's middle ground does seem untenable. He cannot escape
his beginnings, cannot merge his humanism with his sense of the prose
world, and thus seems condemned to nostalgia or to another version
of the enclave theory so common to humanists from Arnold through
Eliot. Oppressed by the residue of his Christian expectations, he can
never face the prose world without a sense of tragic loss. And driven by
his humanist sense that a viable culture depends on the active presence
of collective myths and shared ideals, he can never view his contemporary society without "optimism of will, pessimism of intelligence" (*NB*,
p. 182). If humanism is really to be rejected and if man is to learn
to face the prose world without despair or self-pitying nostalgia, it may

be that we must turn to younger or more alienated poets who never shared Lowell's religious and cultural dreams. Yet the integrity of Lowell's quest leaves for me serious doubts whether these poets might be masking optimism of will as optimism of intelligence. The new myths may well be building new Romes.

Notes to Chapter 2

1. Josephine Miles, *The Primary Language of Poetry in the 1940's* (Berkeley, Calif.: University of California Press, 1951), pp. 384, 408, 466.

2. See, especially for Ransom, his "The Concrete Universal: Observations on the Understanding of Poetry," *John Crowe Ransom: Poems and Essays* (New York: Vintage, 1955), pp. 159–85, and idem, "Poetry: a Note on Ontology," in *Modern Criticism: Theory and Practice*, ed. Walter Sutton and Richard Foster (New York: Odyssey, 1963), pp. 221–33; and for Tate the essays I have over-simplified "Tension in Poetry" and "Three Types of Poetry" in his *Essays of Four Decades* (New York: William Morrow, 1970), pp. 56–71, 173–95.

3. For a good discussion of the problem in philosophically reconciling universals and particulars, see George Lukacs, *History and Class Consciousness* (Cambridge, Mass.: MIT Press, 1969), pp. 114–48. On the importance of the incarnation metaphor to the new critics, see Murray Krieger, *The Tragic Vision* (Chicago: University of Chicago Press, 1960), pp. 238–41, and idem, *The New Apologists For Poetry* (Bloomington, Ind.: University of Indiana Press, 1963). This second book is largely devoted to showing how the incarnation metaphor supports the new critical enterprise of redeeming poetry from the Scylla and Charybdis of naturalism and irrelevance.

4. This change in literary circumstances breeds modern ironic theories of allegories like those of Walter Benjamin and Paul de Man.

5. T. S. Eliot, "Second Thoughts About Humanism," in *T. S. Eliot: Selected Essays*, ed. Ezra Pound (New York: Harcourt, Brace, 1950), p. 433.

6. *The Poems of Richard Wilbur* (New York: Harcourt, Brace & World, 1963), p. 117.

7. See Ralph Mills, *Creation's Very Self; On The Personal Element in Recent American Poetry* (Fort Worth, Tex.: Texas Christian University Press, 1969), and M. L. Rosenthal, *The New Poets* (New York: Oxford University Press, 1967). I must point out that some time and a few suicides have passed; their remarks were accurate when written.

8. Jerome Mazzaro, *The Poetic Themes of Robert Lowell* (Ann Arbor, Mich.: University of Michigan Press, 1965), p. 90. In some versions of the poem (see *For the Union Dead*) the line reads, "Man changed to landscape." Mazzaro also points out the motif of animal imagery and connects it with the problem of finding secular values, but my specific focus on the theme of secular values leads me to reject his claims for corollary stresses on Poundian culture and secular immortality. Hugh Staples has a relevant reading of "Beyond the Alps" in his *Robert Lowell: The First Twenty Years* (New York: Columbia University Press, 1962), p. 72. He points out that the poem's journey establishes a metaphor that

includes many other transitions in the volume and concludes in "Skunk Hour."
Irvin Ehrenpreis makes several interesting comments on the differing functions
of Rome and Paris in the poem in "The Age of Lowell," in *Robert Lowell: A
Collection of Critical Essays*, ed. Thomas Parkinson (Englewood Cliffs, N.J.:
Prentice Hall, 1968). Lowell elaborates on an opposition of Alpine and prosaic
worlds in the opening paragraphs of "I.A. Richards as a Poet," *Encounter* 14
(February 1960) : 77–78.

9. *Lord Weary's Castle* (New York: Meridian, 1946), p. 5. I use the following
abbreviations for Lowell's work: *Life Studies* (New York: Farrar, Straus, &
Giroux, 1959), *LS*; *For the Union Dead* (New York: Farrar, Straus, & Giroux,
1964), *FUD*; *Near the Ocean* (New York: Farrar, Straus, & Giroux, 1967), *NO*;
Notebook, third edition revised and expanded (New York: Farrar, Straus, &
Giroux, 1970), *NB*; "Skunk Hour" in Anthony Ostroff's *The Contemporary Poet
as Artist and Critic* (Boston: Beacon, 1964), *O*; "Interview," *Writers at Work: The
Paris Review Interviews, Second Series* (New York: Viking, 1965), *PR*; "Prose
Genius in Verse," *Kenyon Reivew* 15 (1953), *PG*; "A Talk with Robert Lowell,"
Encounter 24 (1965), *AT*; "Robert Lowell in Conversation with A. Alvarez," *The
Review*, no. 8 (August 1963), *RL*.

10. This view of the novel is supported by George Lukacs, *Theory of the
Novel*, trans. Anna Bostock (London: Merlin Press, 1971), by Ian Watt's famous
Rise of the Novel: Studies in Defoe, Richardson, Fielding (Berkeley, Calif.: University of California Press, 1957), and by J. Hillis Miller, *The Form of Victorian
Fiction* (South Bend, Ind.: University of Notre Dame Press, 1968), who stresses
the horizontal nature of the novel world as a Victorian phenomenon arising from
the death of God. However, the contrast between *Paradise Lost* and, say, Defoe's
work, a contrast pointed out to me by my colleague Roy Roussel, makes one
locate at least the roots of Miller's description of the novel in the very beginnings
of the form. Also relevant is Herbert Schneidau, *Ezra Pound: The Image and the
Real* (Baton Rouge, La.: Louisiana State University Press, 1969), which studies
Pound's debt to Ford Madox Ford and the aesthetics of prose realism.

11. The best treatment of Lowell's early style is contained in Jerome Mazzaro,
"Robert Lowell and The Kavanaugh Collapse," *University of Windsor Review*
5 (Fall 1969) : 1–24. Lowell's own comments on *Life Studies* stress his move from
a symbolic to an experience-oriented style and equate this new style with prose
and with a reliance on the secular world. In the *Paris Review Interview*, he
discusses the novel as "the ideal modern form" (*PR*, p. 343) and claims that
prose is freer from rhetoric than poetry and closer to experience and vitality (*PR*,
pp. 345–46). In his essay on "Skunk Hour" and again in an interview with
Alvarez, he talks about the prose of Flaubert, and especially of Chekhov, as
models for his new style (*O*, p. 108; *RL*, p. 36). Some of the terms for this paragraph
also derive from Frank Kermode, *The Sense of An Ending: Studies in the Theory
of Fiction* (New York: Oxford University Press, 1967), pp. 133–50.

12. Charles Altieri, "Poetry in a Prose World: Robert Lowell's *Life Studies*,"
Modern Poetry Studies 1 (1970) : 182–98.

13. I take the terms *metaphor* and *metonymy* from Roman Jacobson and Claude
Levi-Strauss. Marjorie Perloff, "Realism and the Confessional Mode of Robert
Lowell," *Contemporary Literature* 11 (1970) : 470–87 uses the shift in Lowell from
metaphor to metonymy to discuss the artistic use of realistic details in *Life Studies*
and to suggest that this metonymic poetry marks a major postmodernist break
with the symbolist styles of Romantic and modernist poetry. She uses Jacobson
but not Levi-Strauss, who makes possible a more philosophical reading of the

difference between metaphor and metonymy. In *The Savage Mind* (Chicago: University of Chicago Press, 1966), pp. 228 ff., Levi-Strauss links metaphoric organization of experience with societies essentially outside history (so absolute homology is possible between different events seen in terms of a larger structure) and metonymic organization with societies involved in history and thus condemned to seeing events as at best only contingently related to each other. The distinction is important for at least three reasons: (1) it helps explain the deep connections between the novel, realism, and a culture turning toward secular, historicist perspectives on experience; (2) it underlies the necessity felt by the Coleridgean tradition to reconcile and unify opposites and thus, at least within art, restore a metaphorical frame for otherwise contingent and ultimately irreconcilable events (incarnation, especially in Augustine, is the metaphor for the possibility of a timeless reality informing the flux); (3) it clarifies why even the contemporaries, despite Ms. Perloff, seek to find universals like "Being" or "Gottnatur" within secular experience that essentially deny the reality of historical process and allow otherwise contingent events to share a common and timeless reality. See my "Objective Image and Act of Mind in Modern Poetry," *PMLA* 91 (1976): 101–14, for fuller discussion of metonymy.

14. Jay Martin, *Robert Lowell* (Minneapolis, Minn.: University of Minnesota Press, 1970), p. 35, cites a letter from Lowell to M. L. Rosenthal shortly after the completion of *Life Studies*: "Something not to be said again was said. I feel drained, and know nothing except that the next outpouring will have to be unimaginably different—an altered style, more impersonal matter, a new main artery of emphasis and inspiration." I suspect that Lowell reprints "Beyond the Alps" in *FUD* not just to satisfy John Berryman's desire to have an omitted stanza restored, but to relate this volume with its different orientation to the same crisis inspiring *Life Studies*.

15. Two interesting studies of the relation between the private and the public in Lowell deserve mention here: R. K. Meiners, *Everything to be Endured: An Essay on Robert Lowell and Modern Poetry* (Columbia, Mo.: University of Missouri Press, 1970), and Patrick Cosgrave, *The Public Poetry of Robert Lowell* (London: Victor Gollancz, 1970). Both authors engage the question of Lowell's significance as an emblem of the gap between public and private modes of experience in our time, but Meiners is too Christian and Cosgrave too much a student of Yvor Winters really to sympathize with Lowell's dilemmas. Also neither had the time to attend to *Notebook*, where even the most political subjects like the March in Washington against the Vietnam War achieve their emotional resonance and glimpses of value only in terms of personal acts of kindness and moments of shared alienation. Lowell's own comment on these poems is instructive: "It was mainly the fragility of a person caught in this situation," he says, which dominated his perceptions of that march and makes his own renderings of it so different from Mailer's. See an interview with V. S. Naipaul, "Et in America Ego," reprinted in *Profile of Robert Lowell*, ed. Jerome Mazzaro (Columbus, Ohio: Charles Merrill, 1971), p. 78.

16. In addition to Cosgrave and Meiners, see Mazzaro, *Poetic Themes*, pp. 121–35, and Thomas Parkinson, *"For the Union Dead,"* *Salamagundi*, no. 4 (1966–67), pp. 90–95.

17. John Reed, "Going Back: the Ironic Progress of Lowell's Poetry," in *Profile of Robert Lowell*, ed. Mazzaro, pp. 81–96; Robert Boyers, "On Robert Lowell," in ibid., pp. 97–104.

3

Varieties of Immanentist Experience:
Robert Bly, Charles Olson,
and Frank O'Hara

i

To reject one poetic for another requires some implicit set of standards, or at the very least a complex of needs not satisfied by the current orthodoxy. I have shown how the New Critical aesthetic could not satisfy Lowell after his loss of faith in the symbolic, form-creating imagination, so that Lowell's existential crisis also entailed a poetic one. Now I shall attempt to explore why Lowell's solutions did not satisfy other poets similarly disaffected from the epistemological and cultural implications of the New Critical aesthetic. The various forms this disaffection took can be clarified by describing three basic self-consciously postmodern positions—those of Robert Bly, Charles Olson, and Frank O'Hara.

Those three positions are united by a single theme—an emphasis on what I call *radical presence*, the insistence that the moment immediately and intensely experienced can restore one to harmony with the world and provide ethical and psychological renewal. The term *presence* is dangerously abstract and requires further definition, but that definition will best emerge in the process of my treating the specific forms of presence elaborated by the poets.[1] One way of beginning to define presence is by its opposite—by the idea of *absence*—and here Lowell's poetry plays an important role, for it is the constant pressure of loss and separation in his poetry that leads contemporaries to reject his work as a useful model.

In *Life Studies*, for example, the culminating crisis is a moment of intense emptiness—"I myself am hell; / nobody's here." Lowell richly combines two versions of hell, Satan's absolute individualism and the modern sense of complete inner emptiness, a collocation that provides an excellent gloss on the spiritual problems involved in confessional poetry. Beginning with his realization that traditional value structures are no longer operable, Lowell in *Life Studies* seeks to make present and possess at least his own psychic reality. However the quest for self-possession without any trustworthy reference points outside the self generates only a despairing awareness of how empty, how fictive and self-generated, the isolated individual is.[2] At the volume's most intense moment of self-conscious presence ("I myself am hell"), there emerges also the deepest sense of inner emptiness. The individual consciousness threatens always to become what Sartre calls a principle of sheer negation, unless it recognizes processes it shares with other modes of life. The poem "Skunk Hour" does manage to survive this crisis by discovering a principle of continuity with the natural instincts of other living beings, but one sense of absence will soon be replaced by others. In Lowell's later contemplative poems there remains a constant pressure of loss and anxiety that at times mocks and at times—in the tragic poems—intensifies whatever the present affords. There is in Lowell the constant pressure of memory, of the mind seeking to be free of its involvement in material processes that are quite sufficient without it, and finally of the separation of his particular self from the society and from others. Finally Lowell's ultimate values stem from culture, not nature, and are thus doubly removed—first from the present as immediate experience and then from the perverse and distorted contemporary culture so different from the imaginative ideals he envisions as a true culture.[3] And despite his alienation from American culture, Lowell here presents a form of what may well be its basic experience of absence, for there is a pervasive sense that contemporary culture is a dying and inadequate one, wasting even the potential it has for improving the quality of the lives it controls. Instead of living confidently within it, man finds himself continually denying his cultural role in nostalgic dreams of happier pasts or wishful fantasies of a better future.

For many postmodern poets, then, one needs what Wallace Stevens called "a cure of the ground / or a cure of ourselves that is equal to a cure / of the ground." Even imagining a cure, the poets feel, will entail changing one's fundamental perspectives on experience. Where humanist cultural ideals were, there some form of immediate contact with natural energies must be restored. But this restoration cannot follow even the example of Romantic nature poetry, for Romantic views of a purposive and numinous force immanent in nature are derived from a renewal and reinterpretation of Christianity. Now the challenge is to imagine non-Christian sources of immanent value. This leads to the themes whose logical geography I tried to map in my first chapter. Now it is time to see how specific poetic strategies are developed to disclose what might be numinous sources of value in immediate experience and, more important, to show how postmodern poets articulate states of mind exemplifying ways these values can be apprehended and can dispose one to action.

Bly, Olson, and O'Hara, represent three distinct typical postmodern modes for articulating these states of mind. None of these poets approaches canonical status among his peers, but they do take up and reflect abstractly upon positions that others adapt and experiment with. In fact, one could, without much distortion, define most of the poetry of the sixties that is neither "academic" nor confessional by mapping its relationship to coordinates provided by Bly's poetics of the deep image, Olson's objectivist or projectivist aesthetic, and the New York school that O'Hara most fully represents. And because these poets have roots in marginal aspects of modernism—Bly in theosophically inspired poetry and surrealism, Olson in Williams and objectivism, and O'Hara in Dada, surrealism, and expressionist painting—they help make clear how contemporary poetics flowers from earlier seeds never really central to modernist English and American poetry.

Intellectually, postmodern poetics derives from Romanticism, but equally important is the characteristically American quality of its search for authority in modes of immediate presence. As one explores the ways poets of the sixties seek to go beyond Lowell, it will be useful to keep in mind how closely the entire process reenacts what D. H. Lawrence has described as the recurrent form of classic American literature—both for its cultural interest and because Lawrence used America to define his own highly influential vision of presence as a source of value dependent neither on Romantic theology nor on Paterian aestheticism. Lawrence sees the central American experience as a flight from the spiritual authority of Europe—an authority characterized by doctrines of eternal truth only partially within experience and by reliance on hierarchical structures of value. American literature, then, continually enacts a process of negation, and negation is frightening because it casts man into a void. Without masters it can accept, American literature vacillates continually between submission to the land and a retreat to even more extreme and destructive embodiments of the European ideals. Only with Whitman does the destructive journey end. And the two stages Lawrence sees in Whitman's career nicely parallel the movement from Lowell to Bly, Olson, and O'Hara. Whitman first explores a radical possibility for retaining the dream that consciousness and the human ego can create forms nature obeys. He tries to make his ego an all-embracing consciousness, possessing all beings and possessed by them. (Lowell's ego exhibits, of course, a more limited and ironic version of the same strategy). But he soon comes to see that the desire to identify with all that lives is the equivalent of a desire to die and to merge with an infinite emptiness. Through his imaginative experience of death, however, Whitman emerges reborn with a radically new vision, the vision of the "Open Road." The "Open Road" is for Lawrence the way of presence, and he carefully distinguishes it from any vision of experience that seeks to define value by relating experience to the universal categories of individual or collective consciousness:

> It is a new great doctrine. A doctrine of life. A new great morality of actual living, not of salvation . . . [Whitman's] morality was no morality of salvation. His was a morality of the soul living her life, not saving herself.
> The Open Road. The great home of the Soul is the open road. Not heaven, not paradise. Not "above." Not even "within." . . . The journey itself, down the open road. Exposed to full contact. . . . Towards no goal. Always the open road.
> It is not I who guide my soul to heaven. It is I who am guided by my own soul along the open road.[4]

The morality of ends require a conscious ego determining the meaning of experiences by referring them to phenomena not immediately present —for example, to schemes of salvation, or even to social and philosophical systems. (Kant's categorical imperative is a perfect model for the morality of ends.) Authority, then, is not immediately within the energies of experience. The morality of the open road, on the other hand, allows no absolute; morality, or authentic action, depends on a constant adjustment of the ego to the energies of the moment—in nature or in forces exerted by the human beings with whom one comes into contact. Consequently, there is little sense in ethical or poetic visions that perpetuate the Victorian dream of improving society by creating imaginative models of ideal behavior or appealing to men's sense of duty and self-regard. Perception and not reflection is the primary means for developing a man's capacities for an authentic life. The second aspect then follows logically; if perception is primary there must be something humanly significant to be perceived. Some principle of authority must be conceived as residing in the energies of the moment, so even if one seeking a philosophy of presence rejects Lawrence's theories about the gods, he must describe ways in which the present is numinous and something more than simply intense energy. That energy must have some kind of purposiveness, some way of influencing behavior and determining authentic modes of interrelationship among an individual, his environment, and other men. By exploring the various ways in which presence can be adapted to these axiological needs, the poets of the sixties in effect break with an immediate past only to recover what may be the true American heritage.

ii

The heirs of Whitman, of course, are Roethke and Williams, both of whom can be considered spiritual fathers of the poets I am studying. But it is to those writers heavily influenced by them, to Robert Bly and Charles Olson, one must turn if one wishes to see how their visions are carried over into postmodern poetics. Bly is a particularly fruitful figure with whom to begin because so much of his critical theorizing is an explicit attack on Lowell and on the reasons why Lowell can express the death of a poetic tradition but not break through that death to a new life. Moreover, Bly's poetic is outspokenly, almost simple-mindedly, moral and ontological; it begins with the opposition between absence and presence, between a world of dead facts and one of numinous realities, and goes on to explore ways one can recover a suprahuman ground for establishing a basis for value at once immanent and public.

Lowell's poetry is for Bly a perfect example of the absence or empti-ness that plagues so much contemporary experience. Lowell's very at-tempts to intensify the present moment, both in his choice of poetic detail and in his presentation of emotional experience, only call attention to how dead a world even the best poets are forced to inhabit. Like the body of Charles Bovary at the end of Flaubert's novel, Lowell's poems offer the appearance of vital life only to yield up, on investigation, a horrifying glimpse of how empty is the world as one now normally experiences it. Lowell's poems, Bly argues, have no poetic center, no radiating presence that gathers and gives an appropriate relevance to the specific details; instead they include facts simply because they happened: "A flood of objects comes and buries the poem's project of living inside a certain emotion."[5] Facts are separate from emotion in Lowell because he has no way of conceiving the unity of man and nature, no way of opening himself to see how the facts can speak to and call for the human emotions which might complete them. Lowell's only intensity is psychological; he pretends "to have a poetic excitement when all he has to offer is nervous excitement" (RL, p. 96). "Poetic" to Bly means a sensitive awareness of the "soft ground" of experience and is radically opposed to the elaborate dramatic and psychological sensa-tionalism Lowell requires to give his details any resonance at all:

For the confessional poet anything less than an abortion or a cancer operation really doesn't justify the machinery. A poem becomes a tank that can't maneuver on soft ground without destroying it [*DW*, p. 6]

For Bly genuine poetic excitement depends on the union of poetic feeling with some deeper, nonsubjective reality. Lowell's failure ultimately stems from an existential crisis—he cannot link the aesthetic with the ontological, experience with its ground, or intense moments with secure bases for value. His poetry vacillates between the prosaic and the sensational because it is exclusively centered in man and in the individual ego: "The human being is not studied in relation to non-human lives" (*DW*, p. 4).[6] In true emotional experience man feels in himself the "*Gott-natur*" (a term taken from Georg Groddeck) and "senses the interdependence of all things alive, and looks to bring them all inside the work of art" (*DW*, p. 3). Authentic experience, then, is concentrative (cf. *WT*, pp. 33–34; *DW*, p. 6); it draws together events in the unity of emotion. The psychological emphases of the confessionals, on the other hand, create a diffusive, fragmenting effect. Caught in the flux of isolated subjectivity, and feeding off the most problematic aspects of that selfhood to create poetry, the confessional poet flirts always with complete "disintegration of [the] personality" he or she so desperately seeks to understand (*WT*, pp. 41–42).

Bly's opposition to the homocentric universe as the mere residue of a world once resonant with ontological depth leads one to the central quest in Bly's own work. His poetic theory concentrates on the possibility of the poem recovering that resonance by once again putting readers in touch with the *Gott-natur* and restoring their awareness of the life man and objects share. His central strategy is to define a theory of imagination that demonstrates how the Romantic organicist poem makes visible latent orders of being where nature and consciousness, existential facts and the metaphor or poetic image, share the vital life. There are some parallels here to Coleridge's faith that the creative imagination participates in a level of reality beneath that of mere appearances. But, as I shall soon show, Bly remains radically postmodern by insisting on the imaginative act as a denial of the ego and by pointing to the immediate act of sympathetic perception as the source of one's participation in this deeper life. The poetic imagination does not create unity but finds attitudes or modes of attention that station the mind in levels of reality deeper and more organically unified than those which conscious art can create.

Bly works out his idea of the imagination by developing two corollary terms—*intuition* and *image*. *Intuition* is the creative faculty that can generate the poem once it learns how to inhabit its experiences, and *image* is Bly's term for the resultant work. Both terms are carefully chosen to combine the art of making with the art of seeing, and both allow Bly to adapt the organicist tradition without subjecting himself to a New Critical interpretation of it. Thus *image* refers to the poem as an organic entity, yet the term calls attention to the work not as artifact but as a specific way of seeing or of participating in experience. In a similar way, *intuition* is often used by aesthetic critics like Croce, but Bly's own insistence on the metaphysical implications of the term brings him closer to the Thomism of Maritain. *Intuition* is by definition the creative union of emotion and its ground in the *Gott-natur* (cf. *WT*, p. 34). Neither psychology nor nature by itself can save man from despair and its corollary violence; there is needed instead "a poetry that goes deep into the human being, much deeper than the ego, and at the same time is aware of many other beings (*DW*, p. 6). Poetic intuition then allows consciousness to enter a "field" (analogous to Olson's) where reside the secrets man and objects share:

> In the poems of Neruda, Vallejo, Jiminez, Machado, Rilke, the poem is an extension of the substance of the man, no different from his skin or hands. The substance of the man who wrote the poem reaches far out into the darkness and the poem is his whole body, seeing with his ears and his fingers and his hair. Impersonal poets construct; great poets merely are sensitive. [*WT*, p. 38]

To enter this condition of experience, intuition must penetrate the merely factual truths of experience in the "outer world." Thus Bly's *image* responds to very different needs from those met by Imagism:

> Imagism was largely "Picturism." An image and a picture differ in that the image, being the natural speech of the imagination, cannot be drawn from or inserted back into the real world. It is an animal native to the imagination. [*WT*, p. 40]

The true image, then, is a concentration of outer and inner energies into a single intense state of feeling whereby the poem (and, by implication, the audience) "is released from imprisonment among objects" (*WT*, p. 47).

Bly's poetic treads a delicate and often shifting boundary line between traditional Romanticism and the more secular ontological strategies of other postmodern poets. To combat the split between value and fact, between the isolated human consciousness and more universal energies that might serve as a source of value, Bly returns once more to a series of oppositions that plagued the Romantics. Bly often seeks to separate and then integrate notions of the artist as maker and the artist as seer, of outer and inner experience, of a sense of one's mere facticity and a sense that one feels his interdependence with the universe. And all these oppositions come into play with respect to his central polarity—that of the ordinary public language and a true visionary language. He is nowhere so Romantic as in the epigraphs from Boehme he gave to his two most influential volumes in the sixties:

We are all asleep in the outwardman. [SS]

For according to the outward man, we are in this world, and according to the inward man, we are in the inward world . . . Since then we are generated out of both worlds, we speak in two languages, and we must be understood also by two languages. [LB]

In so distinguishing inner and outer worlds as the basis for his theory of poetic and public languages, Bly comes dangerously close to the most naive Romantic and Symbolist restatements of Christian theology. But without such an insistence, Bly could find himself trapped in T. E. Hulme's Bergsonian version of the two-language theory, which authorized the Imagist poetic Bly despises. And at his best, Bly adapts his theological model in thoroughly secular terms: the grounds for a language of the inner life can be discovered in familiar processes if one learns to look beneath manifest appearances: "A human body, just dead, is very like a living body except that it no longer contains something which was invisible anyway" (WT, p. 46). This force, because invisible, can only be known by the imagination, but it is not therefore outside of nature. Furthermore, since this force is both shared by all beings and life-enhancing, it has a moral function; it makes man aware of what he shares with all life, and thus it can help combat the egocentric violence of American culture. The unconscious, then, that the *deep image* brings into play is as much an ontological as it is a psychological entity. It is man's way of experiencing the nonsubjective depths of his own being alive, and thus is the manifestation in man of the *Gott-natur*.[7]

Bly's poetry functions in terms of the same basic oppositions as his poetic. His characteristic themes and stylistic strategies come back again and again to the tension between dead and live worlds, public versus visionary language. And these oppositions in turn generate his two basic lyric modes—a satiric one when the dead world dominates and a surreal one expressing momentary breakthrough into the interpenetrating energies of psyche and landscape. The satiric mode concentrates on the blindness and moral failings that follow from trusting public rational models of thinking. Here the poems concentrate on the blocking aspects of paternal authority whose ultimate prop is the reality principle. The second mode is a poetry of metamorphosis—not from object to object but from one level of being to another. These poems gradually subvert the authority of a public descriptive language and "slip suddenly inward" to a version of Lowell's "downward and vegetating Kingdom" that Bly envisions as the dark, soft, feminine ground of true imaginative life. The poems begin with a casual event like walking through a field and then dramatize the imagination transforming the scene into a mysterious and evocative presence. The goal is to achieve a point where the radiant present abolishes all distinctions between imaginary and real, metaphor and fact, so that the reader is led to inhabit a world where aesthetic awareness blends with a sense of ontological resonance.

For Bly, then, the poet's role is to absorb the limited public language and leave the reader with a new level of awareness. To do so he repeats the characteristic movement of individual poems in the structure of his volumes by gradually moving from satiric to visionary modes. *The Light Around the Body*, for example, develops like a five-act drama, moving from a survey of the paralysis afflicting those caught in the public language, through the war in Vietnam as a summary exemplum of the effects of a culture's depending on that outer life, to a third part devoted to surrealistic explorations of the psychological pains created by those events. Through suffering, one learns in the fourth part to participate imaginatively in death and realizes by that participation a sense of the unity of all that lives. Then in the last section the speaker becomes secure in what Bly elsewhere calls "the masculine sadness of true poetry" (*PP*, p. 70) and learns the stance that allows poem after poem to slip inward to a vision of *Gott-natur*. Three poems from that volume—the first central to the crisis in public life and the other two illustrating two different strategies of metamorphosis possible once one can move to visionary language—should suffice to illustrate the kinds of imaginative strategies and experiences of value made possible by Bly's poetic.

"Counting Small-Boned Bodies" is Bly's finest poem in the satiric mode:

> Let's count the bodies over again.
>
> If we could only make the bodies smaller,
> The size of skulls,
> We could make a whole plain white with skulls in the
>   moonlight!

If we could only make the bodies smaller,
Maybe we could get
A whole year's kill in front of us on a desk!

If we could only make the bodies smaller,
We could fit
A body into a finger-ring, for a keepsake forever.

(*LB*, p. 32)

One notices first of all how Bly's sense of collective consciousness allows him readily to assume the voice of a whole culture, and his secure sense of values justifies a biting criticism of that culture, not only for its actions (as in Lowell) but for the modes of consciousness that support those actions. Three specific aspects of the public consciousness are dramatized in the poem. First Bly plays on the idea that counting, the manipulation of elements in the outer world, can ever be an adequate measure of events. (The history of body counts provides adequate empirical data to support Bly here.) Counting then leads to a second empty form of public measurement: the poem's tone and grammatical mood express a technological fantasy inspired by the false language of advertising. Finally, the concluding line allies the violence of war with perverted and simplified visions of love. It establishes and casts back over the rest of the poem a purposive role for the irony as intensifying the gap between public desire and the lack of a true inwardness that might define and direct that desire. These distortions then combine to present an inverted version of Bly's typical concentrative movement. The more compressed the bodies become the more the reader approaches the ring, the central unifying symbol of the horror involved in this exercise of perverted love. And the horror is deepened by the fact that advertising's words for this particular union are literally true, though of course in an unexpected sense: those dead bodies will remain intimately involved with our lives for a terribly long time.

The other poems present Bly's two most significant ways of embodying his sense of the true vision of inner man—one dramatizing the process of expansion through concentration and the other the process of interpenetration or, in rhetorical terms, analogy. Visionary concentration in Bly's work serves as a structural response to some of his deepest fears. Not only are there moments of ironic concentration in poems like "Counting Small-Boned Bodies," but the radical splits of inner and outer man continually threaten Bly with disintegration. One need only consider the images of explosion and fragmentation that permeate *Light Around the Body*.[8] But beyond, and probably through, the tension there are moments of exquisite union. Take for example "Looking Into A Face":

> Conversation brings us so close! Opening
> The surfs of the body,
> Bringing fish up near the sun,
> And stiffening the backbones of the sea!
>
> I have wandered in a face, for hours,
> Passing through dark fires.
> I have risen to a body
> Not yet born,
> Existing like a light around the body
> Through which the body moves like a sliding moon.
>
> (LB, p. 53)

Through conversation here the speaker experiences at once an intense union with the other and an "opening" into a larger reality (one can look "into" and not "at" a face). In the natural context of the first stanza the other person functions as a sun drawing toward itself the submerged, cold parts of the poet, while in the second the containing force of the intense union becomes the contained as the mysterious forces of the moon control, define, and illuminate the existential body in a space at once cosmic and human. Bly's own act of concentration in the poem combines the expansive depth of spirit sought by so many in the mystical and Romantic traditions with a sense of security and equilibrium achieved by very few. Psychic depth and cosmic force, the Romantic dream of the redeemed human body and the contemporary quest for a vision of cosmic harmony based on natural law, interpenetrate and reinforce one another.

This union of psychic and cosmic energy is realized most frequently through a rhetoric of analogy. Bly quietly builds the poem through a series of muted analogies between psyche and world to a final moment where an image or series of images express and insist that the reader attend to the completely realized interpenetration now blossoming forth. In other words, Bly the poet slips inward before he asks the same slip of the reader, and the sustained analogy then gives depth and a sense of secure grounding to the moment of insight. This preparation, I think, is the key to the remarkable sense of illumination and peace one experiences at the close of Bly's best poems. There is neither the shattering disharmony felt in Lowell's epigrammatic insights nor the forced discovery found in Bly's less successful poems or in his many imitators. Even soft ground requires an elaborate foundation.

"A Home in Dark Grass" illustrates the processes I've been discussing:

In the deep fall, the body awakes,
And we find lions on the seashore—
Nothing to fear.
The wind rises, the water is born,
Spreading white tomb-clothes on a rocky shore,
Drawing us up
From the bed of the land.

We did not come to remain whole.
We came to lose our leaves like the trees,
The trees that are broken
And start again, drawing up from the great roots;
Like mad poets captured by the Moors,
Men who live out
A second life.

That we should learn of poverty and rags,
That we should taste the weed of Dillinger,
And swim in the sea,
Not always walking on dry land,
And, dancing, find in the trees a saviour,
A home in dark grass,
And nourishment in death.

(LB, p. 44)

The poem derives its energy from a complex synthesis of the human and
the natural leading to a concluding paradox that embodies the significance of those relationships. The first two stanzas dramatize man and
nature exchanging roles; in the first nature is seen in human terms—
perhaps the reason that there is nothing to fear—while in the second
the speaker is naturalized in the metaphor of the trees. The third stanza,
with its shift to the subjunctive, presents the condition of desire generated by the speaker's awareness of the relationships in the first two, a
desire culminating with the slip to a new generalized sense of inwardness in the last line. The last three lines frame that shift of levels with
a marvelously complex restatement of nature and man. Three natural
terms (trees, grass, and, in context of the preceding two, death) are
posed as possible satisfactions for three human needs, and the penulti-
mate lines further emphasize the relationships by arranging them in a
chiasmus (trees saviour) (home grass). The last line then progresses
a step further. While death completes the series of natural terms satisfying human needs, it is itself a general condition in which man shares.
At the same time "nourishment" is a human need shared by natural life.
"Nourishment in death" is dangerously close to cliché, but the poem by
now has established a basis of exchange in which the phrase (at best,
initially a paradox) is sustained on several literal levels—from the level

of natural cycles to one where consciousness can see all being participate in "the impersonal stillness in things."[9] To develop further the implications of these metaphors of exchange, the poem presents opposite progressions in the two categories: the natural terms grow more general and symbolic or psychological (between trees and death, "dark grass" appears both more extensive than trees as a natural phenomenon and, with the adjective, clearly more suggestive), while the human ones grow more specific and closer to those needs man shares with all of life (a "saviour" fills a mythic need; nourishment, a universal physical one). By the last line there is again intense concentration as the human and natural meet at the point of death and, through that concentration, a sense of expansive opening into another realm of being shared by death. As all natural beings come together in death, all human needs return to the natural where they enable one to imagine the secure ground shared by all life.

Bly's analogical method demands a use of metaphor very different from Richard Wilbur's. Bly's poems are at least as metaphoric; without metaphor one is left with only the outer realities of objectivism. The structure of analogy, in fact, often borders on the conceit, but attention is not focused on metaphor as a verbal act. Instead the metaphors frequently ask to be taken as literally true relationships.[10] The links between man and trees and grass and death appear not fictive but natural. The metaphysical conceit suggests wonder at the powers of mind and its playful creative ways of illuminating events and their meanings, a wonder John Crowe Ransom tried to describe with the term *miraculism*. In Bly, on the other hand, the extended analogues focus on the miraculism of natural processes or the *Gott-natur*, which creates and sustains the relationships. Nature is "that synthetic and magical power" which "blends, and (as it were) fuses, 'each into each.'" The poet then need not strive to unify opposites; he need only open himself to that second language of imaginative vision which places man in the condition where unity is the basic ontological reality.

The relevance of the term *miraculism* to Bly's work, however, raises a crucial question: can an ontology based in the soft ground of imaginative association provide also the secure base in nonfictive reality needed so desperately by Lowell and others? Can so special a form of vision, "released from imprisonment among" the objects of the prose world (*WT*, p. 47), claim truth for itself within that world? Might not Bly in his claims for the truth of his poetic visions be confusing art and life, taking the unity of art as symbol for nature, and treating as experiences of ontological value what are really responses of the aesthetic faculty to human creations? How separate are the two languages of outer reality and inner vision? These questions become more pressing when analysis shows how skillfully Bly's analogical rhetoric sustains his moments of vision. Are will and imagination doing for Bly the work best reserved for perception and analysis?

The questions, of course, do not admit of "yes" and "no" answers. For one thing, they beg other questions like the relationship of aesthetic experience to the possible ways one's sense, if not his conceptual grasp, of values realized within art can be operable outside it. But the questions do, nonetheless, enable one to see why many poets cannot be content with Bly's articulation of value and, fearing that soft ground may also be quicksand, insist on more objectivist, less privileged moments of experience as the necessary poetic base for a believable value frame. Moreover, these questions demand that one try to be more precise about the ontological status of poetry like Bly's. Such precision is possible, I think, by adapting some of the argument of Maurice-Jean Lefèbre's *L'Image Fascinante et Le Surréel*.[11] (I say "adapt" because Lefèbre tries to explain only the fascination of images and not the additional qualities in Bly of serenity and the sense of cosmic unity—qualities I think also explicable in Lefèbre's terms.) Following Sartre, he argues that the image is by definition never a present reality but the construct of imagination, precisely because it *is* the making present in the mind what is absent in perception. The image, in other words, is by its nature free "from imprisonment among" objects, and this condition, Lefèbre continues, is the reason why images seem to fascinate readers and project an infinite mystery. This image at once absent and present evokes in one an ambivalent state toward the world known as real. The more one attends to the image, the more one is dissatisfied with the real world that does not include it and the more one tries to see what the image might mean were it real and filling the gap it has created in one's sense of the real. In Bly's dichotomy between the two languages, the image mocks the self-sufficiency of the "outer world," yet the second language containing the image cannot so much replace the language of the outer world as trouble it and provoke the reader's desire to go beyond it. Perhaps the image in Bly's sense so fascinates one because it occupies a mental space on the horizon of experience—always offering a full presence but, when one seeks to grasp it, evaporating into a silent void. Lefèbre offers as the nearest analogue to the image the discipline of metaphysics, for it too is based on one's fascination with entities that are in fact absent but that, once created, trouble the reader with a sense of the insufficiency of the world of facts. One comes more and more to dwell on the absent and hopes to find through it ways of extending the unsatisfactory reality. But where metaphysics tries to deny absence and claim its projection as real, the poetic image is content to revel in its own ambiguity; the image "n'est pas le repos dans une verité, c'est une passion," "la metaphysique du coeur."

Bly, of course, would accept neither Lefèbre's characteristic French dualism nor his academic's realist insistence that poetry is only "la metaphysique du coeur" and not "la verité revelé dans le coeur." Like so many contemporary poets, he must try with images to do the work of metaphysics, even if his poems stagger under this burden. In Bly's particular case, the quarrel with those willing to resign poetry to the heart may also have deeper significance. Lefèbre defines a problem that helps clarify both Bly's contribution to contemporary poetry and his two basic weaknesses—a terribly small range of subject matter and attitudes and a recurrent insistence that value can only be recognized by one metaphorically at the point of death. (This second characteristic is, of course, justifiable as a metaphor, but its recurrence seems almost pathological; at best it manifests an attitude surprisingly alien from the activist voice of Bly's prose.) Both these weaknesses stem from Bly's attempt to have his poems occupy the space Lefèbre defines as the place of the image, but at the same time, to insist that the interpenetrations glimpsed and the mystery realized are actually present within experience for one who has learned to see with the vision of the inner man. Very few experiences, and an even smaller range of attitudes, can consistently occupy this space without pushing the material into either conscious artifice or ironic interplay with an inadequate reality.

The one human experience, in fact, that most obviously exists in the space between simple reality and an absent, mysterious stillness of things is death. For death is at once an undeniably real experience and the entrance into a state of being eternally involved in the continual processes and energies of life. Only when nourished by death can one both possess his own real being and feel himself surrendering to a merger with the universal condition never experienced among the brute particulars and fragments of normal experience.

Death is a state of absence, a state calling forth images that can only fascinate and never be tested for their truth. Yet, as I shall demonstrate more fully in considering Merwin, death is also probably the most absolutely real and present phenomenon man is acquainted with, since all animate life is subject to its power. Death, like the poetic image, occupies a threshold space between absence and presence, calling man beyond his empirical sense of facts but only famishing the craving it creates for deeper, more intense forms of knowledge.[12]

Bly's work, then, seeks to preserve two basic aspects of Whitman's vision. It images an ideal state of consciousness as one in which the ego merges in all being by meditating its death, and it takes that mode of awareness as grounding the understanding and the confidence necessary to appreciate life as a journey along the open road. But because he becomes so obsessed with the means for attaining this vision, one must turn to other poets if one wishes to appreciate what the actual journey might be like.

iii

Charles Olson was not a man to be content with fascinating images. Arrogant, confusing, paralyzed at times by his perpetual struggle with the language of the tribe, Olson nonetheless is the prototype for those contemporaries who insist that "arguing a world which has value" forces one beyond imagination to direct perception, to the cutting edge where man and the world are in perpetual interchange. What vanity it takes, Olson would claim, to say with Lowell "only in touch with what we touch" without exploring just what the mysteries of touch entail. What poverty to escape from objects into inwardness without coming to grips first with the "dogmatic Nature of Experience" at every moment.[13] Only by absolute attention to this experience can we "restate man" in such a way as "to repossess him of his dynamic," to face the failures of humanism and rationalism and to create a postmodern definition of reality answering Rimbaud's, "what is on the other side of despair" (*HU*, p. 114):

> Hanging over into the present from the old cosmology are three drags, each of them the offsets of the principle desire of man for Kosmos during the two millenia [*sic*] and a half preceding us. And the three hang about people's necks like dead birds. They are Void, Chaos, and the trope Man. Or to put them down in the order of their occurrence, Chaos, Man, Void; that is Chaos was the imagined unformed on which the order Kosmos set form. Man was the later child of the same act—teleology of form as progressive was the hidden assumption of the old cosmology, and void is what's left when Kosmos breaks down as the interesting evidence of order. Man falls when that purpose falls, and so Void is the only assumption left; that is, Kosmos infers Chaos as precedent to itself and Man as succeeding, and when it goes as a controlling factor, only Void becomes a premise of measure. Man is simply filling an empty space. Which turns quickly by collapse into man is skin and flesh surrounding a void as well. Void in, void out. It is the counsel of despair. [*SVH*, pp. 47–48]

Any cosmology that looks to only a specific part of itself, like man, as its measure and ultimate purpose borders always on despair; there are always potential contradictions between the multiplicity of the whole and the limitations of that measuring agent. One thinks, for example, of Lowell's humanism: when in "Beyond the Alps" the contradictions between cosmos and human fictions become inescapable, there are left only restricted possibilities for human knowledge and the continual battle against the void within and without. Olson requires instead a cosmology in which the multiplicity provides for its own measure, in which meaning and value are functions of events and not of underlying fictions.

Olson's dream, then, is a total revaluation of values, and, like Nietzsche, the first to make such a claim, he has a vision complex, confusing and at times contradictory. Yet, as also in the case of Nietzsche, there are important rewards if one has the patience to sort out his thoughts and to imagine their possible coherence. The first reward is an obvious one—Olson's thought has been very influential, and if one understands him one comprehends the relationships among a set of concepts basic to much contemporary poetry. More important, though, is the kind of speculation Olson offers. Like Nietzsche's, his vision is radical and total; it gives no quarter to the compromises normally made to preserve many humanist values but demands instead that one envision human values only as the extension of the conclusions science has made and probably will make about man's relationship to natural forces. We usually do not think that way. Our commonsense assumptions about the ego, the mind, human freedom, and many other phenomena are a complex blend of humanism, Christianity, and awareness of practical exigencies. To me this blend is necessary if we are to live in the society our traditions have prepared for us, but it is a tenuous one capable of being altered in numerous ways. And nothing opens possibilities so effectively as imaginative participation in radically different conceptual schemes derived more or less logically from reflections on the direct implications of scientific thinking on human behavior. Finally, Olson's basic dream was to be an epic poet, and the great epics, he saw, always tried to render the human significance of the cosmology of their age. It is likely now that such a project is impossible because modern cosmology is so complex and so apparently isolated from ordinary experience. The attempt even to imagine its possibility, however, deserves some attention, even if Olson's epic itself is too complex a subject for this study.

The easiest entrance into Olson's thought is by way of his theory of meaning. Meaning, he feels, is unmediated and depends neither on concepts of representation nor on the dichotomy between descriptive facts and interpretive values. Meaning, Olson is fond of repeating, is "that which exists thru itself" (*CM*, p. 2), that which emerges as active presence or defined energy in an event. In Chinese, *meaning* is translated *Tao*, a religious term that in the West becomes both the *Way* and "how" (*PT*, p. 61). As "way," meaning is part of a structured process, while "how" points to its dynamic emergence in and through action. "How" (in the sense of "how it is" not "how it works," which is a question like "why") must be opposed to the Western "why." "Why" asks one to locate meaning in explanation; it suggests that to understand a present reality one must refer to a system of causes and relations not immediately "here." Like many modern philosophers, Olson locates the problem of absence in this desire for referential explanation, for it demands the distinction between an event there and interpreting mind here, stimulus or matter there—response and secondary qualities here. It necessitates, in addition, a gap between temporal flux and the permanent and hence limited and inadequate interpretive structures in the mind (cf. *HU*, pp. 96–97). Consciousness of value, then, also must depend on reference to universals, which, without faith in a transcendent Logos, are always problematic. The ground for values becomes relative; one seems bound to accept either the primacy of individual fictions or the conservative claims for social and traditional codes supported by history, if not by God. But either way, man stands deprived of cosmos and choosing in a void without valid support for his choices.

To fault referential theories of truth is easy, to provide alternative models far more difficult. Yet here the poet has an advantage over the philosopher because he works in a tradition only rarely committed to the primacy of reference. Poetic theory has perennially honored the qualities of poetic discourse as unique dramatic events, and it has always been more willing than philosophy to grant that meaning is ultimately not discursive or explanatory but depends on the integrated response of mind, emotions, and bodily rhythms. MacLeish's "A poem should not mean / But be" expresses what most poets have always known and what Romantic poetics made it possible to articulate. The poem's full meaning is never in its references outward to interpretive systems but lies in the multidimensional interplay of forces that constitutes the event of reading the poem. Yet for Olson poetic theory that brings one to this point has not completed its task because it has not created the bridge between aesthetic events and ordinary experience. This was the real Romantic dream—to construct that bridge, to conceive ways in which one could find in the world of ordinary experience the fullness, the significance, the intensity, and the harmony of mental and natural energies found in art. The Romantics, however, all pulled back, seeking Platonic or incarnational models to justify transferring the harmony of mind and world perceived in art back into experience.

Olson's poetic occupies this liminal place between aesthetic and ontological experience. That is one reason one is tempted to adapt his concepts to conventional Romantic or New Critical ideas. Yet to halt at these parallels is to overlook the genuine radicalism in Olson's enterprise. Olson always seeks naturalistic definitions in order to extend terms usually limited to an aesthetic vocabulary.[14] In discussing form, for example, he begins with what are by now truisms, but continually seeks out natural, scientific, and mythological analogues to obliterate the gap between aesthetic and existential values. To those trained in the New Criticism there is certainly nothing surprising in Olson's famous formula (taken from Creeley, he says) "Form Is Never More Than An Extension of Content" (*HU*, p. 52). Yet few in that same tradition would accept the literal way Olson applies this formula. Form is literally within the event as dynamic union of world and acting agent; in no way is it the structuring of an event by a responding, interpreting mind. Form is the property of an event as experienced by a responding consciousness; it does not depend on an interpretive arrangement by consciousness in reflective tranquility once the event has been completed. In other words, form is radically organic and within experience. Form is really the unity of that which, existing through itself, has meaning. So Olson rejects as allegorical refusal of the secular world any attempt to refer experience to orders of significance either hidden beneath it or imposed upon it (*HU*, pp. 83–84).[15] In practice this leads Olson to deny the priority of ideas as the agents by which man imposes order on his world. Ideas do not adequately capture the form of events because they are the constructs of discourse and only follow after the form-event and allow one to deal with it as a completed and dead entity:

> So long as a sentence stayed a "completed thought"—and I'd guess it got that way when the Greeks did impose idea (to see) on act (dran, drama, to act)—it ceased (because ideas are not what we act to, however much we do see afterwards); therefore, form is before ideas. [*HU*, p. 65]

If ideas do not inform action, morality requires a new base—not in consciousness but in qualities of attentiveness, in the only kind of knowledge or contact that matters:

> For the truth is, that the management of external nature so that none of its *virtu* is lost, in vegetables or in art, is as much a delicate

juggling of her content as is the same juggling by any one of us of our own. And when men are not such jugglers, are not able to manage a means of expression the equal of their own or nature's intricacy, the flesh does choke. . . . Value is perishing from the earth because no one cares to fight down to it beneath the glowing surfaces so attractive to all. [*HU*, p. 8]

The Renaissance morality of form gets turned on its back, and the content of poetry becomes essentially all that matters. Then, if value is to be kept from perishing, that content can be treated as neither idea nor dramatic event; it is nothing less than the real itself, the multiplicity or relationships coming together in a single event or connected series of events:

> What makes most acts—of living and of writing—unsatisfactory, is that the person and/or the writer satisfy themselves that they can only make a form (what they say or do, or a story, a poem, whatever) by selecting from the full content some face of it, or plane, some part. And at just this point, by just this act, they fall back on the dodges of discourse, and immediately, they lose me, I am no longer engaged, this is not what I know is the going-on (and of which going-on I, as well as they, want some illumination, and so, some pleasure). It comes out a demonstration, a separating out, an act of classification, and so, a stopping, and all that I know is, it is not there, it has turned false. For any of us, at any instant, are juxtaposed to any experience, even an overwhelming single one, on several more planes than the arbitrary and discursive which we inherit can declare. [*HU*, p. 5]

Olson's entire poetics and ontology follow from his redefinition of form and content. One might notice first of all what becomes of the ideal of reconciling opposites. For Olson such an ideal is at best empty and at worst destructive. In so far as the full event is realized, it contains within itself the opposites and hence determines their true relationship. Beyond the human consciousness, which usually creates rather than reconciles opposites, "is direct perception and the contraries which dispose of argument" (*HU*, p. 4). (Lowell is paralyzed by opposites, Olson would say, because he does not trust his awareness and relies instead on will. He ends then with despair and with arbitrarily created associations.)

But if one cannot trust the synthesizing imagination, how is one to apprend the possible unity of an event? Bly's unconscious will not do (at least for the earlier, more influential Olson) because it cannot be conceived objectively. Olson turns to the most physical aspect of the poem—its rhythm—and redefines that to fit his sense of experience. Our bodies are the place where the fullest union of man and world take place, and it is within them that the unity of experience can be grasped. Discussions of rhythm must be taken out of formalist contexts and related most explicitly to the acts of the body:

> There is only one thing you can do about kinetic, re-enact it. Which is why the man said, he who possesses rhythm possesses the universe. And why art is the only twin life has—its only valid metaphysic. Art does not seek to describe but to enact. [*HU*, p. 10]

Olson's elaborate (and questionable) arguments for breath as the rhythmic measure of poetry have their source in this need to link a poetics of event with a full and active mode of human response.To further sustain the links between the body and complex experience, Olson redefines complexity; he substitutes for mystical metaphors of depth, the physical metaphor of intensity. Rhythm becomes "a pumping of the real" (*HU*, 117–19), and breath the physical measure of intensity. Rhythm allows one to participate in experience, not to control it.

Given the primacy of content over form and of body over consciousness, Olson must redefine human creativity. Once poetic intuition becomes so closely linked with "the dogmatic nature of experience," once poetics also becomes ontology, there is little room for the traditional doctrine of poet as artificer or self-expressive genius:

> What seems to me a more valid formulation for present use is "objectism," a word to be taken to stand for the kind of relation of man to experience which a poet might state as the necessity of a line or a work to be as wood is, to be as clean as wood is as it issues from the hand of nature, to be as shaped as wood can be when a man has had his hand to it. Objectism is the getting rid of the lyrical interference of the individual as ego, of the "subject" and his soul, that peculiar presumption by which western man has interposed himself between what he is as a creature of nature (with certain instructions to carry out) and those other creations of nature which we may, with no derogation, call objects. For a man is himself an object, . . . if he stays inside himself, if he is contained within his nature as he is participant in the larger force, he will be able to listen, and his hearing through himself, if he is contained within his nature as he is participant in the larger force, he will be able to listen, and his hearing through himself will give him secrets objects share. And by an inverse law his shapes will make their own way. It is in this sense that the projective act, which is the artist's act in the larger field of objects, leads to dimensions larger than the man. For a man's problem, the moment he takes speech up in all its fullness, is to give his work his seriousness, a seriousness sufficient to cause the thing he makes to try to take its place alongside the things of nature. [*HU*, pp. 59–60]

Despite Bly's contentions (*WT*, p. 36), Olson does not oppose inwardness, or even the idea of man as maker if interpreted properly. Rather, both Bly and Olson share a distrust of subjectivity, which confuses psychology with inwardness, and both call for a poetry of interchange between creative nature and human response. Even Bly, though, with his emphasis on inward reconstruction of events trusts (in theory at least) too much in mediation to satisfy Olson. What is crucial is the moment of contact. Man's creative being then is best considered as a "pressure" on experience (*HU*, p. 127), rather than a recasting of it. In other words, man is the world's limit (*HU*, p. 115); he allows events to assume their full meaning and hence their value by pushing through "the glowing surfaces" to the presence of nature's energy and hence her measures. As Heidegger says, consciousness is not the center or *telos* of being, but it is necessary for the full creative nature of the real (for the gods perhaps) to emerge. For Olson the creative consciousness intensifies the real in two ways— by exerting pressure on the surface of things ("de-creation") and by becoming a focus for large complexes of energy freed from space time and caused to "interact" (*HU*, p. 127) in a nexus of conflicting forces. Intensity is a measure of tension, and it depends on the power of consciousness to gather or fold together the multiple aspects of the real (cf. *HU*, pp. 93–94).[16]

As breath is a physical measure of intensity; its intellectual counterpart for Olson is the image: "As the Master said to me in the dream, of rhythm is image / of image is knowing / of knowing there is / a construct" (*HU*, p. 121). Like so many moderns, Olson uses the idea of image to draw together the various strands of his poetic. The concept then functions as a useful way to see how Olson tries to synthesize his predecessors. He shares first of all their sense that the poem must ultimately be conceived as a single intensive entity, in a sense free from the sequential displacements of ordinary discourse. And like them, he stresses the nondiscursive quality of that unified entity. But Olson makes clear his difference from the symbolist proponents of the Romantic image by insisting on the image as the intensification of objective reality, not a transcending of it.[17] Image does not, like symbol and allegory, refer beyond itself to conscious intentions and thus disperse energy away from the emerging present (*HU*, p. 121). Instead, image gathers those energies, which might otherwise be dispersed into the independent fictive mind, within a single dynamic movement. Yet that movement must be more intellectual, more related to imaginative archetypes than it is with his objectivist masters: "Image, therefore is vector. It carries the trinity via the double to the single form which one makes oneself able, if so, to issue from the 'content' " (*HU*, p. 97). Form is the unity of the event; the double is the awareness that man is always both subject and object of experience (*SVH*, p. 32); and the trinity, whose tensions are held in balance by the vector, Olson describes as *"topos/typos/tropos."*[18]

That trinity in turn summarizes the way Olson hopes poetry can recover Cosmos. It functions to explain the forces balanced by the image and helps Olson reconcile the metaphysical and archetypal dimensions of the Romantic Image with objectivist concerns to preserve the energies of immediate experience. *Topos*, a term that behaviorists might equate with environment, refers to the effects of the ground upon consciousness (*PT*, p. 42). *Typos* refers to those energies deriving from the metaphoric book one reads to find names; it calls one's attention to recurrent forms, be they in psychic archetypes or in the "imprints" of nature (*PT*, p. 55). Behind Olson's naturalized sense of typology lies Whitehead's definition of the "primordial" aspect of God as the nexus of all eternal objects, the locus (or Logos) of all potential forms to be realized in the processes of history:

> It's type, and is typology, and is typification, and is, in a sense, that standing condition of . . . I mean standing, really, in the very literal sense of substantive or object or manifest or solid or material. We get our word type—which interests me, I suppose, as a writer—from it. If any of you have ever seen a piece of movable type, at the bottom is the letter and the block is above. So that in order, really, to imagine a printer doing it . . . he's under your words in order to make the letters of them. Which always delights me, literally, as a problem of creation. In fact, literally, I would go so far—if you will excuse my Americanism—to think that you write that way. That you write as though you were underneath the letters. And I take that a hell of a lot larger. I would think that the hoof-print of the creator is on the bottom of creation, in exactly that same sense. [*PT*, pp. 42–43]

Finally, Olson uses the idea of *tropos* to describe the force that reconciles the energies of place with the forms of typological consciousness. *Tropos* is tropism, a dynamic force at once "ourselves" (*PT*, p. 43) in our response to the influx of cosmic energy and the power by which we obey cosmic laws; it depends on the deepest subjective response of particular beings, yet demands as well obedience to cosmic rhythms: "I mean, obey yourself and in obeying yourself kneel or lean to the sun, or whatever that heliotrope, like, is" (*PT*, p. 50). Tropism is itself a marvelous trope; it combines a process of cosmic desire and nourishment with the dynamic processes of human rhetoric seeking imaginative constructs that might reveal to consciousness its own place in cosmos. Scientific and imaginative orders now share not only Bly's "stillness of being" but also the dynamic properties of desire. *Cosmos* returns to its original Greek meaning as both "order" and "the entirety of what is."

The metaphors of *tropism* and *Cosmos* reflect Olson's ultimate quest to reappropriate for man the divine prerogative of being at once center and circumference of the Cosmos (*SVH*, pp. 36, 44).[19] Two conceptual and ethical obstacles must be overcome: man must be defined in such a way that each individual can be a relative creative center of Cosmos without that relativity turning Cosmos into Chaos, and man must be repossessed of a less egocentric and narrowly willful sense of his own centrality (or Cosmos and Chaos become merely human orders). Olson confronts these problems by constructing a dialectical model of three stages of feeling, which lead to a state of satisfied balance between objective and subjective forces:

> In the first stage of feeling, the chaos of physical enjoyment is both the reality and the process, but as process (in other words, as in motion) already Spirit (which is pneuma and means breath—wind, air) is operative. In the second stage, when the individual impresses his or her sense of order on the multiples, already Desire or Eros has begun to leaven the matter; already the vision of form (Kosmos, order harmony the world) is operative. And in the last stage, satisfaction, when both the enjoyment and the desire are one (the desire for form is the creative force, or what has been usually called God), the process of feeling becomes the reality and man is "satisfied." But such a satisfied man is never possibly the trope Man. The trope Man, like the sliding concept Chaos . . . is only the creature at the second stage of feeling, which amounts to no more than the creature crowing over his own triumph over incoherence. It is not the thing man when he has the thing in hand, which is any one of us in the face of satisfaction. And at that point any man or woman recedes as God does from his creation. [*SVH*, pp. 51–52]

Man exists in multiplicity; he gathers that multiplicity into the unity of an event; and then he must actively recognize that interpenetration of world and self as only a single moment in a universe he creates as it creates him. Humanism, in reaction against the chaos of the first stage of feeling, locks man into the second where the will to power "collapses back to the subjective understanding—tries to make it by asserting the self as character." If humanism is to be overcome, one must be able to replace the asserting function with an "obeying one," based on the trust "that the actionable is larger than the individual and so can be obeyed to" (*SVH*, pp. 44–45). One can recognize that the possibility of action depends on the world's eliciting desire in the very process by which consciousness chooses to do something. In other words, what the phenomenologists call *intentionality* witnesses to the fact that choosing is also in a sense affirming and obeying man's tropistic relation to Cosmos.

Olson, I think, is the central figure of postmodern poetics. Because of his difficulty, Olson's direct influence has not been very great outside limited circles. Yet even without grasping the full doctrine, young poets could not but be struck by both its suggestive image of an ontological project to be undertaken by postmodern poetry and by the numerous flashes of insight it provides as useful means for realizing that project. The tropism metaphor, the theory of feelings, or the discussion of selectedness in *The Human Universe* point beyond themselves to new ways of seeing and to fields for metaphoric exploration. More important is Olson's exemplary relation to Lowell's prose world: he neither resists (as do the modernists), nor despairs over, nor evades the fact that so much of our lives must be explained in terms of natural law. Instead he rejoices in the fact that dynamic energy remains subject to law, and at the same time he explores natural science for analogues with human feeling. The task is to have natural law without behaviorist determinism, to find the spirit within the letter; and the method is imaginative participation in what all beings share by being alive. And beyond the method there is the presence of the man—combining with his vitality an intense awareness of the moral demands life makes on all if its richness is to be realized. For nourishment Olson turns not to death but to life, not to concentration and a sense of the stillness in things but to the active expansion of energies interpenetrating one another.

Olson's poetry, on the other hand, is neither so influential nor so central. First of all, its content is often private or recondite, and the poems for the most part are difficult to see as coherent human experiences. And it just does not bring "the news" as the prose does. Moreover, in his best lyrics Olson is trying to enact certain qualities of his metaphysic not easily assimilated into one's expectations about the modern lyric. We usually consider the lyric poem as an individual's creating a particular form to capture, intensify, and often to interpret experience. For Olson, though, such ideals reflect only his second stage of feeling. (In mocking "the triumph over incoherence" he refers explicitly to Yeats's sense of lyrical form as the individual's means for mastering chaos.) Olson feels that he must go further, must find ways of embodying in his work the third stage of feeling. He insists that "the actionable is larger than the individual," and consequently verse must again "carry much larger materials than it has carried in our language since the Elizabethans" (*HU*, p. 61). This task requires a rejection of the dramatic lyrical ego and the more difficult and original feat of eliminating the lyrical exhibitions of that ego. Olson distrusts and tries to eliminate all forms of striking ornate language and emphatic resolving images, for both involve the reduction of energy to the gathering power of the individual poet. Olson wants his lyrics to have at once more particularity and greater distance—particularity in the specificity of objects and energies in no way changed to metaphor, and distance through a consciousness that transcends the ego's desire for synthesis and actively thinks and accepts the interpenetration of subjective and objective forces. For Olson poetry is the relationship of things and uses, not of images and dramatic subjects. Hence, in his poems, there is not only the paucity of lyrical images that his critics point out, but language is asked to carry a special burden. Olson does not use a particularly fresh language, but he invests syntax with enormous significance. That is where energy manifests itself, in the processes of mind appropriating nature and adjusting itself to her orders. Moreover, he emphasizes the etymological rather than the dramatic qualities of language. For in asking readers to reflect on the etymological layers of a word, Olson calls attention to qualities of the interchange between mind and nature that have collective significance. He points to the history of the way a word has been used and thus leads readers to see their own speech as at once participating in a historical process and readapting the energies of the past to the demands of the present. He makes them aware that consciousness is a force more expansive and more intensive than is normally recognized by those who see the individual as the source of meaning.[20]

"Variations Done For Gerald Van de Wiele" (D, pp. 86–89) is more clearly structured than most Olson poems, but that less-than-typical structure provides access to the characteristic lyric workings of Olson's sensibility. The poem presents its speaker's involvement in the natural energies of spring and his gradual process of aligning human consciousness with those energies. One can interpret its structure in terms of Olson's triads, or perhaps more accurately in terms of the Romantic triad—innocence, experience, higher innocence: part 1 ("Le Bonheur") moves from the natural vitality of spring to the bewildered presence of human consciousness trying to adapt to it; part 2 ("The Charge") presents that human consciousness coming to know what the charge (the blend of orders and energies) is it must adapt to; and part 3 (beautifully given the generalized title "Spring") embodies the active taking thought created by the full interpenetration of consciousness and natural energy. The poem, like spring itself, takes the musical form of Variations— within a basic law or structure of repetition a wide variety of phenomena are allowed an apparent free play that ultimately makes one appreciate the complex possibilities of the informing structure. The opening lines illustrate this dynamic variety within an informing unity:

dogwood *flakes*
what is green

the petals
from the apple
blow on the road

mourning doves
mark the sway
of the afternoon, bees
dig the plum blossoms

the morning
stands up straight.

The five one-syllable verbs I have italicized, each in the same grammatical structure and four also in parallel positions in the line, present
an emerging energy at once shared and manifest in diverse particulars.
Within the parellelism Olson stresses the opposite directions the energy
can take: the bees dig down while the morning stands up. But when the
reflective human consciousness enters the scene, it cannot at once achieve
full participation. Instead it only sees men and the birds as vaguely
"busy," and proceeds to reflect on the separation of the individual soul
from the fullness of natural process:

What soul
is without fault?

Nobody studies
happiness

Every time the cock crows
I salute him

I have no longer any excuse
for envy. My life

has been given its orders: the seasons
seize

the soul and the body, and make mock
of any dispersed effort. The hour of death

is the only trespass

The protagonist sees unity as an ideal, but cannot reconcile his awareness
of individual death with spring's offer of vitality. He sees that there can
be no excuse for envy (envy is essentially the insistence on individual

difference from a universal process), but his vision of order remains in the passive voice, and the theological overtones link an outworn mode of consciousness with the fear that awareness of death irreconcilably alienates man from unity with nature (while also mocking the Christian use of natural symbols to express a betrayal only man is capable of).

The second section presents "The Charge" consciousness must comprehend if it is to be reconciled with spring. But the same reflective activity necessary to comprehend death also transforms and confuses the natural scene:

> the birds are so many they are
> loud, in the afternoon
>
> they distract, as so many bees do
> suddenly all over the place
>
> With spring one knows today to see
> that in the morning each thing
>
> is separate but by noon
> they have melted into each other
>
> and by night only crazy things
> like the full moon and the whippoorwill
>
> and us, are busy.

Given a purposive human consciousness seeking its own unity, natural energy gets dispersed in unresolved conflict and contradiction (both birds and bees "distract"). The unified multiplicity of the first section breaks down into the sheer particularity of morning and the complete lack of distinction at noon. Again the speaker separates his own activity from the collective process. Now he tries as active subject to study happiness:

> can you afford not to make
> the magical study
>
> which happiness is? do you hear
> the cock when he crows? do you know the charge,
>
> that you shall have no envy, that your life
> has its orders, that the seasons
>
> seize you too, that no body and soul are one
> if they are not wrought

in this retort? that otherwise efforts
are efforts? And that the hour of your flight

will be the hour of your death?

To study happiness the mode of address must be second person; the self
must objectify its being and stand apart questioning it. Yet this alienation is the necessary condition for reconciliation. Now the speaker
recognizes that unity depends on his own active retort. The charge is
both to recognize that effort is not the struggling of alienated self-consciousness but part of the process and to imagine death as not inevitable
but as the result of a "flight" from harmonious action.

To know the charge, however, is still only the act of a single consciousness. That consciousness must learn to act within the scene and
to achieve a larger perspective in which it can see itself as object acted
on and as creative synthesizing force. The key in the third section is
the active role of the body, which the speaker can come to see as his
own mode of participation; the body thus can "whip the soul" to the
reflective salute and the summarizing epithet that conclude the poem.
After the opening stanzas suggest the completeness that returns to the
landscape (birds, for example, now have the religious unity of a multitude), Olson makes a surprising shift to a series of rape metaphors, two
of which are in the passive voice:

The flowers are ravined
by bees, the fruit blossoms

are thrown to the ground, the wind
the rain forces everything.

The passive voice suggests that the unity of action in section 1 must
now be seen in a larger context where natural entities are objects of
larger forces. Where the active verbs in section 1 shared a common
position, the verbs now share a single auxiliary and lead up to the
unifying sexual power of the generalized forces of wind and rain.

Now the active verb can return in a total vision. And this sexual
energy starts also to work on the speaker as his body and consciousness
come together to take their place in the scene. He recognizes that man
is only "as busy" as the other creatures (as his death must also be
only the equivalent of all the other deaths), and the poem consequently
breaks out in a hymn of sexual verbs embodying the union of natural
energy, body, and consciousness:

even the night is drummed
by whippoorwills, and we get

as busy, we plow, we move,
we break out, we love.

The earlier sequence of paralleled verbs expressing sheerly natural acts
gives way to a series blending the human and the natural. Moreover, the
rich parallelism between natural acts like breaking out and human acts
of love manages to "naturalize" and objectify the human without reducing
it beyond freedom and dignity. The "I" of section 1 and self-reflective
"you" of section 2 give way to the collective "we." And having achieved
unity there can be no need to study happiness. Instead of the "magical
study which happiness is," there is only the actual magic of spring's
"transmutations" and the transformation of study into the active unity
of soul inspired by body:

And we rush
to catch up. The body

whips the soul. In its great desire
it demands the elixir

In the roar of spring,
transmutations. Envy

drags herself off. The fault of the body and the soul
—that they are not one—

the matutinal cock clangs
and singleness: we salute you

season of no bungling

Fault here is the key term, for a fault is a gap or emptiness in a rock
structure. Faults can exist in nature as well as in the relationship between man and nature, but conversely faults can be conceived as part of
a more inclusive unity, an inclusiveness now sustained by the poem's
admitting such an abstraction as "singleness." The final gestures then
complete the sense of singleness. "We salute you" brings all the beings
of the poem together and allows the consciousness of the "we" realized
earlier to result in a specific action. Finally the last line embodies that
totality. The statement predicates without employing the subject-object
form, and the objective genitive allows an abstract term like *season* to

appear concrete and to transfer predicative force. Even death has its place in such a scene.

"Variations Done For Gerald Van de Wiele" is essentially a pastoral poem in the Romantic meditative mode whereby consciousness tries to define for itself an adequate relation to a satisfying and often numinous external scene. Yet unlike the Romantic pastoral there is almost no movement inward to symbolic psychic landscape. Olson's goal has been to lead readers out to the objective scene and ultimately to its "singleness," not to make subjective reflections on its meanings for them. The ending is neither a sharply realized celebratory image, nor the more frequent Romantic sense that this moment too must pass; rather it is a simple action, one the poet shares with the entire landscape, complemented by a reflective act—itself simple, complete, and beyond the bungling of isolated egos.

iv

Frank O'Hara's verse play, *Try, Try*, provides the most ready access to many characteristic qualities of his fictive world.[21] On the surface, and the play is all surface, it appears merely a reminder of how far verse drama has slipped even from Eliot's not very successful attempts to bring dramatic verse to the world of contemporary cocktail parties. *Try, Try* presents two lovers, Violet and John, whose delightful provocations of each other are rudely interrupted by the return of Violet's husband, Jack, from the war. Jack, though, proves not much of an obstacle to their love. Asked by Violet to leave, he calmly accepts his fate, and the play ends with the lovers triumphantly in each other's arms. The play is farce, or better pop art, deliberately refusing Eliot's symbols and portentous psychological probings; the play, in fact, even refuses the conventional means for theatrical action in the love-triangle plot. There is no violence, no passionate confrontation, and no insight or recognition of any truths, profound or otherwise, by the characters—if such undifferentiated dramatic agents can be called characters.

Yet the play is both entertaining in itself and indicative of O'Hara's world view—precisely in the way O'Hara manipulates absolutely trivial and conventional materials. One realizes first of all that such materials are a comment on contemporary reality and on the materials that reality affords the artist. Traditionally, verse was called for in drama only when the materials were of the greatest importance, when the playwright wanted to project the nobility of his characters or have at his disposal linguistic and rhythmic means capable of rendering serious and complex materials. In *Try, Try,* on the other hand, verse is required because the material is so slight; only elaborate and witty language can interest one in such painfully insignificant and typical people and situations. Like many other pop artists, O'Hara is reminding his audience that this age has lost whatever it was that allowed people to think that certain materials were intrinsically significant and fit material for serious artistic exploration. The world no longer sustains or inspires powerful language. Yeats once said that modern tragedy was impossible because modern man, when deeply moved, did not indulge in emotional outbursts but stared quietly at the fireplace. Now, as Ionesco reminds us, even the man moved enough to stare at the fireplace seems somehow ridiculous. Powerful language is no longer a response to the intensity of experience but to its poverty; man needs the artifice of witty and elaborate speech because without it he would have only the pressure of an absurd and oppressive reality. In one of his poems, O'Hara is eating a cheeseburger in Juliet's Corner when he fantasizes an association with Giulleta Massini, "e bell' attrice" (*CP,* p. 258). In this situation, "e bell' attrice" is a contemporary version of Beatrice, now not a light leading one through the world to a transcendent informing principle but a goddess of illusion redeeming one only momentarily from the stereotyped trivia dominating contemporary life (cf. also "Galanta" [*CP,* pp. 463–64]).

As a poet, O'Hara explores facets of the pop aesthetic that complement and confute the thinking of Bly and Olson. In *Try, Try* the lover, John, does not win the girl from her husband, Jack, because of any inherent character traits. The men are almost exactly alike (as the names indicate), and if anyone were to have moral claims it would be the husband, who is also returning from service to his country. John wins simply because he has been living with the girl; wins, that is, because he has been present, there, while the husband was absent. Here is Violet's rejection of her husband: "I wish you'd/go away and stay away. All you've done is kept me/looking out windows, wondering what things were/really like. Get out!" (*AT,* p. 39). The lover's seconding remarks are as philosophical as O'Hara will allow himself to be:

> You've got a claim on it, but I've got it
> These things don't happen temporarily . . .
>
> I suppose I'm the snake-in-the-grass but
> I can't say I'm sorry. Someone has to smile
> at her as she comes back from the bathroom.
> Do you think everything can stay the same,
> like a photograph? What for?

(AT, p. 41)

Presence then is a central value for O'Hara; but what kind of presence is it he affirms? First and foremost it is a demystified one stripped of the ontological vestments with which Bly and Olson endow it. For O'Hara the open road has lost its resident gods capable of mastering and directing the ego. There remains only the present as landscape without depth, satisfying only by contrast to the anxiety Violet felt when she tried to refer her condition to the needs and demands of an absent master. And if the present is without depth, whatever vital qualities it has depend entirely on the energies and capacities of the consciousness encountering it. Olson had opposed the dangerous tendencies toward passivity (the merger with the all that is death) in poetics like Bly's by insisting that man fulfills himself only in action. Yet this active creative self is always grounded in a cosmos at once lawful and itself continuously emergent or creative. With O'Hara, the self must be creative without such a ground; value depends entirely on the vitality with which one engages his experiences:

> You are of me, that's what
> and that's the meaning of fertility
> hard and moist and moaning[22]

(*CP*, p. 387)

In "Fantasy," the concluding poem in *Lunch Poems*, O'Hara tells his readers: "The main thing is to tell a story. / It is almost/very important," and he ends the fantasy with the playful reminder, "Never argue with the movies" (*CP*, p. 488). Literally the lines refer to a movie, *Northern Pursuit*, which, because it is either in his memory or on television, keeps intruding into his consciousness as he prepares medicine for Allen Ginsberg and converses with him. Seen, however, as figurative comments on the poetry of the entire volume, the lines become much more resonant. One notices first of all, in this poem titled "Fantasy," the emphasis on story, an emphasis I take to be a way of summarizing the necessary and superficial creative intelligence celebrated in *Try, Try* and in the exuberance of *Lunch Poems*. The story is only "almost" very important both because the movie, *Northern Pursuit*, is a trite one, and, more significantly, because, given the centrality of stories or fictions, there are no acceptable structures of value to define genuine hierarchies of importance. And without terms that can distinguish the important from the trivial, there is a concomitant breakdown in one's sense of the necessary boundaries between fantasy and reality. Why privilege reality, even if one can distinguish it from fiction? Matters of truth then merge with matters of the creative imagination, and the imagination itself can no longer assume its noble form-creating role but tends instead to be conceived as story-maker whose major media is the B movie, the public equivalent of private daydreams. The movies, then, are at once emblem of contemporary views on the nature of reality (who hasn't seen his life as a B movie and himself as seedy director powerless to do more, with the budget and script he's been given?) and moral witness of our times. It is folly to argue with them for two reasons: one's arguments have no grounds not themselves as fictive and superficial as the movies, and (as the poem "Ave Maria" suggests [CP, pp. 371–72]) one stands to lose more than he would gain if he successfully argues with the movies. The movies at least engage one's imagination and enliven experience; most of the forms of argument used to refute movie truth are themselves analytic and sterile ways of returning one to the poverty of a present emptied of all vitality.[23]

The way out of this emptiness is the story, but story in O'Hara requires careful definition since he is in no way a traditional narrative poet. Possible forms of story, of course, are fantasy and the witty artifice of Try, Try, forms O'Hara normally equates with pop art (see "Poem" on Lana Turner [CP, p. 449]). But for O'Hara life provides fictions both more superficial and more interesting than pure fantasy or artifice. The poet keeps his story alive by a loving fidelity to the specific facts and qualities of his daily experience—seen for themselves and not as the building blocks of larger, more significant wholes traditionally called poems:

> I am mainly preoccupied with the world as I experience it, and at times when I would rather be dead the thought that I could never write another poem has so far stopped me. . . . What is happening to me, allowing for lies and exaggerations which I try to avoid, goes into my poems. I don't think my experiences are clarified or made beautiful for myself or anyone else. . . .
>
> It may be that poetry makes life's nebulous events tangible to me and restores their detail; or conversely, that poetry brings forth the intangible quality of incidents which are all too concrete and circumstantial. [CP, p. 500]

It is in this context of life continually providing materials for the story that one must understand O'Hara's love affair with New York City (cf. "Steps" [CP, pp. 370–71]). For the city is a continual source of interesting and engaging details. Moreover, the city is a perfect metaphor for O'Hara's sense of the value in these details. Presence in the city is antithetical to presence in nature. City details, after all, have neither meaning, hierarchy, nor purpose not created absolutely by man. And more important, the city is committed to perpetual change; there are no enduring seasonal motifs or patterns of duration underlying and sustaining the multiplicity of city phenomena. They exist completely in the moment. And they exist superficially. In the city, as in O'Hara ontology, interesting and engaging details are continually becoming present. Yet not only do these momentary apparitions promise no underlying significance or meanings to be interpreted, they actually resist any attempt on one's part to know them better. City life offers a series of phenomena to notice, perhaps to play with in one's own psyche, but very rarely do these phenomena inspire or welcome any attempt to participate in their lives. O'Hara's analogue for the specific form of presence manifested by the city is his way of naming. His texture of proper names gives each person and detail an identity, but in no way do the names help the reader understand anything about what has been named. To know a lunch counter is called Juliet's Corner or a person O'Hara expects to meet is named Norman is a reminder for the reader that the specific details of another's life can appear only as momentary fragments, insisting through their particularity on his alienation from any inner reality they might possess.

What makes O'Hara so interesting a poet is his sense at once of the necessity for story, of its superficiality, and of the pain potentially lurking in every moment. The dialectic between presence and alienation found in his use of names is more strikingly evident in the larger rhythms of his work. Coexisting with O'Hara's evident joy in a kaleidoscopic rush of details and encounters are frequent perceptions of a lurking anxiety ready to seize him if the flow of events should give it a moment's foothold:

I ducked out of sight behind the saw-mill
nobody saw me because of the falls the gates the sluice the
                                        tourist boats
the children were trailing their fingers in the water
and the swans, regal and smarty, were nipping their "little"
                                        fingers
I heard one swan remark "That was a good nip
though they are not as interesting as sausages" and another
reply "Nor as tasty as those peasants we got away from the
                                        elephant that time"
but I didn't really care for conversation that day
I wanted to be alone
which is why I went to the mill in the first place
now I am alone and hate it
I don't want to just make boards for the rest of my life
I'm distressed
the water is very beautiful but you can't go into it
because of the gunk
and the dog is always rolling over, I like dogs on their "little" feet
I think I may scamper off to Winnipeg to see Raymond

but what'll happen to the mill
I see the cobwebs collecting already
and later those other webs, those awful predatory webs
if I stay right here I will eventually get into the newspapers
like Robert Frost
willow trees, willow trees they remind me of Desdemona
I'm so damned literary
and at the same time the waters rushing past remind me of
                                                    nothing
I'm so damned empty
what is all this vessel shit anyway
we are all rushing down the River Happy Times
duckling poling bumping sinking and swimming
and we arrive at the beach
the chaff is sand
alone as a tree bumping another tree in a storm
that's not really being alone, is it, signed The Saw

                                        (*CP*, pp. 428–29)

To be "alone" is also to be all one, but again, like city life, O'Hara has only the unity of mad process trying to make up in motion what it lacks in meaning. The self threatens always to dissipate into the surfaces it contemplates, to become merely a "skein of lust" (*CP*, p. 403) unwinding in time. Yet one need only recognize the dangers to overcome them, to reaffirm his commitment and love of the processes he is engaged in: one must maintain, he says in his essay on Nakian, "a kind of despairing sensual delight" by achieving "a relation with physical truth that is both stoic and sybaritic."[24] Notice how in the poem I have quoted, O'Hara never dwells on the problems but keeps turning instead to the details of the scene or his own fantasies of future possibilities. "Naptha" offers an even better example of a conclusion nicely capturing both the underlying sterility of his experience and the rich union of stoic and sybaritic roles he creates in response.

> how are you feeling in ancient September
> I am feeling like a truck on a wet highway
> how can you
> you were made in the image of god
> I was not
> I was made in the image of a sissy truck-driver
> and Jean Dubuffet painting his cows
> "with a likeness burst in the memory"
> apart from love (don't say it)
> I am ashamed of my century
> for being so entertaining
> but I have to smile

                                        (*CP*, p. 338)

He "has" to smile—because he has no alternative, but· also because his and his century's absurd situation are genuinely entertaining. O'Hara has to smile, not to laugh, and in that small difference one can realize the distance between his genuinely sybaritic stoicism and the less humane anguish of the black humorist.

Ontologically, O'Hara's demystified sense of process is very close to the tragic Lowell of *Notebook*, but there are two major differences. First there is O'Hara's exuberance; his awareness of lurking emptiness generates neither a constant sense of how forced pleasure is nor the limited context of personal experience that is all Lowell can trust. All O'Hara's poems are intensely personal, but they retain, even celebrate, the necessary public dimension and shared quality of the surfaces that constitute his story.[25] The more important contrast lies in O'Hara's treatment of anxiety. For O'Hara the tragic themes so celebrated by the existentialist tradition are both ridiculous and dangerous. The tragic seems ridiculous because of its exalted and probably false sense of the heroic embattled ego—even if the ego is in the cathartic process of learning cosmic pity: "The strange career of a personality begins at five and ends/forty minutes later in a fog the rest is just a lot of stranded/ ships honking their horns full of joy-seeking cadets in bloomers" (*CP*, p. 392). The goal is not meeting or defying fate but "avoiding it" (*CP*, p. 365), and tragic themes are dangerous because they encourage one to think he or she can turn on anxieties and successfully wrestle them to the ground. But people are more like Actaeon than Hercules, more prone to be devoured by anxiety than to conquer it in direct conflict.

"Adieu to Norman, Bon Jour to Joan and Jean-Paul" summarizes most of O'Hara's poetic strategies and makes evident the differences from Lowell:

It is 12:10 in New York and I am wondering
if I will finish this in time to meet Norman for lunch
ah lunch! I think I am going crazy
what with my terrible hangover and weekend coming up
at excitement-prone Kenneth Koch's
I wish I were staying in town and working on my poems
at Joan's studio for a new book by Grove Press
which they will probably not print
but it is good to be several floors up in the dead of night
wondering whether you are any good or not
and the only decision you can make is that you did it

yesterday I looked up the rue Frémicourt on a map
and was happy to find it like a bird
flying over Paris et ses environs
which unfortunately did not include Seine-et-Oise
                                        which I don't know

as well as a number of other things
and Allen is back talking about god a lot
and Peter is back not talking very much
and Joe has a cold and is not coming to Kenneth's
although he is coming to lunch with Norman
I suspect he is making a distinction
well, who isn't

I wish I were reeling around Paris
instead of reeling around New York
I wish I weren't reeling at all
it is Spring the ice has melted the Ricard is being poured
we are all happy and young and toothless
it is the same as old age
the only thing to do is simply continue
is that simple
yes, it is simple because it is the only thing to do
can you do it
yes, you can because it is the only thing to do
blue light over the Bois de Boulogne it continues
the Seine continues
the Louvre stays open it continues it hardly closes at all
the Bar American continues to be French
de Gaulle continues to be Algerian as does Camus
Shirley Goldfarb continues to be Shirley Goldfarb
and Jane Hazan continues to be Jane Freilicher (I think!)
and Irving Sandler continues to be the balayeur des artistes
and so do I (sometimes I think I'm "in love" with painting)
and surely the Piscine Deligny continues to have water in it
and the Flore continues to have tables and newspapers
                                    and people under them
and surely we shall not continue to be unhappy
we shall be happy
but we shall continue to be ourselves everything
                        continues to be possible
Rene Char, Pierre Reverdy, Samuel Beckett it is possible isn't it
I love Reverdy for saying yea, though I don't believe it
                                    (*CP*, pp. 328–29)

Just as one has no grounds to measure adequately good and bad and so must look only at the qualities of his life as process (ll. 10–11), the poem can only counter the anxieties that continue to oppress by turning time and again to the details and possibilities to which one can keep saying yes, even if one does not believe them. O'Hara's characteristic strategies are clearest in the fourth stanza. In the initial line he tries to encounter his present sense of emptiness with an escape into fantasy and a possible future, but the escape does not work. By the third line he is returned to a dangerously static vision of himself as object (instead of as actor playing a creative role in process), one he escapes only by completely changing his vision and his theme to an awareness of the weather. And even here O'Hara is careful to avoid any illusion of depth. He swiftly metamorphoses spring's melting ice into the ice at cocktail parties so that none of spring's traditional symbolic overtones can emerge. For to admit spring as a symbolic entity is to remain on the symbolic generalized level of discourse where the problem of rootlessness is most pressing. While symbolic solutions might convince one for the moment he's overcome a philosophical problem, they also tempt his consciousness to continue operating on levels where further anxieties are inevitable. Symbolism perpetually promises qualities of experience that are not present and hence problematic.

O'Hara himself is one whom other poets love for saying "yes" but do not actually believe. His influence and popularity are considerably greater than his achievement—a phenomenon attributable to many factors including his sheer entertainment value and the notoriety of his pathetic and unexpected death. But most of all I think his popularity stems from his sybaritic stoicism, or perhaps affirmative skepticism, and from his articulation of strategies, attitudes, and values that other poets find themselves momentarily sharing. In addition, many of O'Hara's strategies can be adapted to qualities of experience less camp and aggressively superficial. While O'Hara reduces the present to sheer surface and the creative play of the individual consciousness, he also points to materials and attitudes that might constitute a genuine moral vision free of the systematic and abstract distortions of most philosophical attempts to define value.

Take as an example of O'Hara's centrality the question of how poets can handle moral materials within a philosophy of radical presence no longer able to lean on Bly and Olson's ontological crutches. Given the insistence on the open road and the denial of referential moral systems, it is impossible for the poet to affirm a morality stressing contents. The poet cannot recommend specific actions to be universally imitated, nor even propose very specific moral criteria individuals can use in defining their own rights and wrongs. All he can do is offer a set of moral attitudes. The poet illustrates and exemplifies modes of engaging whatever experiences a person might have, and his work becomes testament to the kind of effects these attitudes might bring about.[26] This sense that poetry is moral through the attitudes it embodies permeates postmodern poetry, and O'Hara is an influential example of both a specific strategy and the general framework supporting such an emphasis: think, for example, of poets like Gary Snyder, Allen Ginsberg, Bly, and W. S. Merwin who seek to embody modes of consciousness that one can or must inhabit to intuit moral truths; or consider others like John Logan, Bill Knott,

David Ignatow, and John Ashbery (O'Hara's close friend whose ironic and disembodied voice suggests a mode of living almost exactly opposite O'Hara's, though the two share the same ontology) whose attitudes are more directly moral, more concerned with ways of acting in relation to suffering and to other people, than they are with leading readers to ontological truths. What all share, though, is a tendency to expand traditional lyric modes so that they become existential strategies. Lyric poetry has always had as its primary function the invention and testing of attitudes toward experience, and *persona* was a primary critical category for critics of the fifties. But within the tradition, attitude was always supplementary to the moral qualities of the experience itself. Thus critics and poets could conceive *persona* ironically and contemplate the gap between ideal modes of response suggested by the experience and the specific moral or intellectual failures of the specific voice in the poem. Contemporary poets cannot afford to be ironic about their *personae* because they cannot trust, either in the poem or in reality, that the experience itself provides norms for judging the response. Rather only the response itself—its appeal for the reader and the possibilities it offers for keeping him open to the reality of his own experiences—can be the measure of the poet's moral value.

O'Hara's specific attitude is also very influential—not only on those New York poets who continue in the pop-art tradition but on others more taken by his humility and affirmative skepticism. The qualities of skepticism and humility in fact often go hand in hand, for it is always tempting, if not always possible, to extend one's skepticism about external values to skepticism about the self. And O'Hara's poetry does just that: one so aware of the arbitrary creativity he requires to keep the present vital is not apt to take either himself, his poetry, or his world view as possible salvation for everyone. So O'Hara presents demystified views of both the reconciliation of opposites and the poetic image. The high Romantic doctrine of the form-creating imagination unifying and reconciling opposites promises a solution at once unlikely, without distorting experience, and undesirable. For what makes life interesting is precisely confusion, contradiction, and the constant presence of alternatives. O'Hara approaches Olson's contention that only the multiplicity of the real can reconcile images, but he remains aware that this multiplicity will always seem contradictory to human consciousness. Yet like Donald Barthelme, his counterpart in prose fiction, O'Hara celebrates just this ironic reality of human experience. In a similar way, O'Hara presents a skeptical view of the poetic image: it is neither means for capturing the *Gott-natur* nor collocation of *topos, typos,* and *tropos.* Most often it is merely *topos,* the accurate and engaged description of interesting facets of experience, but when topology is not creative enough the poet self-consciously creates startling images and metaphors. O'Hara never allows himself, or his readers, to confuse will and perception or to mistake careful rhetorical construction for discovered ontological or psychological truth.[27]

O'Hara's resultant universe may be superficial and impoverished, but it is also fun—and fun with a strong measure of truth. The second of O'Hara's "2 Poems from the Ohara Monogatari," with its skeptical attitude toward created images and monistic world views, exemplifies both the truth and the fun:

> After a long trip to a shrine
> in wooden clogs so hard on the muscles
> the tea is bitter and the breasts are hard
> so much terrace for one evening
>
> there is no longer no ocean
> I don't see the ocean under my stilts
> as I poke along
>
> hands on ankles feet on wrists
> naked in thought
> like a whip made from sheerest stockings
>
> the radio is on the cigarette is puffed upon
> by the pleasures of rolling in a bog
> some call the Milky Way
> in far-fetched Occidental lands above the trees
> where dwell the amusing skulls

(CP, p. 213)

The poem is never really meditative, but given its oriental setting and religious overtones the first two stanzas could be a slightly cranky version of modish Western poems about Eastern religion. Even the transformation of the wooden clogs into stilts need not yet suggest an equation between humble Eastern religions and Yeats' self-conscious creative poet on his stilts. It is only in the third stanza that the irony takes over and reminds one that religion, Eastern or Western, is a creature of the fictive imagination. At the moment when the meditative state seems realized ("naked in thought"), O'Hara introduces the metaphor of a whip made of sheer stockings. The metaphor is high camp, at once completely arbitrary and an ironic reminder of how out of tune urban Western man is with whatever natural and religious energies he hopes to experience in the setting. Finally, this intrusion of self-consciousness leads to the last stanza's presentation of the pain and death willfully overlooked in turning to Eastern monistic visions of cosmic unity—a unity mocked, one might add, by the obvious way the poet's mind cannot satisfactorily merge into the scene.

There is, however, another sense in which O'Hara's materials are at least as important as his attitudes to his influential position, not in their camp specifics but as indications of areas in human experience not often mined by poets. For O'Hara is quintessentially a poet of the domestic and the quotidian. Few poets, thank God, share his sense of what the domestic and quotidian entails, but the success of any domestic poetry encourages others to look freshly at the immediate experiences that matter to them and to ask poetically why they matter. As John Ashbery asks, "Have you begun to be in the context you feel?" Moreover, the philosophy I have extracted from O'Hara can be used to rediscover the moral content of domestic experience. For one need not believe in numinous forces in order to recognize specific values in all sorts of prereflective and prephilosophical forms of life—in one's choices, in commitments, and even in compromises and acceptances.[28] If one can become aware of how important these energies, desires, and commitments are to one's enjoyment of life, one can realize how fully man in fact does live in a present charged with value contexts very difficult to define philosophically. In effect, O'Hara encourages readers to take Olson's admonitions about use and man's necessity to recover the familiar without the ontological, cosmic, and epic perspectives Olson cloaks them in. These grand ideas, as much of Olson's poetry unfortunately indicates, tend to lead one away from what they encourage one to recover. It is hard not to prefer the joyful, confident humility and honesty so fully witnessed in O'Hara's poetry.

Paul Carroll is the first critic I know to claim a really influential role for O'Hara in the poetry of the sixties. My argument complements and extends his, which deals primarily with the aesthetic aspects of the themes of domesticity and the process of continual creation. O'Hara's influence, he says, stems from three related factors in his work. He makes clear for poets how the dada and expressionist doctrines of creation can work for them, for his poems continually insist that they are not representations of reality but the enactment by the artist of certain attitudes and choices within that reality. Consequently there are no canonical or privileged subjects for poetry: "Anything, literally, can exist in a poem; and anything can exist in whatever way the poet chooses." O'Hara then shows how the poet need no longer feel committed to organic unity as a principle of poetic construction. His details need not be chosen because they enhance a specific lyric point or attitude; the objects chosen can embody the multiple facets of experience, only some of which might be essential to the lyric feeling. This antiorganicist aesthetic Carroll defines as the aesthetic of the "impure poem."[29]

The idea of the "impure poem" is both helpful and dangerous. It is helpful in so much as it calls one's attention to the materials and attitudes the contemporaries try to give poetic expression, but it oversimplifies the texture of relationships in the best poems using such materials. The organic poem need not be the single-minded evocation of simple emotions; "organic" simply means that all the aesthetic choices contribute to the complex effect of the poem. It is true that many of O'Hara's poems do not aim at single lyric effects but focus instead, like Duchamp's urinal and Warhol's Campbell's soup cans, on celebrating the powers of artistic choice and thus reminding one of the simple levels at which value experience continually takes place. But O'Hara's best lyrics employ details both as specific references to an impure, discontinuous texture of experience and as carefully related elements in a complex lyric feeling.

"The Day Lady Died" is Carroll's example of the archetypal impure poem; but that poem to me is one of the finest examples of the rich poetic possibilities in the domestic lyric. The poem not only captures the vitality of prereflective experience but arranges that experience so that it participates in and evokes for consciousness a complex, satisfying, and relatively traditional lyric emotion:

It is 12:20 in New York a Friday
three days after Bastille day, yes
it is 1959 and I go get a shoeshine
because I will get off the 4:19 in Easthampton
at 7:15 and then go straight to dinner
and I don't know the people who will feed me

I walk up the muggy street beginning to sun
and have a hamburger and a malted and buy
an ugly NEW WORLD WRITING to see what the poets
in Ghana are doing these days
                    I go on to the bank
and Miss Stillwagon (first name Linda I once heard)
doesn't even look up my balance for once in her life
and in the GOLDEN GRIFFIN I get a little Verlaine
for Patsy with drawings by Bonnard although I do
think of Hesiod, trans. Richmond Lattimore or
Brendan Behan's new play or Le Balcon or Les Negres
of Genet, but I don't, I stick with Verlaine
after practically going to sleep with quandariness

and for Mike I just stroll into the PARK LANE
Liquor Store and ask for a bottle of Strega and
then I go back where I came from to 6th Avenue
and the tobacconist in the Ziegfeld Theatre and
casually ask for a carton of Gauloises and a carton
of Picayunes, and a NEW YORK POST with her face on it

and I am sweating a lot by now and thinking of
leaning on the john door in the 5 SPOT
while she whispered a song along the keyboard
to Mal Waldron and everyone and I stopped breathing

(CP, p. 325)

One way of seeing how the poem is impure, Carroll suggests, is to recognize that twenty lines are devoted to the casual events of O'Hara's day and only four to the ostensive subject of the poem. He goes on, though, to offer two insights that help explain how the artist's apparently free creative selection of details really creates a single complex lyric emotion:

> I wonder how touching that beautiful final memory . . . would be if O'Hara had preceded it with emotional tributes and "props" customary in most traditional elegies. . . .
> In another sense, "The Day Lady Died" isn't about Billie Holliday at all. It is about the common but sobering feeling that life continues on its bumbling way despite the tragic death of an important artist or some loved one.[30]

But it is not only the general configuration of details, the contrast between bumbling life and the suddenness of death, that unifies the poem. The actual particulars by which the poem captures the vitality of life at the same time constantly call attention to their own contingency and perpetual hovering on the brink of disconnection. O'Hara has plans for dinner but does not know the people who will feed him; he is divorced in space and attitude from the Ghana poets, in time and habit from the writers mentioned in the third stanza (one usually does not "go to sleep with quandariness"—one sleeps from boredom and the lack of choice—but O'Hara wants to suggest connections between multiplicity, lack of connections guiding choice, and forms of death); he encounters probably for the hundredth time a bank teller he has no communication with, yet who also disproves his expectations; and even the apparently most arbitrary item, the reference to Bastille Day, has a curious appositeness in a poem so thoroughly about death, separation, and the fragility of established order. Moreover, the "and" rhetoric so pronounced in the poem further enhances one's sense of the tangential and problematic links between particulars: parataxis calls attention to the rush of time piling up details united only by sequential time alien to specifically human patterns of relationship. The rush of life then embodies also a process of continual death leading to the climactic stoppages of life and breath in the last four lines. But the initial twenty lines also allow the poet to find a meaning in Billie's death. Seeing in her art and his memories of it the experience of connection counters and helps mollify the pains of discontinuity. What he remembers about Billie is a moment of stasis that is at once death and very intense life—death because it so divorces him from the normal (and insignificant) activities of his daily life, and intense life for precisely the same reason since it has been that life which is really involvement in continual deaths. The moment he remembers is one of absolute communication when Billie controlled the entire audience and led them to a single ecstasy ("everyone and I stopped breathing"). And O'Hara's poem is itself an act like Billie Holiday's; the full elegiac effect depends on the reader's union with his memory. Like her singing, the poem also can claim at least for a moment to transcend the contingent multiplicities of daily experience and, through the poem's deliberate slowing in these last lines, allow a brief space where readers all stop that rushing breath always associated with process in O'Hara and realize how art and memory can console in the face of recurrent death.

O'Hara is not often so good; but neither are any other poets of the sixties. Nonetheless, Carroll is correct in insisting that "The Day Lady Died" is a crucial touchstone for postmodern poetry. The poem exemplifies how postmodern literature can thrive, though oppressed on the one side by philosophical nihilism and on the other by the oppressive burden of literary history always reminding poets of how little room there seems to be for meaningful originality. Literature can remain honest and "de-mystified," without succumbing to self-pitying nostalgia or refining away its content in the self-conscious acrobatics of what John Barth has called "the literature of exhaustion." Not only poetry, but even some of the basic values of civilized life can be discovered by pushing further than the past into the manifold particulars and the texture of domestic contemporary life.

Notes to Chapter 3

1. *Presence* and its dialectical opposite *absence*, seem to me very useful terms for defining the quest for immanence in contemporary poetry. First of all, the

terms constitute a way of talking about the immanence J. Hillis Miller so elegantly discusses in *Poets of Reality* (Cambridge, Mass.: Harvard University Press, Belknap Press, 1965) without allegiance to any theology or even philosophy. *Presence* is the term for a condition of experience (or "instress") made possible by a latent or immanent principle of significance (or "inscape") in the objects experienced or in the prehensive act of knowing them. Miller's own preference for the term *being* seems to me at times to warp his analyses of poets like Eliot and Yeats, in whom immanence takes such different forms (one theological, and the other oriented toward participation in the being of a single all-encompassing Adam or unified man, best described as daemonic) into a single Heideggerean mode. *Presence* allows one to define a shared quest for immanence while leaving open the specific form it might take. In a similar way *absence* can be defined in many ways, both by poets and by competing conceptual systems, without one's being forced to use a single interpretive scheme. Lowell's experience of absence, for example, can be interpreted in numerous ways: a Freudian would speak of sublimation, an existential psychiatrist of anxiety, a religious thinker of anxiety caused by the death of God, an epistemologist of the separation of mind and object, and a Marxist of alienation. All are true at times, and to separate one from another requires intellectual skills I do not possess. I know I have particular favorites among the alternatives, but hope that the abstractness of my basic term allows me some flexibility even within my preconceptions to see how the poet himself interprets his experience.

Let me also point out that I use the term *presence* in a slightly different way from that of Jacques Derrida and those influenced by him. Derrida takes *presence* in two complementary ways. First, *presence* is an illusion fostered by one's taking speech as the primary model for understanding the mode of being of language. Thus one ignores the displacements created by the arbitrary and oscillating qualities of linguistic codes. And second, presence serves as a term for any metaphysical desire for terms to have clear and distinct objective referents— present as it were by being pictured in language. My own position, articulated in the essay in Wittgenstein cited above, is that scholars need to explore the ontology connected with speech-act theory in order to clarify the way presence is a condition of man's ways of acting in the world, not of some abstract pictorial connection between words and things. *Presence* in short is a condition of perception and a quality of certain modes of reflective or dramatic action. Poems do not make the world present but create imaginative stances in which one can envision how the world might be present in some form of numinous vitality. Hence in poetry one can reflect upon the idea of presence and the qualities of craft and vision exhibited by the poet's articulation of his dramatic stance.

2. See Kierkegaard's discussion of the despair of being a self in *Sickness Unto Death* (New York: Anchor, 1954), pp. 146 ff., 207 ff.

3. For the importance of culture as basis of Lowell's value system, see "Robert Lowell in Conversation with A. Alvarez," *The Review*, no. 8 (August 1963), p. 40.

4. D. H. Lawrence, *Studies in Classic American Literature* (New York: Viking, 1961), pp. 172–77.

5. Robert Bly, "Review of Lowell's *For the Union Dead*," *The Sixties* 8 (1966): 96. In this study I will use the following abbreviations for Bly's essays and poems: "Review of Lowell," *RL*; "A Wrong Turning in American Poetry," *Choice* 3 (1963): 33–47, *WT*; "The Dead World and the Live World," *The Sixties* 8 (1966):

2–7, *DW*; "Prose vs Poetry; *Choice* 2 (1962): 66–67, *PP*; *Silence in the Snowy Fields* (Middletown, Conn.: Wesleyan University Press, 1962), *SS*; *The Light Around the Body* (New York: Harper and Row, 1967), *LB*. For Bly on Lowell, see also *WT*, pp. 43–45.

6. What Bly takes as refusal of nonhuman experience can be seen more sympathetically as an unwillingness to mystify or indulge in any fictions. Lowell's reticence about nonhuman energies is remarkable, even within the prose tradition that is his heritage. For even Pound expanded imagism into Vorticism in order to take into account the natural energies evoked through art, and Pound always saw the prose tradition as means for a genuine recovery of the Gods he glimpses so often in the *Cantos*.

7. If one follows Bly's argument that openness to the *Gott-natur* will have ethical effects, there is no way to explain how James Dickey, whose openness to the *Gott-natur* in his earlier poetry earned Bly's deepest praises, could support the Vietnam War. Like many other poets of the sixties, and unlike Lawrence, Bly refuses to grant the possibility that presence in a world without God can be as much demonic as it is ethical. Violence, as Yeats's prayer for war in his time testifies, is perhaps the most immediate form for creating intense present moments. For the comments on Dickey see *PP*, pp. 66–67, and a review of *Buckdancer's Choice*, in *Sixties* 9 (1967): 70–79, which viciously attacks Dickey's support of the war.

8. William Matthews, "Thinking about Robert Bly," *Tennessee Poetry Journal* 2 (Winter 1969): 53, discusses the images of explosion and fragmentation in terms of the tendency in Bly for the inner and outer worlds to fly apart. One might also notice how Bly's dichotomy between nervous and centered energy develops similar themes.

9. Bly uses the phrase praising David Ignatow, in *Sixties* 10 (1968): 22.

10. W. K. Wimsatt, "The Structure of Romantic Nature Imagery," in his *The Verbal Icon* (New York: Noonday, 1958), pp. 103–16, discusses this suppression of self-consciousness about metaphor as characteristic of Romantic poetry. If Bly differs from the Romantics at all in his use of metaphor, it is in his tendency to emphasize the space of analogy. He is as interested in the kind of attitude necessary to perceive analogically as much as he is in the actual analogical processes in nature. See also the important and timely essay by Ronald Moran and George Lensing, "The Emotive Imagination: A New Departure in American Poetry," *Southern Review* 3 (1967): 52–67, which uses the term *emotive imagination* to describe the way Bly, Simpson, Wright, and Stafford all base their work on metaphors juxtaposing the objective with images evoking a profound subjectivity. (The essay is very useful in describing the various rhetorical strategies that make this emotive imagination come alive.)

11. Maurice-Jean Lefèbre, *L'Image Fascinante et Le Surréel* (Paris: Librarie Plon, 1965), especially pp. 17, 29, 259, and the two quotations below, pp. 271, 267. Lefèbre, like Jacques Derrida and Paul de Man, finds the dialectics of absence and presence most useful in discussing the illusory nature of the Romantic quest for poetry that captures a higher reality (especially p. 67).

12. For another, darker view of death as the central theme in Bly's poetry, see Richard Howard's chapter on him in *Alone with America: Essays on the Art of Poetry in the United States Since 1950* (New York: Atheneum, 1971).

13. This phrase is the subtitle of Olson's *Poetry and Truth* (San Francisco,

Calif.: Four Seasons Foundation, 1971), and the quotation above is from p. 54 of that text. For Olson I use the following abbreviations in the text: *Poetry and Truth, PT; Human Universe and Other Essays,* ed. Donald Allen (New York: Grove, 1967), *HU; The Distances* (New York: Grove, 1961), *D; Causal Mythology* (San Francisco, Calif.: Four Seasons Foundation, 1969), *CM;* and *A Special View of History,* ed. Ann Charters (Berkeley, Calif.: Oyez, 1970), *SVH.*

14. One might contrast the New Critics with Olson here, for they either absolutize aesthetic truth as a unique mode of knowing (this is the theme of Murray Krieger's study of New Criticism, *The New Apologists for Poetry*) or try to oppose artistic knowledge to operational moral and practical truths. This second argument is an attempt to refute Arnoldian humanism and to keep the aesthetic realm distinct from faith. See as a good example Cleanth Brook's famous dispute with Douglas Bush over Marvell's "Horatian Ode" in *Seventeenth Century English Poetry,* ed. William Keast (New York: Oxford University Press, 1962), pp. 321–58.

15. The last few sentences have been a paraphrase of a section in "Quantity in Verse, and Shakespeare's Late Plays," *HU,* pp. 83–84.

16. It is this idea of man the gatherer of being that lies behind Olson's desire for epic. The point is to make verse, and hence man, handle and bring together larger areas of being than the traditional lyric does (cf. *HU,* pp. 127–28, 61). By a similar logic Olson laments what history has lost of the high energies once captured in the past (*HU,* pp. 8–12).

17. Frank Kermode, *The Romantic Image* (New York: Vintage, 1964), especially pp. 43–44.

18. Olson also sees the metaphor of vectors to describe how all history can be seen as the resolution of four basic forces—millennia, process, person, and quantity. See *A Bibliography on America For Ed Dorn* (San Francisco, Calif.: Four Seasons Foundation, 1964). One might also note how Olson's coming later in his career to fuller definitions of terms like *typos* and *tropos* manifests the basic mode of his development as a thinker. He begins with a basically behaviorist emphasis on the body and comes gradually to see the specific body as essentially a participant in larger mythic forces best expressed in Blake's Albion, the body that is also a mythic integration of the cosmos. I simplify Olson by emphasizing his more mundane earlier speculations (except at the end of my discussion) because of my own inadequacies, but also, I hope, because this earlier thought has been the more influential—even on people as close to him as Creeley. Creeley's edition of his *Selected Writings* (New York: New Directions, 1966), is in fact an interesting example of selective influence: not only does Creeley stress Olson at his most empirical, but he leaves out many of the essays in Allen's edition that express Olson's concerns for the hero and the epic—concerns Creeley does not share.

19. For fuller discussions by Olson on the themes of tropism and Cosmos see "A Syllabary For a Dancer," *Maps* 4 (1970).

20. William Aiken, "Charles Olson: A Preface," *Massachusetts Review* 12 (1971): 49–68, offers the best analysis I know of how Olson's poetic tries to adapt traditional modes to a metaphysic of process. "Olson's main theme," he argues, "is the definition of the self as an extension of the processes of nature" (p. 58), but he neither elaborates what "extension" involves nor adequately defines the dynamics of Olson's lyrics.

21. *Try, Try* is published in *Artists' Theatre in New York: Four Plays,* ed. Herbert Machiz (New York: Grove Press, 1960), pp. 15–42. O'Hara's poems and essays are collected in *The Collected Poems of Frank O'Hara,* ed. Donald Allen (New York: Knopf, 1971). The two works will be cited in the text as *AT* and *CP.*

22. O'Hara's differences from Olson on creativity is analagous to the difference between pop and Dada acts of creativity, which endow the objects with importance (Duchamp's urinal, for example) and the abstract expressionist creativity whereby one is both subject and object of the forces realized in the act of creating. O'Hara, though, as I shall show, often goes beyond pop creativity to merge his own creative acts with the energies of the city. But even then there is an emphasis (foreign to Olson and to Pollock) on the surface qualities of the object.

23. "To put it very gently, I have a feeling that the philosophical reduction of reality to a dealable-with system so distorts life that one's 'reward' for this endeavor . . . is illness both from inside and outside" (*CP,* p. 495). Nonetheless, my own analysis of O'Hara, particularly the discussion of story, is based on a philosopher, Jacques Derrida, who tries to work out the epistemological and ethical implications of a postmodern reality without depth and impossible to interpret. I use the term *story* as literary embodiment of what Derrida calls "free play," in a world whose givenness is all one can have. And central in that givenness is one's own creative play among the phenomena one encounters. (Derrida insists far more than O'Hara on the strictly verbal qualities of this given reality.)

24. Quoted in Richard Howard's fine essay on O'Hara in his *Alone with America,* p. 403.

25. Derrida, in his essay "Structure, Sign, and Play," *The Languages of Criticism and the Sciences of Man,* ed. Richard Macksey and Eugenio Donato (Baltimore, Md.: Johns Hopkins University Press, 1970), pp. 247–65, distinguishes between the "nostalgia" of most Western poetry and metaphysics seeking a center or source of reference and value that can define and interpret the value of specific phenomenal experiences and a kind of Nietzschean free play that, rather than lament the continually displaced quality of phenomena, accepts and revels in the freedom of their lack of external or referential definition. Lowell is a poet of nostalgia, while O'Hara keeps one aware of the potential nostalgia but refuses to submit to a suffering that seems even more purposeless than the phenomena he possesses. (To see how close O'Hara is to Derrida on this theme, consult his refutation of Lionel Abel's "nineteenth century" expectations that Pasternak should exhibit the "grief-expression of the romantic hero," [*CP,* p. 504].)

26. This is precisely what Robert Motherwell does in O'Hara's collection of his work and his reflections, *Robert Motherwell* (New York: The Museum of Modern Art, 1965), p. 53.

27. We might distinguish four attitudes toward the image-imitation—two traditional ones, and two adapting expressionism to an aesthetic of immanence. Almost no contemporary poet has an imitative aesthetic; poetry for them is an act in experience, not a copying of it. Nor are many poets self-expressive, in the sense of the Romantic or religious lyric. But many have a slightly different attitude toward expression: in expressing himself the poet presents an event in which the energies of experience find definition, form, and resonance through the poet's language. Poetics of immanence usually exhibit this conception of the poet as at once subject and object, as creative medium for the immanent qualities of

experience always there but only brought to consciousness in poetic language. The danger of this conception, however, is that the poet often confuses his own will with genuine immanence. Self-expression makes itself an expression of the world, a phenomenon one finds recurrent especially in deep-image poetry where often the most arbitrary images are proposed as dynamic experiences of creative objective energy coursing through the poet. The fourth approach to the image accepts, and often revels in, the self's freedom to endow experience with imaginative significance. O'Hara, like few other contemporaries, uses both the expressive and created images without confusing the two.

28. Kenneth Rexroth, in *Assays* (Norfolk, Conn.: New Directions, 1961) and *The Alternate Society* (New York: Herder and Herder, 1970) is the poet and critic most conscious of how significant the contemporary emphasis on domestic materials can be. Opposing Williams to the poetic defenders of "civilization," he reminds readers that the true "power" and "almost inextinguishable life" of civilization "consists of things like your cats stepping over the window sill." Williams had so much to give because he knew what he had already (*Assays*, p. 204). Few of us, Rexroth points out, are called to imitate the lofty actions of the world's great books, but "we are all called to be human" and can imitate a poetry of attention and reverence (*Assays*, p. 207).

29. Paul Carroll, *The Poem In Its Skin* (Chicago: Follet, 1968), pp. 157–65; quote from p. 163.

30. Ibid., p. 160.

4

Process as Plenitude: The Poetry of Gary Snyder and Robert Duncan

i

I have dealt abstractly with the themes that unite such disparate enterprises as Bly's, Olson's, and O'Hara's. Now I want to concentrate on the careers of Gary Snyder and Robert Duncan in order to clarify pure or naive (in Schiller's sense) poetic visions that assert a radical faith in the aesthetics of presence as the ground for a postmodern religious attitude. These poets are significant craftsmen, worthy of attention strictly in terms of their own achievements, but I also find them very useful figures for articulating the possibilities and the limits in the sixties' dream of using poetry to transcend the realm of aesthetic questions and concerns. First, the more fully one appreciates their ideals, the more one can understand the doubts, the struggles, and the skepticism of other poets who examine some of the ironies and contradictions involved in pursuing a faith in process. Duncan and Snyder represent the comic pole of postmodernism, and hence if one is at all drawn to a map of imaginative structure like Northrop Frye's, they help define the ideals producing the tensions and struggles of more complex and cautious poets. And second, both writers illustrate the burden placed on traditional stylistic aspects of poetry when poetry is asked to express and testify to values capable of sustaining a religious faith.

Wendell Berry offers a succinct statement of this stylistic burden.[1] Speaking of postmodern nature poetry, he argues that the poet's primary aim is to render "a religious state of mind," which affords "a sense of the presence of mystery or divinity in the world." But to do so, the poet must take as his antagonist a long history of thinking and of conceiving language in terms separating the Creator from Creation and hence of imaging the holy as a transcendental principle easily susceptible to the attacks of positivist thought. For a postmodern religious vision to be possible, poets must find styles capable of presenting "a new speech— a speech that will cause the world to live and thrive in men's minds." Berry suggests, in short, that a religious perspective can escape positivism only if it foregoes transcendental claims and grounds its assertions of value in particular dramatic ways of attending to the objective world of secular science. The numinous is not symbolic, not a vision of a reality beyond the familiar; rather it inheres in particular stances toward natural facts that exhibit the mind adjusting and accommodating its energies and its needs to the energies and structures disclosed by science. Religious awareness in poetry, then, becomes a matter of syntax rather than of symbolism, a matter of forging through language models of an attentive mind that sustains certain types of balances between its own ways of connecting perceptions and relationships manifesting the world's capacity to satisfy desires for value.

The lyric can carry this syntactic burden because it is a form traditionally dependent upon syntax for a good deal of its power and significance. Authority in the lyric normally depends on the manner in which linguistic structures figure forth acts of mind and imaginative stances. What makes lyrics potentially universal or typical is less their arguments or ideas than their way of articulating the mental act that produces or applies ideas. Romantic nature lyrics, then, are essentially new, more meditative ways of relating traditional lyric strategies to a particular set of stances involving the mind's stances toward nature. And the postmodern religious nature lyric, in turn, manifests the same tendencies under the greater pressure of a vision that cannot rely on symbolism or theological metaphors but instead depends entirely on the quality of mental acts dramatized in process. One can see both the similarities and the differences from the traditional lyric if one notices the two further requirements placed on relational structures by the specific claims of postmodern religious nature poetry. To the degree metaphor is distrusted, pressure is placed on syntax to satisfy a reader's desire for significance and aesthetic pleasure, and to the degree poets reject abstract themes or formal patterns, there is a need to make specific lyric poems and isolated moments of lyric vision cohere in some larger system of internal connections. Hence Lowell's strategies for creating unified volumes must be adapted to different ends. The unified volume must serve as testimony that religious faith involves a coherent and complex range of attitudes. Faith must be a "way" of being in the world and not simply a response to isolated moments of intense lyric vision.

Snyder and Duncan have very different stylistic manners for creating and testing their religious stances. Snyder's lyric poetry is concrete and dramatic, developing specific Romantic and objectivist strategies for focusing the full energies of mind in moments of intense attention to familiar scenes so as to bring out their numinous aspects. Duncan, on the other hand, concentrates primarily on acts of reflection rather than acts of attention. His goal is to naturalize the processes of mythic thinking and to recover traditional Western hermetic visions in contemporary terms. The two poets thus represent the two basic poles between which one can place the work of other poets seeking to render religious attitudes defensible in a thoroughly secular and empirical culture.

Both poets, however, share numerous values, as defined in my first chapter, and both share a fundamental model for correlating style and religious belief. In provisional general terms (to be developed in the ensuing analyses), one can say that they reverse the modernist quest to make art out of the flux of experience in order to explore ways in which aesthetic modes of perception might parallel and reveal possible organic relationships between the mind and nature. Both poets ground their religious claims on the ontological status of analogies between natural, mental, and aesthetic patterns of relationship, and both seek to make the idea of organic unity a testimony to a unifying force linking various particulars and revealing shared properties in nature, in the mind, and in imaginative aesthetic acts of reflecting upon the creative mind at work in nature.[2] For Snyder, this project involves extending the aesthetics of organicism into a religious model of "Communionism," while Duncan tries to make the processes of allegory testimony to the continuing vitality of the traditional analogical vision of the world as the book of God.

It is extremely difficult, however, for the secular mind to accept these elaborations of aesthetic metaphors. When one clearly sees the aesthetic roots of conceiving the world as religious text, he finds it hard not to take the metaphysics as mystified aesthetics; one sees the book of God as one permutation of man's continual aesthetic enterprise of adapting nature to his own textual strategies. One need not give full rein to his suspicions. At their best Snyder and Duncan do create stances one can accept as possible ways of correlating aesthetic vision with natural and mental processes. But once the ironic potential inherent in their fundamental metaphors becomes clear, one can recognize how skeptical poets of process like O'Hara and John Ashbery can (perhaps must) coexist in essentially the same logical place. Then one can also see how other poets like Creeley and Merwin are continually torn between asserting moments of presence and questioning their own beliefs, so that the very dream of presence seems a fantasy requiring equally extreme explorations of the modes of consciousness involved with disillusioned self-awareness and a terrifying sense of absence.

Ashbery is the clearest antithesis to Snyder and Duncan. His most recent work, *Self-Portrait in a Convex Mirror,* makes it clear that the journey of his poetic career has led him gradually from a totally ironic sense of presence as realizable only in a book, in the artifice of imaginative structures, to a tenuous and rich exploration of the way the folds of that book implicate moments of presence that have a kind of religious plenitude. In this chapter, however, I shall only refer to some of Ash-

bery's work in the sixties in order to demonstrate the ironic reversals
to which any postmodern religious vision is susceptible.

ii

Gary Snyder is one of the very few poets since 1900 to command
both a large popular appeal and considerable respect from his peers.
The reason for the former is his articulation of a possible religious faith
at a time when cultural alienation was pushing many people to experiment with various non-Western metaphysical systems. The reason for
the latter is evident if one compares Snyder with other poets responding
to the same quest for alternate religious doctrines. On the one hand
there are poets like Cid Corman and Philip Whalen who directly translate Zen materials and forms into English, and on the other there are
those like Allen Ginsberg or Jerome Rothenberg who achieve the intense
and dramatic religious emotion the former lack, but only at the cost
of a considerable sacrifice of secular intelligence. Consider Ginsberg's
"Wichita Vortex Sutra," which so accepts Eastern idealism that it equates
abolishing war in one's head with the claim that the Vietnam War has
been literally transcended. Snyder differs from Corman and Whalen by
exercising care to adapt his Eastern meditative habits to concrete dramatic experiences and to make his syntax reflect those habits of vision
which justify and give resonance to his religious assertions. And unlike
Ginsberg, Snyder tries to limit his affirmations to claims he can support
or at least embody within the affective context and attitude created by
his dramatic lyrics. When he goes bad, Snyder's work collapses into one
or the other of the types I have mentioned, but he normally avoids them
by basing his religious vision on dramatic techniques and situations that
manifest their relevance to Western culture.

Snyder, in short, repeats the central strategies of Dante and Donne,
conceiving his religious vision as a repetition in a finer tone of what
the imagination in fact does and discloses when it constructs a set of
metaphoric relationships attesting to some ideal unity not readily evident
to the discursive logical mind. This same principle led John Crowe Ransom to define the successful poem as a form of "miraculism" because
of the way it blends discrete particulars into a dynamic whole and
reconciles the multiplicity of phenomena with the coherence of logical
abstraction. Ransom, however, had too much faith in the mind's powers
to trust his own metaphor and could never reconcile for himself the
contrary pulls of aesthetic naturalism and faith in a transcendental religion. By naturalizing the mind and placing it at once within and beyond
natural process, Snyder can more easily accept the organic poem as

testimony to an organically unified cosmos. Notice how close to aesthetic theory his fundamental religious insight is:

> The Australian aborigines live in a world of ongoing recurrence-comradeship with the landscape and continual exchanges of being and form and position; every person, animals, forces all are related via a web of reincarnation—or rather, they are "interborn." It may well be that rebirth (or interbirth, for we are actually mutually creating each other and all things while living) is the objective fact of existence which we have not yet brought into conscious knowledge and practice.
>
> It is clear that the empirically observable interconnectedness of nature is but a corner of the vast "jewelled net" which moves from without to within.[3]

For the skeptic or half-believer, the real miracle is the skill with which Snyder uses the aesthetic devices of lyrical poetry to sustain his religious claims. His basic achievement is his power to make his readers reflect on the ontological core of the lyrical vision by calling attention to the way it can be things or processes themselves, and not merely the elements of a poem, which mutually create one another's significance and suggest a unifying power producing, sustaining, and giving meaning to these relationships.

Snyder's lyrics have always sought the state described in the above quotation, but his earliest lyrics make clear by their lack of full inter-relationships how difficult it has been to achieve the easy, confident sense of interbirth in more recent poems. These early lyrics concentrate more on the moral task of achieving freedom from Western ways than on realizing the goal of a new religious vision. What freedom they achieve from the struggle to escape slavery to "culture" is expressed primarily in the form of naming particulars, not of discovering relationships. Particulars come to function as riprap, marking and securing the way to a religious vision of the stillness at the heart of change:[4]

> Down valley a smoke haze
> Three days heat, after five days rain
> Pitch glows on the fir cones
> Across Rocks and meadows
> Swarms of new flies
>
> I cannot remember things I once read
> A few friends, but they are in cities
> Drinking cold snow-water from a tin cup
> Looking down for miles
> Through high still air.

(RR, p. 9)

The poem dramatizes a sense of place and a sense of cosmos, but that cosmos is backdrop and not active agent. Similarly, the language is essentially nominal (Olson's hated push to the nominative) and neither active in itself nor alive with interrelationships. Snyder has escaped into the territories, but not yet mapped their ecology.

The opening poems in *The Back Country* provide the first maps. Interbirth here is not yet a cosmic dance, but one does see its genesis in Snyder's sense of the way particulars require one another if they are to be appreciated fully. The resultant mode of consciousness, in poems like "A Walk," might best be described as an ecological one— bringing the "vast 'jewelled net' " to "conscious knowledge and practice":

> Sunday the only day we don't work:
> Mules farting around the meadow,
> Murphy fishing,
> The tent flaps in the warm
> Early sun: I've eaten breakfast and I'll
> take a walk
> To Benson Lake. Packed a lunch,
> Goodbye. Hopping on creekbed boulders
> Up the rock throat three miles
> Piute Creek—
> In steep gorge glacier-slick rattlesnake country
> Jump, land by a pool, trout skitter,
> The clear sky. Deer tracks.
> Bad place by a falls, boulders big as houses,
> Lunch tied to belt,
> I stemmed up a crack and almost fell
> But rolled out safe on a ledge
> and ambled on.
> Quail chicks freeze underfoot, color of stone
> Then run cheep! away, hen quail fussing.
> Craggy west end of Benson Lake—after edging
> Past dark creek pools on a long white slope—
> Lookt down in the ice-black lake
> lined with cliff
> From far above: deep shimmering trout.
> A lone duck in a gunsight pass
> steep side hill
> Through slide-aspen and talus, to the east end,
> Down to grass, wading a wide smooth stream
> Into camp. At last.
> By the rusty three-year-
> Ago left-behind cookstove
> Of the old trail crew,
> Stoppt and swam and ate my lunch.

(BC, p. 19)

The poem at first seems flat until the reader perceives a dynamic process at work. The key to the poem's significance is the exclamation, "at last," when the speaker reaches his destination. The phrase demands that the reader see some kind of completion in the concluding details. As one thinks about these details, one comes to realize that the whole poem is a balancing: it holds in solution the speaker's difficult journey over an expanse of space in the mountains and the comfort and security of the secluded rest, the swim, and the lunch that conclude the hike. The phrase "at last" points to the emotional importance of these last details, an importance created only by the exertions of the journey. In other words, the balanced elements each achieve their full significance, obtain their fullest life, only when seen as a dialectic unity: the lunch and swim are only fully appreciated because of the exertions of the hike, and the hike is only truly appreciated through the conclusion it makes possible. Snyder's habit of loading his poem with detail is neither frivolous nor without artistic consideration, for the paradox of relationship is that it returns the reader to the particulars with a greater appreciation of them ("the other becomes the lover through whom the various links in the net can be perceived" [*EHH*, p. 34]). This is especially true for the concluding detail in the poem, the lunch, which is redeemed from its quotidian triviality and reconstituted as one of the most fulfilling aspects of one's normal life. Snyder restores some of the sacramental significance of a meal—a significance not the result of a unique transcendental act but implicit in the normal secular event. This particular lunch, like the Christian sacrament, is an event participating at the same time in other, deeper levels of reality. The rusting cook-stove stands as a memorial that other travelers have shared his experience, have probably come to appreciate a similar sense of satisfaction, and, finally, have left a reminder of the way nature itself is partially shaped by and preserves traces of its interactions with men.

Snyder here builds from the fact that the organic poem is a kind of ecological system to make the poem illustrate moral qualities basic to an ecological perspective on experience.[5] First of all, there is the tone that by its quiet casualness denies the traditional assumption (taken to extremes in confessional poetry) that lyric poetry is the expression of unique moments charged with extraordinary intensity. Second, the syntax of the poem supports its ecological intent, for as the speaker becomes more involved in his actions he forgoes any explicit references to himself as subject. The reader gets instead a series of verbs and almost dangling participles that tend to blend actor and action, man and world. Finally, the preponderance of concrete details has two effects. So much pointing asserts the referential power of language and denies the self-reflexive implications that accompany more metaphoric styles. It is not words but things that are being related to one another. And these concrete relations enable Snyder to communicate a non-Western frame of mind without references to occult philosophy or a series of abstractions. Ecology deals not with ideas, but with modes of action and with the unity of inter-relationships in nature, and its verification is the fullness of the environment it creates. In a poem that realizes Snyder's ecological perspective, myth and text no longer require separate statement; they are unified in one's quiet reverence at the depth of connection suggested by the poem.[6]

"Six-Month Song in the Foothills" (BC, p. 17) puts the ecological sense of experience into a larger framework that incorporates the active reflective mind into its pattern of relationships:

> In the cold shed sharpening saw.
>   a swallow's nest hangs by the door
> setting rakers in sunlight
> falling from meadow through doorframe
>   swallows flit under the eaves.
>
> Grinding the falling axe
> sharp for the summer
>   a swallow shooting out over
> over the river, snow on low hills
> sharpening wedges for splitting.
>
> Beyond the low hills, white mountains
> and now snow is melting. sharpening tools;
>   pack horses grazing new grass
> bright axes—and swallows
>   fly in to my shed.

Again the poem is constructed around balanced spatial elements whose interactions suggest the meaning of spring. Snyder's own space objectified as his shed, the space of the natural world about the shed, and the expanse of the natural world introduced in the third stanza enter a complex relationship evoking the balance of inner and outer life, smallness and infinity, created by a full awareness of the force of spring. Spring in the poem is the bringer of vitality: it sets the birds flying, the horses grazing, the snow melting, and Snyder to the spring ritual of sharpening his tools. This sharpening becomes metaphoric or, better, analogous to both the general quickening of life produced by spring and to Snyder's awakening mind. Spring sharpens the "razoredge," where man's attention meets the world (EHH, p. 41; see also p. 34). The shed then, as it encloses the swallows without impeding their actions, objectifies the new state of mind, which Snyder calls *"That* level of mind—the cool water—not intellect and not—(as Romantics and after have confusingly thought) fantasy—dream world or unconscious. This is just the clear spring—it reflects all things and feeds all things but is of itself transparent" (*EHH*, p. 57). The syntax of the last stanza and the emphatic position of "fly into my shed" in the last line go on to produce complex spatial relationships. Grammatically each of the last three nouns in the poem might fly into the mind, and without the punctuation (i.e., in the rush of oral presentation) all the objects in the stanza can enter the mind. The shed remains a limited place, but at the same time becomes capable of entertaining even the mountains with the same freedom that it entertains the swallows.

The free interchange of awakening mind and nature is beautifully sustained by Snyder's use of participles in the poem. The participle is a verbal noun representing both a state of action and a state of being. Its repeated use evokes the metaphysical state described by Fenollosa and Whitehead where what one tends to see as entities are in fact states of action; verbs approach substance and nouns become active. Moreover, participles blend human and natural action; both share the same verbal form and share the single action of spring. Snyder reinforces this by refusing, as he did in "A Walk," to supply explicit referents to the participles modifying his own actions, so that they appear as if freed from the limits of subjectivity. The first explicitly subjective reference comes only in the last line and there it serves primarily to stress the blend of subject and object in the free space of the shed. The whole poem serves to set off Snyder's subjectivity, to preserve it while showing that it achieves its fullness only when in total harmony with the processes of the world in which it dwells.[7]

The shed here can serve as a perfect metaphor for this kind of Snyder lyric: the shed is a small enclosure and yet it contains an infinite depth created by the relationships it contains and forms. The poem then becomes an enclosed space that is not a limiting space; relationships are manifest without being forced and without reduction of or tension between any of the elements. This lack of tension is important because it distinguishes Snyder's lyrics from the expectations created by modernism. Insofar as his poems are based on dialectic and juxtaposition, Snyder remains traditional, but the lack of tension leads to radically different emotional and philosophical implications. Yeats's gyres are a perfect emblem of the traditional dialectic. The elements held in relation by the typical Yeats poem are in violent, often unresolvable conflict. Only superhuman heroic enterprise can make a sphere of the gyres and reconcile or resolve such tensions—thus Yeats's stress on the power of the artist and later on the tragic hero. Similar senses of the heroic enterprise entailed in reconciling opposites lead Pound and early Eliot to their belief in the importance of traditional cultures and Eliot to his ultimate reliance on a transcendent still-point. For Snyder, on the other hand, the purpose of the poem as dialectic is to reduce tension by affirming the opposites' need for one another.[8] Snyder, then, does not require heroic enterprise; reconciliation of the opposites is possible for all because the reconciliation need not be imposed; it exists in fact. Man does not have to transcend nature; he has only to recognize how that flux itself generates meaning. He need only regain for himself what the primitive has, "this knowledge of connection and responsibility" (*EHH*, p. 121).

The knowledge of connection, in turn, prepares a possible meditative mode where one can construct an imaginative space in which particular balances reveal a deeper unity: " 'Beyond' there lies, inwardly the unconscious. Outwardly the equivalent of the unconscious is the wilderness: both of these terms meet, one step ever further on, as *one*" (*EHH*, p. 122). But, as "Burning the Small Dead" makes clear, the path these steps follow is not an intense symbolic dialectic but a quiet return to the dynamics of spatial relationships:

> Burning the small dead
>   branches
> broke from beneath
>   thick spreading
>   whitebark pine.
>
>   a hundred summers
>   snowmelt   rock   and air
>
> hiss in a twisted bough.
>
>   sierra granite;
>
>   mt. Ritter—
>   black rock twice as old.
>
> Deneb, Altair
>
> windy fire
>
>   (*BC*, p. 22)

The process of the poem up to the last line is a continual pushing outward in time and space until the contemplative mind reaches the stars Deneb and Altair, which combine age, the coldness of stone, an immensely large body of fire, and the appearance of mere points of light. The last line then creates a fusion of two forces: it is a return to the limited space of the burning branches, but it is also a continuation beyond the stars to a kind of essence of fire. The reader is present in a particular locale, still contemplating the physical distance of the stars, and gradually moving into a third windy fire that unites the two spaces in the back country of the poet's mind.

That third space where spatial expanse and interior depths coalesce is for Snyder the space of "the mythological present" (*EHH*, p. 117). There mind and matter interpenetrate one another and distance becomes depth. Much of Snyder's work manifests a movement like that of "Burning the Small Dead," a movement out to an awareness of self in cosmos complemented by the perception of cosmos contained within the self. His volumes, for example, tend to expand their frame of awareness —from localized Western contexts and images of the individual in nature, through journeys to the East and exercises in Eastern philosophy, mythology, and meditation, to a synthesis in which these materials all are restored within a simple domestic context. Such a movement is evident in *Myth and Texts'* gradual union of logging, hunting (with its emphasis on Indian mythology), and burning (with an emphasis on Eastern thought) till a particular fire becomes text for an all-encompassing mythic vision of distances within and without ("the mountains are your mind") :

> The black snag glistens in the rain
> the last wisp of smoke floats up
> Into the absolute cold
> Into the spiral whorls of fire
> The storms of the Milky Way
> "Buddha incense in an empty world"
> Black pit cold and light-year
> Flame tongue of the dragon
> Licks the sun
>
> The sun is but a morning star.[9]

(*MT*, p. 48)

Earth House Hold begins with Snyder as lonely wanderer in the American west, imaginatively explores several cultures, and concludes with a traditional communal celebration of a marriage between Western man and Eastern woman set in the context of all human time and embodying a relationship with the elements to be developed poetically in *The Regarding Wave*.[10]

The unified volume exemplifies the metaphoric gathering of otherwise contingent elements and expands lyric states of awareness into a general style of life.[11] Snyder's fullest dramatic achievement of these goals occurs in *The Back Country*, where the first part of the volume employs poems like those I have discussed in order to represent a state of innocence characterized by Snyder's self-sufficiency in the American wilderness. But a full religious vision must encounter other cultures and come to terms with a sense of loss and evil. Hence the second part of the volume takes Snyder to Japan and confronts him with his own rootlessness (the Robin poems) and, more important, with his differences as an American from other men. Those differences are manifest first of all in his own limited vision of nature's values, "thought nature meant mountains" (*BC*, p. 97). The first poem of section 2, like the first one in the concluding section, presents instead the Japanese, feminine sense of natural value residing in minute detail and composed spaces. Subsequent poems raise this sense of difference to a moral level; for Snyder is not only different in appearance from his hosts (*BC*, p. 41), but he carries in his appearance traces of a national identity that destroyed millions of the natives. Sharing his nakedness with others in the public bath, Snyder is overcome by the distances between them:

> squatting soapy and limber
> smooth dense skin, long muscles—
> I see dead men naked
> tumbled on beaches,
> > newsreels, the
> > war

> (*BC*, p. 42)

Here Snyder's eye for concrete detail yields to abstraction as he is overwhelmed by the historical burdens one carries and by the immensity of modern warfare. "Six Years," the section's final poem, then moves toward resolving some of these tensions by dramatizing a rhythm of repetition and a gradual absorption of Snyder into his new environment and of the environment into him. The poem's last section compresses Snyder's six years in Japan into the rhythms of a year's seasonal movement and parallels that temporal order to the daily cycle of life in a Zen monastery. The joyful acceptance of discipline (the road to a deeper freedom than he had known in the territories) and the sharpness of detail, especially of the poem's final perception, then summarize what those six years have meant. "A far bell coming closer" literally promises the beginning of a new day exactly like the one recorded, but that coming closer has profound psychological reverberations as Snyder internalizes what this essence of Japanese life can offer him. The last line recapitulates the poem's first two, but now in the form of a single line that reinforces and calls attention to the single meditative state

Snyder achieves. The entire six years can be focused in the quality of a moment's inner awareness. Time is recapitulated and extended as the capacity for action in concert with a new, more reflective environment.

In the third section, the fear is that cycles might not have any progression, that the Hindu vision of all as fleeting illusion bound to the wheel of Maya might be a true one (the section is titled for Kali, the Hindu goddess of destruction).[12] India provides the landscape of evil previously only glimpsed—both in its religion and in the economic and social conditions of the people (cf. *BC*, pp. 93, 74, 75). And this sterility in turn throws Snyder back upon the failed love that is the volume's emblem of the loss one must undergo to be saved. Now, however, that love evokes in Snyder images of his own psychic sterility as a creature too caught in words, self, and memory to love another (cf. *BC*, pp. 67, 73, 88, 91). The section's final poem directly expresses the ultimate tensions and overcomes them only by an assertion that it will be the burden of the fourth section and *The Regarding Wave* to prove:

> Arms shielding my face
> Knees drawn up
> Falling through flicker
> Of womb after womb,
>   through worlds,
> Only begging, Mother,
>   must I be born again?
>
> Snyder says: you bear me, nurse me
> I meet you, always love you,
>   you dance
>   on my chest and thigh
>
> Forever born again.
>
>   (*BC*, p. 94)

Having broadened his experience and internalized what knowledge his travels could bring, Snyder in the fourth section can assume a cosmic perspective and a prophetic stance. The universe as illusion becomes the universe as cosmic play within which no loss or failure need be final:

> we have all trippt and fallen.
>   surf rough, and full of kelp,
> all the ages—
> draw a line on another stretch of sand—
>   and—
>   everybody try
> to do the hop, skip, and jump.
>
>   (*BC*, p. 107)

The poet who passively witnesses social evil can now give political advice to both West and East. And the failed lover discovers another whom he can love and who embodies a ground or "field for experiencing the universe as sacramental" (*EHH*, p. 124). Particulars blend not only with one another but with the infinite energies beyond and "below":

> What my hand follows on your body
> Is the line. A stream of love
>   of heat, of light,   what my
>   eye lascivious
>   licks
>   over, watching
>   far snow-dappled Uintah mountains
> Is that stream.
> Of power.   what my
>   hand curves over, following the line.
>   "hip" and "groin"
>
> Where "I"
>   follow by hand and eye
>   the swimming limit of your body.
> As when vision idly dallies on the hills
> Loving what it feeds on.
>   soft cinder cones and craters;
>   —Drum Hadley in the Pinacate
>   took ten minutes more to look again—
> A leap of power unfurling:
>   left,   right—right—
> My heart beat faster looking
>   at the snowy Uintah mountains.
>
> As my hand feeds on you
>   runs down your side and curls beneath your hip.
>   oil pool; stratum; water—
>
> What "is" within   not known
>   but feel it
>   sinking with a breath
>   pusht ruthless, surely, down.
>
> Beneath this long caress of hand and eye
>   "we" learn the flower burning,
>   outward, from "below".

(BC, pp. 108–9)

Even the words themselves (through the awkward device of the quotation marks) seek to burst out of their nominal functions to participate in those energies leaping forth to meet the poet's hand as it traces the

line where love through desire generates form and gathers all the burning
into a collective and expanding " 'we.' "

The volume ends, though, with a less triumphant note; for too intense a conclusion would return the reader to the world of individual
lyrics and the dialectic of intense presence emerging from a neutral or
dead context and thrusting one back there when the visionary force is
expanded. To push the lyrical consciousness into nature demands that
one also adapt it to continuing process (another reason, perhaps, for
a unified volume of lyrics). One must be left with a quiet joyful acceptance, at once open ended and returning the reader to the simplicity
and style of the volume's opening poems—now with a cosmic perspective
informing the image of eating ("loving what it feeds on") :

> First   Samish Bay.
>   then all morning, hunting oysters
>
> A huge feed on white
> wood State Park slab-plank bench-
>   and table
>   at Birch Bay
>   where we picked up rocks
>   for presents.
>
> And ate oysters, fried—raw—cookt in milk
>   rolld in crumbs—
> all we wanted.
>
> ### ALL WE WANTED
>
> & got back in our wagon,
> drove away.
>
> (*BC*, p. 112)

Snyder is dealing here in concrete terms with the perennial philosophical
and theological problem of reconciling the achievement of plenitude with
an acceptance of change. Christianity tends to promise plenitude at the
cost of renouncing flux, while Eastern religions often come to terms
with flux by an ascetic rejection of all desire for plenitude (hence there
can be no Eastern *Divine Comedy*). In this poem, however, Snyder's
dialectical method shows how one can have both plenitude and change.
In fact the two conditions are necessary if one is to appreciate either.
Full satisfaction with the feast is possible only because the act can be
enjoyed entirely on its own terms, as an absolute present unspoiled by
desires to prolong or transcend it. The plenitude cannot be imprisoning,
cannot "hook" the actors so that they become unwilling to move on

(see "Oil," *BC*, p. 26). At the same time, when the present is completely accepted, there is nothing to fear from change. The actors can move on without anxiety and open to future moments of fullness.

Snyder reinforces the affirmative dialectic here by picking up and reversing in the last line one of the symptoms of cultural malaise he had presented earlier in the volume. In the book's second poem, he records watching "thousands of cars/driving men to work" (*BC*, p. 16). Liberated now, he overcomes the passivity of Western man trapped by his possessions and the culture that supports them. He moves on, content and in control of his own destiny. To have all one wants is the American dream, and Snyder with his innocence, pragmatism, vitality, and perpetual wandering Eastward or into the wilderness belongs in the tradition of American romanticism. But the contrast created by the last line and, more important, the tone of the poem suggest a new way of realizing that dream. All one wants cannot be achieved by the way of self-transcendence, for every triumph depends on another failure and adds a new possibility of failure. Only when one learns to control the desire for plenitude by a sense of the simple necessities whose satisfaction constitutes one mode of that plenitude will one free the dream and the dreamer from the bitter disillusionment that often torments self-consciousness.

Snyder's next volume of lyrics, *The Regarding Wave,* follows thematically from the last section of *The Back Country.* The images of cosmic play and the sacramental body of the beloved woman, which embodied Snyder's enlarged perspective, are central to the new volume, but the more recent poems try to enact a vision Snyder only described or projected in *The Back Country.*[13] Interbirth is no longer the controlled mutual dependency of specific events; rather it is universal intercourse or "Communionism" (*RW*, p. 39), a dance of energy permeating, informing, and transforming all particular phenomena. There is no absence and no contingency. All particulars retain their identity and even find it reinforced through their functioning as dynamic parts of a single whole. "The Way Is Not A Way" (or "away") but the continual presence of all ways within a single process:

> scattered leaves
>   sheets of running
>   water.
> unbound hair.   loose
>   planks on shed roofs.
> stumbling down wood stairs
>   shirts undone.
> children pissing in the roadside grass

(*RW*, p. 51)

Let me count the ways: while each fragment is a unique perception, some are more clearly linked than others in their modes of acting and in the ways the action is grasped within the poetic structure (leaves and hair, running water and pissing, loose planks on the roof and stumbling down stairs), and all ultimately share qualities of motion caught in stasis, in part by being given similar linguistic weight (for example, each object of a preposition is modified by a qualifier balancing the action and substance).

Snyder is trying to create poetically not so much a system of references that will articulate "The Way" as an emotional consciousness of what it feels like to know oneself as a part of such a total system. To achieve his vision he enacts a style considerably different from that of *The Back Country*, and he creates a carefully unified volume not as dramatic context but rather as an exemplum of the dynamic intercourse of concrete and universal typified in his own sacramental roles as poet, husband, and father within a universe suffused with creative love. The stylistic shift is most readily described as the movement from an essentially dramatic, psychological style to a meditative, religious one. The specific interchanges between a mind localized in time and space and its environment give way to a sense of mind as recording, praising, and gathering energy while only slightly tied to a specific personal context. The goal is to put mind more directly into the impersonal processes of the world and still be true to its powers of encompassing those processes. (These generalizations will be reversed in the volume's climactic central section.) Thus instead of dramatic contexts there are numerous songs gathering various manifestations or "transformations" (*EHH*, p. 128) of phenomena like seeds or clouds or taste. The mind is a point of focus, not an active agent locked in events. Moreover, attention to mind as a gatherer of being allows Snyder to stand partially outside the particular acts of mind within process and to see them as aspects of a deeper connecting principle. Behind individual acts of perception lie the experiences of the collective mind captured in language and myth and recoverable through etymology. Words are treasure-hoards, records of the mind's sense of the rhythms it shares with nature and of its own active participation in that interchange:

    Wave   wife.
            woman—wyfman—
   "veiled; vibrating; vague"
     sawtooth ranges pulsing
              veins on the back of the hand.

> Ah, trembling spreading radiating wyf
> > racing zebra
> catch me and fling me wide
> To the dancing grain of things
> > > of my mind!
> > > > (RW, p. 3)

And as is often the case in poetry, sound patterns become an even more subtle record of deeper transformations between world and mind. In "Kyoto Born In Spring Song," for example, the celebrating poet's linguistic craftsmanship is really a religious act praising and articulating the forces set into action and balanced by spring:

> O sing   born in spring
> the weavers swallows babies in Nishijin
> nests below the eaves
>
> glinting mothers wings
> swoop to the sound of looms
> > (RW, p. 18; see also RW, p. 81)

"Hiking In The Totsugawa Gorge" nicely dramatizes mind's place in the "dancing grain of things":

> pissing
>
> watching
>
> a waterfall
> > (RW, p. 74)

A poet like Cid Corman might write something like "Pissing/by a waterfall," and the poem would resonate the rhymes of flowing waters and suggest a harmony between human and natural acts. But Snyder not only incorporates this vision into a volume whose central theme is "Running Water Music," but he also complicates and enriches the rhyme by adding "watching." For watching is the structural center of the poem, Pound's unwobbling pivot, making mind participate substantially in the processes of things. As a participle, "watching" links verbally and semantically with "pissing," and thus inner and outer human actions exist on a single plane. Moreover, the "wa" sound links mind directly to the waterfall and the series of short a's in the last line, so both the transient acts of the first lines are joined in the more substantial and recurrent processes of the falls. Not only are there no ideas but in things, there are no ideas that do not exist as things in action. Yet on another level it is the mental act that structurally and thematically stands at the center of the three phenomena, gathers them together, and makes possible the reader's sense of their shared substance. The more one contemplates the poem, the more that central act takes on a power of its own—not only gathering the phenomena but absorbing them into another infinite space, "the dancing grain of things/of my mind" (*RW*, p. 3).

The volume opens with the image I have just quoted, and the second poem, "Seed Pods," also works very hard to make mind a part and even the ground of the dance. Seeds throughout the volume are the productive, creative agents of the dancing wave, and "Seed Pods" catalogs the ways of seeds, building to this conclusion:

> seed pod burrs, fuzz, twist-tailed
> nut-babies
>
> in my fucking head.
>
> (*RW*, p. 4)

The "fucking head" is both father and mother of the process—spreading and gathering the seeds that perpetuate the dance. Mind is the "regard" of the wave—a power coextensive with things, but that in gathering them projects a reality beyond what is imaged. Snyder's basic metaphor for this regarding mind is the mirror (cf. the two pages of *EHH*, 124–25, which summarize the themes of *RW*). For in one respect the mirror expresses Snyder's mimetic ideal: he portrays himself as revealing or disclosing rather than creating significant relationships in experience. But Snyder adds a further epistemological aspect to the image of art as a mirror not often recognized in imitative theories of poetry. The way to the cosmic perspective of section 4 in *The Back Country* is through the inverted mirror image (*BC*, p. 95), which allows one to return "back" to his earlier experiences with a more comprehensive view. The mirror gathers and reflects what it regards without disturbing or altering it, yet it also creates another dimension, a composed and peaceful surface apart from what it contains. In possessing what is before it, the mirror creates a wholeness and a reality beyond what is imaged. The mediation of an act like "watching" creates a space similar to that of the poem, apart from and transcending the particulars—not into any symbolic depth "beyond" but into another ground of relationships inverted and infinite, though not symbolic. The mirror is an analogue of the Zen void, which is not emptiness but a one-dimensional plenitude. Everything is contained in a single surface that in another sense is not really there at all.

The particular person who participates in acts of mind is, like mind, essentially a mediator, not a creator; he gathers, particularizes, and even fertilizes energies ultimately beyond and informing his act. *The Regarding Wave* is carefully structured to bring out that role of selfhood as concrete agent and mediator of universal energies. The ultimate purpose is sacramental—to dramatize how a person in his ordinary actions participates in and makes visible deeper cosmic forces. The "Table of Contents" provides the first clue to the volume's sacramental structure when it separates "It Was When," the central poem in the central section of the volume, from the poems that follow. That poem is a poem about conception, the moment when a particular form is engendered by the universal dance of seeds. "It Was When" recalls four dramatic scenes of intercourse, all satisfying in themselves but also all possibly the source of Kai's conception and hence a link between human intercourse and cosmic creativity:

> That we caught: sprout
> took grip in your womb and it held.
> new power in your breath called its place.
> blood of the moon stoppt;
> you pickt your steps well.
>
> Waves
> and the
> prevalent easterly
> breeze.
> whispering into you,
> through us,
> the grace.
>
> (*RW*, p. 31)

By linking events full in themselves to a possible relationship with a grander productive process Snyder realizes a fuller evocation of the blend of process and plenitude he dramatized in "Oysters." Each event has its own reality, but certain particular events also partake in a sacramental crossing of ways or become what Pound called radiant nodes of the process. (No wonder Snyder feels alienated from a culture in which *trivial* is the word deriving from the place where ways cross.) Moreover, this cosmic context allows Snyder to be content with reflecting on his self in action. He need not, as the confessionals, confuse value with psychic inwardness and self-consciousness. Depth comes from the physical forces one participates in; one need not strive to create depth and self-importance through *Angst* and the infinite convolutions of self-reflexiveness.

The volume as a whole mirrors the structure of "It Was When": it

moves inward from a general sense of the waves in their various manifestations to the particular sacramental embodiment of this intercourse
in Snyder's own life ("making a new world of ourselves/around this
life" [*RW*, p. 34]), back out to a satisfied sense of his being only a small
part of the process. The opening poems of the volume introduce the
theme of intercourse ("my fucking mind" is one example), and the first
two sections play on its variations ("Eating each other's seed/eating/ah,
each other" [*RW*, p. 17]). These poems provide a specific thematic
transition from the general pattern to the specifics of Kai's conception.
"Kyoto Born in Spring Song" links several births in terms of the underlying force celebrated in Eastern religions: "Great majesty of Dharma
turning/Great dance of Vajra power" (*RW*, p. 18). "Burning Island"
introduces the central third section with a more elemental pagan celebration of "Wave God," "Earth Mother," and "All" who make his wedding
with Masa a sacramental act:

> O All
> Gods tides capes currents
> Flows and spirals of
>   pool and powers—
>
> As we hoe the field
>   let sweet potato grow.
> And as sit us all down when we may
> To consider the Dharma
>   bring with a flower and a glimmer.
> Let us all sleep in peace   together.
>
> Bless Masa and me as we marry
>   at new moon   on the crater
> This summer.
>
> (*RW*, p. 24)

Even the vowels, each keeping its sharply cut identity and each blending
with several others, realize a form of marriage.[14] Moreover, the final
details—new moon, crater, and especially the emphatic Wordsworthian
"this summer"—all insist on a concrete particularity of scene whose
elements reach out to patterns of spatial, temporal, and historical recurrence and to ages of man's mythic celebrations of precisely this ritual at
this spot at this time in other times. "Shark Meat" then prepares for
"It Was When," the following poem, in a different but analogous context.
Like the moment of conception, the shark one eats comes to the present
"to be part of/this loom" through an almost miraculous congerie of
chance relationships.

After the central section of the volume has described the way the intercourse transforms life, and the child in turn alters the parents' lives, Snyder once again turns outward. He offers a social vision based on "Communionism" (*RW*, p. 39), a renewed sense of the cosmic backdrop to human fertility ("The Voice/is a wife/to/him still" [*RW*, p. 35]), and finally a total picture of the universe as energy in continual interchange. This concluding section, introduced by "Looking For Nothing," which defines the target of "Target Practice," manifests an epistemology best characterized by the idea of play worked out by idealist aestheticians.[15] The game metaphor of "Hop, Skip and Jump" is now made actual; any target, any precise verbal description, is accompanied by a sense of freedom within cosmic security. The self is no longer a mediating force that centers relationships but a faculty of attention loving the flux it feeds on. So interbirth depends no longer on a self in action, but can be recognized in whatever phenomena strike the eye. "Cats Thinking About What Birds Eat" is one of these moments of playful attention:

> the kitten
> sniffs deep
> old droppings
>
> (*RW*, p. 79)

The cat's slightest gesture evokes a relationship between several significant acts—between the physical act of "sniffing" and the conceptual "thinking" of the title, between the caught moment and its continuity with history, and between the inner intensity of sniffing "deep" and the depth of events preserved in the landscape. Snyder as man enters the sacramental field of the cosmos; as poet he at last becomes an embodiment of a great tradition he had long desired to incarnate:

> The archaic, the esoteric, and the primitive traditions alike all teach that beyond transcendence is Great Play, and Transformation. After the mind-breaking Void, the emptiness of a million universes appearing and disappearing, all created things rushing into Krishna's devouring mouth; beyond the enlightenment that can say "these beings are dead already; go ahead and kill them, Arjuna" is a loving, simple awareness of the absolute beauty and preciousness of mice and weeds. [*EHH*, p. 128]

Snyder's achievement is a considerable one. Judged simply in aesthetic terms, according to norms of precision, intelligence, imaginative play, and moments of deep resonance, he easily ranks among the best poets of his generation. Moreover, he manages to provide a fresh perspective on metaphysical themes, which he makes relevant and often compelling. Yet it is impossible for me, perhaps for most academics, to be completely satisfied with his work. One reason may be his ambition. He wants not only to provide poems but to offer a total vision of a new redeemed man at home with himself and celebrating his place in the cosmos,[16] yet the field of experience in his poems is quite limited and it therefore renders problematic his claims to totality. One requires a more complex sense of human nature, of social reality, and of one's own self-conscious awareness of the gaps between desire and realization, faith and works, before accepting his authority as one offering more than moments of metaphysical insight. Moreover, Snyder's dramatized version of himself, especially before *The Regarding Wave*, gives readers a hero from the mythic American past who is closer to their fantasy lives than to their practical needs to give sense and significance to specific situations in society.

This last point, I think, gets to the heart of the matter. One cannot judge poets according to strict philosophical canons of truth and falsity. But especially when the poet himself claims the authority of a wisdom tradition, one must ask whether readers can seriously entertain in their imagination the hypothetical relevance of his values and his dramatic situations for their own basic concerns. This is not simply a question of intellectual resonance. It involves the very conditions for a really deep participation in and commitment to the poet's work. I can achieve this with Snyder only by abstracting from his specific dramatic contexts and his social positions to concentrate exclusively on his treatment of epistemological and metaphysical themes and strategies. This clearly would not satisfy Snyder, and it does not satisfy me; nonetheless it does allow me to see him as considerably more than the poetic Marlboro man he is called by Robert Boyers.[17]

iii

Snyder's poetry can be seen as an extension of Williams's objectivism. The poem on the kitten discussed above, for example, echoes one of Williams's most famous poems at the same time as the references to depth and to traces of history preserved in nature adapt Williams to Snyder's concern for linking landscape to larger rhythms of nature and of reflective mind. Robert Duncan shares Snyder's faith in process as plenitude and even pays homage to the same objectivist tradition, but Duncan's is a very different religious project. Where most postmodern poets are content to render dramatic instances of the mind satisfied in process, Duncan has grander ambitions. His aim is to reinterpret the aesthetics of presence in terms that can recover the contemporary significance of the Romance and hermetic imaginative traditions. Hence myth assumes a very different status in his work than it does in Snyder's, and consequently the two poets explore very different styles. Snyder can conceive his task as primarily a mythic one and yet remain essentially a lyic poet because he feels little need to be discursive; his myth is ultimately a way of life and a set of attitudes that can be dramatized within the lyric. Duncan, on the other hand, conceives myth as a far more abstract and philosophical venture. The mythic poet, he argues, cannot simply be open to the present; "he must reflect himself upon that which he is a reflection of."[18] Thus the poet must take on the difficult task of making poetry of reflective thought and the emotions it can create.

Duncan, then, raises very different problems from those I suggested are raised by Snyder. When critics notice him at all, they comment on his weaknesses as a lyric poet, for his verse is often diffuse, boring, and without vitality in language or imagery. Moreover, like Olson, his work is often difficult and apparently remote from contemporary concerns because his mythic enterprise requires that he incorporate a good deal of abstruse learning into his work. Yet once one accepts him as a poet whose primary task is to reflect on what others express directly, one can, I think, forgive some of the lyric weaknesses and learn to read him for his intellectual interest and for those moments when he develops those interests into intense lyrical passages. Duncan is at the least a very important influence on other poets like Creeley and Levertov and at best he rivals his stylistic master, Pound, in integrating historical and mythic meditations with lyrical exaltation.

Duncan is perhaps best approached by first trying to articulate his own central myth and the particularly contemporary twists that he gives to its traditional forms. "Passages," the title he has given to his attempt to rival Pound's open-ended epic, provides one key term whose multiple meanings can allow the reader to enter that myth. *Passages* is essentially a term referring to thresholds or motion between boundaries, and it nicely links a sense of the natural process of temporal flux with the power of language to gather and surpass pure duration. The more one considers these two forms of passage, the more the process of analogy between writing and natural energy itself becomes the ground for a final text or passage reflecting a possible synthesis between them.

Duncan's basic myth, then, is the traditional myth of the world as book of God, but several of the traditional elements are transformed to satisfy the demands of the postmodern consciousness. If the poet devotes himself to reading "The Book of the Earth" (*OF*, p. 43), he also keeps in mind the motto " 'Poetry, a Natural Thing' " (*OF*, p. 50). If the earth is a book, its author can no longer be a transcendental self-contained God but one involved in natural process, speaking through the codes science has taught man to read, and recognizing that nature is itself being created in and through the acts of those trying to read and image the Book. Duncan, like the medieval and Renaissance poets who saw the world as a book, writes an essentially allegorical poetry, but it is an allegorical poetry with a modernist twist because the truth of the allegory depends on its incompleteness. Since God is not a Logos defining all the essential properties of being, but a force seeking to realize himself in evolution, Duncan's allegory keeps returning to its own failures, to the *lacunae* in the text, for it is only by encountering what is lost or not present that one can help gather together that divine Being which escapes man.

Duncan renders on a metaphysical level the central tension in the poetry of presence—that in the service of an immanent force it must continually de-create or break down the accepted codes men live by. Meaningful presence is never simply there without a creative act by a responding consciousness. In order to read the text of the world one must write the book of that world as the way of resurrecting its sacramental meanings. In this sense all poets seek to reflect on what they as conscious beings are a reflection of; Duncan reflects on their reflection:

> The universe and our experience in it is a text that we must learn to read if we are to come to the truth of it and of ourselves. . . . This creative life is a drive towards the reality of Creation, producing an inner world, an emotional and intellectual fiction, in answer to our awareness of the creative reality of the whole. If the world does not speak to us, we cannot speak with it. If we view the literal as a matter of mere fact, as the positivist does, it is mute. But once we apprehend the literal as a language, once things about us reveal depths and heights of meaning, we are involved in the sense of creation ourselves. . . . If the actual world be denied as the primary ground and source, the inner fiction can become a fiction of the Unreal, in which not Truth but Wish hides. The allegorical or mystic sense, Dante says in his letter to Can Grande, is the sense which we get through the thing the letter signifies. It is our imagination of what the universe means, and it has its origin in the universe. To put it another way, it is by the faculty of imagination that we come to the significance of the world and man, imagining what is in order to involve ourselves more deeply in what is [*D*, pp. 3, 5]

Once Duncan glimpsed ways of overcoming the various forms of alienation recorded in his earlier poetry, he turned first of all to the basic postmodern pursuit of presence, of "the faces of being" (*OF*, p. 87) emerging in a dynamic multiplicity:

For great life itself uses us like wood
and has no laws in burning we understand,
gives no alternatives. "Is"
we think of as intransitive,
who are exchanged in being,
given over from "I" into "I",
law into law, no sooner breaking
from what we understood, than,
breaking forth, abiding,
we stand
. . . . . .
It's the sense of law itself demands
                        violation
within the deceitful coils of institutions.

What is
hisses like a serpent
and writhes

to shed its skin.

                                        (*RB,* pp. 29–30)

The law here is the necessity to deny established cultural laws, for the reality of Being as it emerges in the present is continually being lost in the loose and ill-fitting cultural forms with which man clothes his perceptions. As Heidegger restates idealist clothes philosophy: to know the energies that make a thing stand man must break down those codes which only carry messages in the past tense (where what "stands" is merely "understood"). Yet Duncan's sense of a creative cosmos depends at least as much on language—on the codes that preserve what man records of his reflections on the world—as it does on his perceptions of presence. Language, of course, is man's way of capturing perceptions, but it also appears to have an origin and a forming energy of its own: "It is the virtue of words that what were forces become meanings and seek form" (*TQ,* p. 70). Thus Duncan's poetry has two orientations that often conflict: he seeks at times to capture fresh perceptions of Being directly, but more often he is concerned with relationships among perceptions, with seeing how the forms man has given to his perceptions reveal the latent interconnections of cosmic design and illustrate man's place in it. He makes clear the priority of this second orientation when he rewrites Denise Levertov's "Claritas"—shifting the emphasis from her precise concreteness to a series of analogical demonstrations that the songs of birds, of men working, and of the poet himself are all "a work of the natural will" (*RB,* pp. 124–26). He tends to see the poem not as an end in itself or as a completed vision but as a reflection of larger synthesizing powers of the cosmos, form seeking to achieve a "Form of Forms":

> Poems then are immediate presentations of the intention of the whole, the great poem of all poems, a unity, and in any two of its elements or parts appearing as a duality or a mating, each part in every other having, if we could see it, its condition—its opposite or contender and its satisfaction or twin. Yet in the composite of all members we see no duality but the variety of the one. [*TL*, p. 63]

Here Duncan adapts a conceptual strategy similar to Snyder's. The aesthetic properties of poetry, particularly of allegorical poetry, become figures of the way cosmic design reconciles the contradictions between the one and the many. The poem is a unique reality, yet it is also one of the transformations possible in a code or structure that includes it. The poem, for example, uses archetypal images and echoes verbal structures that go deeply into the past; thus its particularity depends for its full significance on the other latent dimensions of the code that it figures forth. And as one poem figures others, every event in the universe is related analogically to others. Duncan returns to a medieval cosmology, and he roots that cosmology in scientific discoveries like that of DNA, which propose a single unifying force undergoing analogous transformations in every different creature that shares life. This analogical universe is a cosmic form of the dance, with all the related parts forming a whole that glorifies the creative and sustaining power of its maker.[19] *Symboliste correspondances* are no longer essentially psychological and transcendent but comprise a quality of mystery within what Duncan calls a natural "process of responses" (*BB*, p. ix). That process is the theme of "Roots and Branches":

> Sail, Monarchs, rising and falling
> orange merchants in spring's flowery markets!
> messengers of March in warm currents of news floating,
>   flitting into areas of aroma,
> tracing out of air unseen roots and branches of sense
>   I share in thought,
> filaments woven and broken where the world might light
>   casual certainties of me. There are
>
>   echoes of what I am in what you perform
> this morning. How you perfect my spirit!
>   almost restore
> an imaginary tree of the living in all its doctrines
>   by fluttering about,
> intent and easy as you are, the profusion of you!
> awakening transports of an inner view of things.
>
>   (*RB*, p. 3)

The orange tree functions as a metaphor for the inner life, but more important in the poem is the fact of this analogical relationship that Duncan then extends to evoke a structure of relationships between inner and outer far more inclusive than the initial identification. Like myth, the poem presents "at once things in themselves and things in ourselves" (*TL*, p. 20), and in the process renders evidence of a unifying spirit that redeems isolated facts from their cells, "The part in its fitting does not lock but unlocks; what was closed is opened. . . . I bring the laws that bound me into an aerial structure in which they are unbound as outlines of a prison unfolding" (*BB*, pp. iv–v). Inner meanings, even the creative unifying force, become as rooted in the processes of things as things do in spirit. Duncan then has found a contemporary way to justify the analogical vision. Whatever spirit one wishes to find must be compatible with scientific law, and one of the poet's roles is to ground his vision in metaphoric extensions of those laws. Olson's tropism becomes in Duncan a univeral principle of desire rooted in a set of genetic codes that establishes the modern *Pre-Text* or grounding structure without which the play of analogical relationships soon becomes sheer fiction (as it does in the late Renaissance). Modern science makes it possible for Duncan to propose that as nature is allegorical, allegory is natural:[20]

> Come, eyes, see more than you see!
> For the world within and the outer world
> rejoice as one. The seminal brain
> contains the lineaments of eternity.

>> (*RB*, p. 50)

"Roots and Branches," however, is too simple a rendition of natural allegory because it maintains a closed system of one-to-one correspondences. There are no absences, no room for indeterminancy or play, and no structure to explain suffering. The poem finally is not true enough to the many dimensions in which the world might be seen as a book. One of Duncan's richest puns echoes Augustine and shows the way to a more complex allegorical method. For Duncan, "sentences of force and instrument" (*OF*, p. 83) are the natural analogues of "the unyielding Sentence that shows Itself forth in the language as I make it" (*OF*, p. 12). Ultimately, man's sentence or task is to achieve in time "intensifications" of God's "orders" (*BB*, p. viii), and this involves one's continual re-creating of the book that is found. One is faced, first of all, with Augustine's insight that while the natural order might be a complete mode of utterance, a sentence or a book, man, who is in time, only reads the sentence one word at a time. Man is, in other words, continually faced with gaps in his knowledge and moments when the overall unity seems lost in a series of associations or reveries not controlled by the book as a whole. If, however, one is to intensify God's orders, one must learn to cultivate these gaps, to see what energies they make available not explicitly contained in the unity that was trusted, and finally to regather them into the controlled tensions of the overall structure. Duncan's allegorical poetry, like Augustine's paradoxical meditative style, must seek confusion and complexity if it is to re-create an order that matters and holds:

> So, the artist of abundancies delites in puns, interlocking and separating figures, plays of things missing or things appearing "out of order" that remind us that all orders have their justification finally in an order of orders only our faith as we work addresses. [BB, p. ix]

Duncan's ideal poet must walk in fear of the striking image, for it pretends to a completeness and self-satisfaction with particulars that tempts one to read no more this day:

> This is the great temptation of all true poets to be so enraptured by the beauty of the language in love of which they have been called to their life work, so taken in by the loveliness of words or by the wonder of images and persons that the art projects, that they lose the intent of the whole, the working of the poem towards the fullness in meaning of its form. [D, pp. 11–12]

The poem for Duncan must have "something to do with keeping open and unfilled the urgencies of life" (CJ, p. 15), yet it must complement this fidelity to the hissing energy of what is with a sense of Law working to resolve the contradictions it creates. Duncan's structural model for his lyrics is the modern epic, a form that can only pretend to totality by refusing all imposed structures and continually regathering the complex particulars that alter the emerging structure. The poet, like Jacob, "wrestling with Form to liberate Form" (TL, p. 16), continually remakes his own book in service of the inclusive Book he tries to re-create as he reads.

The sentence not only imitates sentences of natural force but has a structural place in language itself, which taken metaphorically includes all other poets' sentences in the service of that Sentence which shows itself forth in language. This is Duncan's second, self-conscious twist on the surface, if not on the underlying reality of conventional allegory. For the individual poet reads both the book of the world and the book of sentences about the world, which have sought to realize its immanent forms and intensify those energies. If the epic is a poem including history, the poem faithful to the world's sentences is one continually incorporating poetic tradition. Tradition is essentially the history of what Duncan calls "rime," the history of man reflecting on the reflections of God and re-creating that God in terms of imagination and desire:

> Man's myths move in his poetry as they move in his history, as in the morphology of his body all his ancient evolution is rehearsed and individualized; all of vertebrate imagination moves to create itself anew in his spine. Families of men like families of gods are the creative grounds of key persons. And all mankind share the oldest gods as they share the oldest identities of the germinal cell. . . . God strives in all creation to come to himself. The Gods men know are realizations of God. But what I speak of here in the terms of a theology is a poetics. Back of each poet's concept of the poem is his concept of the meaning of form itself. [*TL*, p. 25]

Most of Duncan's best and most characteristic poems (among which "Apprehensions" is my favorite) are too long and diffuse to serve as convenient examples of my generalizations. "The Dance," however, provides in a fairly simple form the recurrent aspects of his style:

> Lovely their feet pound the green solid meadow.
>   The dancers
> mimic flowers—root stem stamen and petal
>   our words are,
>   our articulations, our
>   measures
>
> . . . .
> Lovely our circulations sweeten the meadow
> . . . .
> Maximus calld us to dance the Man.
> We calld him to call
>   season   out of season-
> d mind!

> (*OF*, pp. 8–9)

The dance is a typical metaphor with which to celebrate the analogical universe; one might recall, for instance, John Davie's "Orchestra: A Poem for Dancing," which Tillyard uses to exemplify the *Elizabethan World Picture* and which Roethke echoes in his own celebrations of the cosmic dance. Duncan's poem differs from these others in the disparate elements it tries to hold within his rhetorical play and in his elaborate sound patterning, which dramatizes at the most fundamental level how the numbers have entered the poem's feet. Duncan's content is diversified not only because of the range of materials he refers to, but, even more important, because of the multiple voices, times, and levels of diction and experience he tries to gather within his form. The poem itself enacts a dance of mind utilizing a variety of poetic techniques to at once extend diversity, encounter gaps between disparate modes of experience, and suggest an overall unity informing the variety the poem preserves. The ambiguous grammatical reference of the phrase "root, stem. . . ," for example, manages both to extend the dance, flowers (picking up the flow of "circulation"), and human speech by defining their analogical base and to collapse all three into a single force. Puns operate the same way—extending meaning and then unifying the variety they create. "Circulation" gathers together the movement of the dancers, the life forces of the body, and finally the circulation of the earth whose outward sign is the dew. And the dew is "due" as an element in nature's ordered interchange of night and day, warmth and cold. Learning, Duncan states, is "in re—and in—*turning* that forms a ring" (*OF*, p. 72), and the structure of "The Dance" both depends upon and exemplifies that vision.[21] The structure renders an "inbinding," a drawing into the mind's dance at least six modes of consciousness, all essentially disparate or metonymic. The poet first of all both records a vision of the dance and calls attention to his active re-creation of the dance within the poem ("Writing it down now . . ."). The turn to the present active self also allows different forms of memories to participate in the dance— personal memories of his particular life and loves one summer (a scene saved for the end and put in prose—to suggest both the small part he as a particular plays and the way a consciousness of the dance gives that small part a place); cultural memories of Rubens, Olson, and Whitman; and a reflective memory of the way silence (with its overtones of death evoked by "dead tired") can be seen as an integral part of the dance even though seeming at first only its negation. Finally as the poem is threatened by a silence on the one hand, it reaches toward transcendence on the other. The Lady of Rime, who speaks in italics, is made manifest at the margin of the dance and the vision it and its associations inspire. This presence at the margin, inseparable from the poem's willingness to face the gaps and de-creations that complicate the efforts of the analogical consciousness, seems the ultimate goal that Duncan can only seek indirectly through his reflections. Both *The Opening of the Field* and *Roots and Branches* end with realization of this marginal presence. The lines ending *The Opening of the Field* offer Duncan at his lyrical best:

> Flickers of unlikely heat
> At the edge of our belief bud forth.

As one might expect of Duncan, the poem's struggle to encounter and overcome gaps in the analogical matrix is basic to his ontology as well as to his poetics. Two central ideas—about language and about God—ground the union he develops and lead to a series of meditations on traditional Christian and pagan myths that have always implicitly recognized the analogies between poetic and natural creation. One line from his poetry serves nicely as an epigraph for his entire enterprise: "Poetry . . . is of violence and obedience a delicate balancing" (*OF*, p. 89). In its pursuit of the energy of being, the poetic word must be violent and de-create what is understood that presence might come to stand. Yet, on another level, that de-creation is obedient because it serves a Law whose principle is creative evolution toward a Form of Forms that may well be the cosmos in human shape, as Blake and the theosophical tradition have imaged it. Whatever its end, this process of balancing the violent and the obedient word mirrors on the level of poetic theory the larger synthesis Duncan is trying to realize between pagan, pre-Socratic monism and a Christian ethical and psychological framework. As Heidegger points out, the obedient word honors the Christian ideas of Logos—the idea of the word as God's form-giving command.[22] The poet's word in this Christian framework is incarnational: the poet repeats Christ's redemptive death into nature in order to be reborn with the power to authorize a new law or set of symbolic relationships revaluing a purely empirical order. Lowell's "Colloquy in Black Rock" exemplifies this process. However within this Christian vision, poetry is essentially static. Creation and incarnation take place in ideal form only once, and the allegorical foundation of the book is complete. The Greek Logos on the other hand, is conceived as a mode of violence continually unsettling what is and re-creating it. Etymologically derived from the root to gather, or collect, the Greek Logos (before Plato) is "the unifying unity of what tends apart" and requires of its practitioners the willingness to sustain a continual struggle with the Strife that Heraclitus envisions at the heart of all things. What the Greek word lacks is a form of teleology; without the Christian model of a world moving toward God, the effort to gather and unify strife must be an end in itself and doomed to eventual failure.

Whitehead's cosmology allows Duncan to extend his sense of the dual function of language so that it reflects and defines poetry's role in evolution. God's being, according to Whitehead, consists of two distinct but complementary phases.[23] This being is first of all "primordial," "the unlimited conceptual realization of the wealth of potentiality." God, then, like Hegel's Reason, contains in himself potentially all the "eternal objects" or forms of being and relationships that might be realized within history. This potential being is the ultimate *telos* of all beings, "the lure for feeling, the eternal urge of desire" that informs every being's movement to its own complete development. In the first phase God is a kind of map, a structure of definitions that only becomes realized in the process of experience. The second phase, the God realized within the processes of experience, Whitehead terms the "consequent" phase of divine being. Here God is not potential and complete, but involved in the process of realizing those potentials as actual events in the course of evolution. History with its torturous re- and in- turnings is "the weaving of God's physical feelings upon his primordial concepts." As no idea is real until it becomes part of an event, God's potential being only becomes realized as events make the forms physical. God, then, is a creature man obeys within a kind of violence, for man creates Him as he breaks down and re-forms in experience the book of potential meanings. And like the open-ended book, God's ultimate completeness is the totality of the creative acts of physical experience He inspires.

For Duncan, Christian and Greek mythology preserves a vision made explicit by Whitehead. Catholicism, for example, intuited the multiple phases of God in the figure of the trinity—as eternal form, as act of knowing, and as love or desire attendant upon any full experience of knowledge—within the limits of a Platonic and Hebrew vocabulary that could actually express God only as static unity. What so fascinates Duncan in this myth is the way all being and creating shares the son's suffering to incarnate the "orders" only potential in the Father:

> The configuration of It in travail: giving birth to its Self, the Creator, in Its seeking to make real—the dance of the particles in which stars, cells and sentences form; the evolving and changing species and individualizations of the Life code, even the persons and works of Man; giving birth within Its Creation to the Trinity of Persons we creatures know, within which in the Son, "He," is born and dies, to rise as the morning forever announces, the Created Self, Who proclaims the Father, first known as he named Himself to be Wrath, Fiery Vengence and jealousy, to be made or revealed anew as Love, the lasting reason and intent of What is—this deepest myth of what is happening in Poetry moves us as it moves words. [BB, p. vii; see also TL, p. 24]

The son gathers the potential words of the Father into the physical reality of the dance, the form for all coming together in erotic love. But, as the cross so powerfully reminds one, love requires sacrifice. To enter the dance, the self must die into the creative intent of the whole: "God died from and into all the extensions of Its Self, so that the Resurrection and Revelation is a new Identity of all persons and intentions" (TL, pp. 74–75). Inspiration, the creative loving breath of the Holy Spirit "moving between the creator breathing and the breath of his creature" (*BB*, p. viii), is the continual secular presence created by this sacramental sacrifice. Olson's field and its attendant poetics of breath become analogically figured in traditional meditations on the creative process.

The Greek myth Duncan finds most clearly repeating this same inner drama of the "poetic opus" (*TQ*, p. 67) is that of Eros and Psyche, a myth that serves as the core of "A Poem Beginning With a Line of Pindar," one of his best and most typical poems. I have analyzed this poem at some length in an essay,[24] so here I shall simply summarize the way it correlates the act of writing an allegorical poem with a process of being informed anew by the natural and historical processes the imagination releases. The poem opens with a conjunction of three levels of reality—a quotation from Pindar, an imaginative identification by the speaker with the dance Pindar celebrates, and a brief glimpse of Eros made possible by the participation in the dance. Duncan then extends these visions in order to identify himself with Psyche and to construct a sense of meaning and imaginative depth for his own desperate attempt to reach Eros and a more enduring light than that provided solely by Scientia. Here faith depends on poetry: the more fully Duncan can adapt the myth to his own experience, the more he can trust its structure as a ground of assurance that his own quest has significance and promises at least one psychic resolution.

The Eros myth has value precisely to the degree Duncan can identify with it in the very process of developing an allegory based upon it. And because the identification is successful, Duncan can justify correlating natural desires with archetypal spiritual experiences and can envision poetry as a far more general power, reaching down into nature and back into time, than is possible in any concept of poetry as merely self-expression.[25] Poetry is a being made anew as one tries to make it new:

> The figure of Eros, then, is not only developing from the stone to the winged Homoeros to the divine Bridegroom but also is constantly revealing what It is in Its changes. We have begun to find our identity not in a personality but in a concept of Man, so that all the variety of persons Man has been may be inhabitants of what we are as we impersonate him. [*TQ*, p. 85]

In general terms, the "Story, Herself a mother of sorts" (*BB*, p. 67) replaces that original physical mother, source of man's traumatic fears, in the form of a matrix giving birth to a dance of stories generated by the Father in quest of his own image. Man enters this matrix most completely when he learns to read and create the book of experience in the form of a palimpsest, an overwriting that both displaces and makes evident a text hidden beneath it:

> To read the universe as a palimpsest, *from which one writing has been erased to make room for another,* and yet to find the one writing in the other, is to see history anew as a drama in which the one is in many acts enacting Himself, in which there is an Isis in history, history itself being her robe of many colors and changes working to restore in many parts the wholeness of What Is as Osiris. This is a form that exists only in the totality of being, a form in our art that exists only in the totality of that art's life; so that in any particular work this form appears as a faith or on faith.[26] [*TQ,* pp. 97–98]

Duncan's dance ends on a note very similar to the one on which it begins—in a statement of the necessity for faith that beneath the signs the poet uses there is a coherent set of signatures. That faith is especially important for Duncan because, despite his sharing all the postmodern immanentist values, he differs from his peers in one important respect. Perhaps aware that a vision as inclusive as Snyder's tends to collapse man into the universal energies he participates in, Duncan tries to give a special place to distinctive human moral and psychological traits carried in these signatures. But to do that he must try to recover Western romance traditions and must make mythic claims not as easily captured in specific dramatic moments as the claims Snyder makes. The difference is essentially between deductive and inductive uses of mythis and metaphysical ideas. Most poets of the sixties are primarily inductive in their use of mythic ideas: when they employ supplementary concepts they do so mostly as momentary intensifications of dramatic experience, and thus the only authority they need invoke in their poems is provided by the qualities of thought and feeling they exhibit in these specific poetic experiences. One can view the myths they employ as less hypotheses about general truths than themselves components of a numinous moment for which they are only one possible expression. Duncan, on the other hand, is systematic, at least by comparison to his peers.[27] One can read his ideas in the same provisional way one reads other postmoderns, but if one does, he ignores the ambition Duncan shares with the great modernists to make of abstract poetic thought the materials for speculative visions. He loses the quest to transcend particular dramatic situations and to meditate on the ontological and psychological grounds for the poetic imagination and the values it professes.

Sympathetically read, Duncan's work then has greater imaginative scope than that of his peers. By reflecting on what other poets are reflections of, he achieves a generality and abstractness that articulates the value schemes shared by most postmodern visions of Romanticism.

He makes self-reflexive and systematic the analogical nature of most of the poetry I have been dealing with, and he defines the analogical process in a rich restatement of the Romantic dialectic between creative mind and creative nature. But his ambitiousness creates serious aesthetic problems, exacerbated by the fact that he is more deductive and allegorical in his use of myth than the great moderns and consequently exhibits little doubt or struggle. One cannot simply read Duncan dramatically; one must understand and work to share the beliefs before one can really participate in the poetry. In this skeptical age Whitehead is no Aquinas, and readers find it difficult to pursue abstractions they see as hard to understand and impossible to trust—especially when Duncan's immediate surfaces are so thoroughly conceptual and remote from ordinary existential problems and needs.[28]

Duncan's abstractness and the problematic nature of his imaginative faith make it easy for one to understand how readily a poetics of presence based on analogy or nature as the book of God leads into skeptical and aestheticist models of presence. Romantic dreams of finding the mind reflected in nature are always dogged by the possibility of becoming solipsistic celebrations of mind as the only nature and the most immediate locus of presence. I have shown how Frank O'Hara empties the aesthetics of presence of all metaphysical and ethical residues. Now Duncan makes it possible for one to understand how O'Hara's close friend John Ashbery performs a similar task on a more abstract and reflective level. Ashbery at once participates in the aesthetics of presence and reverses its characteristic ways of balancing creative mind and creative nature. Here I shall speak only of a particular mode Ashbery developed in the sixties, but if one sees its ironic parallels to Duncan's work, one establishes a context for understanding how Ashbery's later poetry could move back out to develop its own sense of analogical nature.

The easiest way to observe the logical link between Duncan and Ashbery is to notice that faith is only necessary if one tries to accept literally Duncan's claims for an interchange between natural and imaginative processes. If, on the other hand, one treats his work as similar to Norman O. Brown's, whom he often echoes, one need only take it as articulating the life of the imagination and no problems arise.[29] His treatments of Eros and Psyche are immediately accessible in ways that his claims for a natural order of energies and signatures informing poetic language are not. The former requires only that one see the myths as expressions of recurrent psychic struggles, while the latter depends on analogical readings of selected scientific discoveries and on accepting a specific theory of nature. Duncan, I might say, wants to claim as grounded in nature an imaginative vision that appeals primarily as a self-contained aesthetic structuring of recurrent psychic events. In trying to combine the allegorical book the mind writes with a set of signatures inscribed in nature, Duncan actually shows why it is so easy to insist on a radical difference between imaginative and natural orders.

Ashbery's response to the dream of natural signatures, then, like Mallarmé's before him, is to make a poetic book that can supplant and displace the problematic book of nature with a self-contained world of verbal signifiers. Here Duncan's vision of a continual allegory, deepening its participation in some virtual Logos or space of total mental activity, makes perfect sense. The mind continually reflects on its own reflections and gathers them into new wholes without being required to adapt itself to an unknowable natural order or to depend on the relative and temporary metaphors of science. Just as O'Hara adapts the poetics of presence to the continually changing surfaces of urban existence, Ashbery takes the imagination itself as the only real city, whose surfaces and folds demand the activity of ambitious poets, devoted to portraying the life of the mind without mystifying it by transforming surface into symbol.

Here is Ashbery's most succinct statement of his own self-image as "ascetic sensualist."[30] Notice the very different, playful use of mythology:

> I took advantage of the fact that it was built like a maze. Whenever you do this, even if the problem is just one in algebra, everything becomes simple immediately. Because then you can sit back and get a picture of yourself doing whatever it is. . . . Before, I might have seemed beautiful to the passerby, I now seemed ten times more so to myself, for I saw that I meant nothing beyond the equivocal statement of my limbs and the space and time they happened to occupy . . . I realized that I now possessed the only weapon with which the minotaur might be vanquished—the indifference of a true aesthete. [*AT*, pp. 47, 52]

There is no aesthetic pursuit of form or transcendence in early Ashbery; rather, his is the ontology of the aesthete seeking to reverse the Romantic dream of erasing art so nature will stand clear. He dreams instead of erasing nature so that the book might stand free as a dynamic interchange of self-referring elements.[31] His goal is a life of process not of forms, but process is most freely and complexly experienced within the self-referring, though not necessarily self-enclosed, book. Negatively, his cold removed voice dramatizes "a kind of fence-sitting/Raised to the level of an aesthetic ideal" (*DDS*, p. 18) so that one might be preserved from the terrible "feeling somebody should act, that ends in utter confusion and hopelessness" (*DDS*, p. 36). Ashbery's keenest insight is that

Western man's long dream of freedom might be realizable only if one is willing to distinguish sharply between world and mind, a realm of action where each move has consequences and limits further possibilities and a reflective realm where an infinite range of transformations and connections remains always possible. His model for this state of freedom is abstract art; his quest is to give poetic language the same freedom from referential demands, so that words can operate as constructions within an essentially two-dimensional space (and yet retain their sensual and semantic qualities within this space, as do the elements in abstract art). Thus Ashbery is drawn to surrealism more because of his aesthetic ontology than because of any myths promising an ultimate reality to be discovered in the unconscious. (For orthodox surrealism is merely another dream of words capturing natural signatures.) Surrealist style renders the work a single nonreferential whole where all the elements are linguistic and merge in a single displaced mode of being where an infinite number of relationships seem possible. Ashbery's style, in fact, echoes the casual freedom of automatic writing as it revels in this space of infinite transformations. In Ashbery's work, Dante's polysemous text becomes linked with Brown's "polymorphous perversity": Eros becomes a force released in the author's and reader's play. Both create Eros as they create a disembodied dance among the whirling transformations of signifiers released from Psyche's onerous tasks in the natural world.

If space allowed, these generalizations could be demonstrated in Ashbery's "Leaving the Atocha Station" (*TCO*, pp. 33–34). Here it must suffice, however, to refer the reader to Paul Carroll's analysis of the way the poem deliberately toys with the readers expectations of coherence and plays with the method of allusion that Duncan takes so seriously.[32] The major action of the poem, which Carroll does not grasp, is a nice reversal of Duncan's continual attempt to ground his allegory in concrete situations. Ashbery's poem is the process of leaving the Atocha station, not dramatically but ontologically. The poem is the act of leaving the demands of the empirical world for one composed entirely of linguistic units responsible only to the order given by a reader's free creation of his own allegories. There is no nature and no objectivity; indeed Duncan's creative *lacunae* become absolute gaps or negations of sense that can only be filled provisionally and differently in different readings "next time around." Most of the clear linguistic units in the poem are those marking the journey as an escape from the claims of one's station in the "real" world. The dance here is not Duncan's human figures metamorphosing into one another but a dance of disembodied signifiers reveling in the freedom from signatures and given a home in Ashbery's **displaced book of antinature.**

Notes to Chapter 4

1. Wendell Berry, "A Secular Pilgrimage," *Hudson Review* 23 (1970): 401–24. I quote below from pp. 402, 408.

2. Stanley Burnshaw's *The Seamless Web* (New York: Braziller, 1970) is a widely read theoretical treatment of poetry arguing the ontological truth of poetic principles. He opposes poetry as the speech of nature and nature's presence with its ecological structure to the mediated speech of "civilization." For an interesting discussion of intrinsic relationships between poetic and ontological values, see Thomas McFarland's appendix "The Connexion between Poetry and Pantheism," in his *Coleridge and the Pantheist Tradition* (London: Oxford University Press, 1969), pp. 274–82.

3. Gary Snyder, *Earth House Hold* (New York: New Directions, 1969), p. 129. I shall use the abbreviation *EHH* for this work in the text and shall use the following abbreviations for other works of Snyder's: *Riprap* in *Collected Poems of Gary Snyder*, ed. Stuart Montgomery (London: Fulcrum Press, 1966), *RR*; *The Back Country* (New York: New Directions, 1968), *BC*; *Myths and Texts* (New York: Totem Press, 1960), *MT*; *The Regarding Wave* (New York: New Directions, 1970), *RW*.

4. Sherman Paul, in an excellent essay on Snyder "From Lookout to Ashram: The Way of Gary Snyder," *Iowa Review* 1, nos. 3 and 4 (1970): 76–89, 70–85, makes the following comments on *riprap* as a metaphor for poetic style: "The imperatives of composition are modernist: the unit of composition is the single word, like rock, a solid particular thing of weight and texture that exists in place and time and appeals to the senses ('body of the mind'); the act of composition is architectural, a building by words, a deliberate handwork" (no. 3, p. 86).

5. Hugh Kenner, *The Pound Era* (Berkeley, Calif.: University of California Press, 1971), p. 128 points out that ecology "is a romantic discovery, in poetics as in biology." The organicist idea of interchanging dynamisms is the nineteenth-century paradigm replacing the eighteenth-century one of the closed system (see p. 126).

6. When I use the terms *myth* and *text*, I am interpreting Snyder's own use of the terms. *Text* represents pure natural process, and *myth* is nature seen in terms of imaginative value. *Text* is analogous to the profane, *myth* to the sacred. Snyder's use of these terms is clarified by Claude Levi-Strauss's definition of *myth* as a way of blending nature and culture. See *The Savage Mind* (Chicago: University of Chicago Press, 1966), pp. 91 ff. Later in this essay I cite the way Snyder brings myths and texts together in the earlier volume *Myths and Texts*. I should also point out that in an "Interview" in *Road Apple Review* 1, no. 4 (1969): 65, Snyder asserts, "I look at most of my stuff as being on a myth-making order as opposed to a lyric order. Or a ritual and magic order as against a pure song order." My argument is that it is precisely by ritualizing lyric elements and extending them to ontological matters that he raises text to myth and song to magic.

7. The sense at the end of the poem that one is now in touch with a new life and is beginning to participate fully in it is supported by the connotations of pregnancy and of the beginnings of a journey in the title.

8. Thomas Parkinson, "The Poetry of Gary Snyder," *Southern Review* 4 (1968): 616–32, was the first to develop the idea of the lack of tension in Snyder's poetry. In this respect Snyder does in nature what O'Hara and Ashbery can do only by withdrawing from the pressure of reality.

9. The allusion to Thoreau in the last line does more than put Snyder in the American tradition; it thrusts the whole American Romantic tradition epitomized in this line into the cosmic perspective of the entire closing passage. The sun and Thoreau are only the foothills of the back country, as the text is but a morning star to the cosmos of myth.

10. On the relationship of simple life-style and expanded consciousness, see *EHH*, p. 143. Snyder realizes in his poems the insight shared by Zen and Kierkegaard that the religious man is outwardly the most normal and regular of men.

11. Snyder differs from Lowell in this because for him (Snyder) the unified volume represents not only the action of consciousness but a unity there for it to gather. In Lowell the volume's unity embodies consciousness working to find and to hold together the condition of a person whose self-consciousness is the only possible metaphoric unity in chaotic experience.

12. See "Interview" in *Road Apple Review*, p. 66, for Snyder's sense of the dangers in Hindu religion.

13. Paul, "From Lookout to Ashram," no. 3, p. 82, has a nice discussion of an earlier three-part version of *The Regarding Wave*. He also points out how the discussion of woman and cosmos (*EHH*, pp. 124–25) summarizes the thematic framework of *RW*.

14. Kenner, *The Pound Era*, pp. 82–85, shows how Pound tried to change the music of poetry so that sounds both hold their own identity (as they do not in Swinburne and Tennyson) and form a whole. In this and many other respects Snyder learned from Pound. My colleague Carl Dennis has pointed out to me how Snyder's rhythms have an effect similar to that of the sounds: by using many spondees and few unstressed syllables Snyder gives his poems tremendous solidity— one is secure in a world of numerous distinct and self-contained objects that also create a unified field of rhythmic energy.

15. The classic texts are Kant's *Critique of Judgment* and Schiller's *Letters on the Aesthetic Education of Man*. See also the chapter on Nietzche and Hegel in Herbert Marcuse, *Eros and Civilization* (Boston: Beacon, 1955) and the discussion of language as erotic play in the opening chapters of Norman O. Brown, *Life Against Death* (Middletown, Conn.: Wesleyan University Press, 1959).

16. Paul, "From Lookout to Ashram," no. 4, p. 70, quotes Robert Bly's application of Whitman's sense of the hero to Snyder: [Snyder's poems embody] "the pervading presence of the poet who simultaneously shares in the process of life and reveals some of its meaning through his actions."

17. Robert Boyers, "A Mixed Bag," *Partisan Review* 36 (1969): 313. I give a more thorough treatment to the question of evaluating Snyder in "Gary Snyder's *Turtle Island*: The Problem of Reconciling the Roles of Seer and Prophet," *Boundary 2* 4 (1976): 761–78.

18. Robert Duncan, *Bending the Bow* (New York: New Directions, 1968), p. 108. I use the following abbreviations in the text to refer to Duncan's works: *Bending the Bow*, BB; *The Years as Catches First Poems* (1939–46) (Berkeley, Calif.: Oyez, 1966), YC; *The Opening of the Field* (New York: Grove, 1960), OF; *Roots and Branches* (New York: New Directions, 1964), RB; "Towards an Open Universe," in *Poets on Poetry*, ed. Howard Nemerov (New York: Basic Books, 1966), PP; *Derivations: Selected Poems 1950–56* (London: Fulcrum Press, 1968), Der; *The Sweetness and Greatness of Dante's "Divine Comedy"* (San Francisco, Calif.: Open Spaces Press, 1965), D; *The Truth and Life of Myth* (New York: House of Books, 1968), TL; "Notes on Grossinger's Solar Journal: Oecological

Sections" (Los Angeles, Calif.: Black Sparrow Press broadside, 1970), *NG*; "Beginnings," *Coyote's Journal*, nos. 5–6 (1966), pp. 8–31, *CJ*; "Two Chapters from HD," *Tri Quarterly*, no. 12 (Spring 1968), pp. 67–99, *TQ*.

19. I take my sense of an analogical universe and the need for a grounding text beneath the surface one from Michel Foucault, *Les Mots et Les Choses* (Paris: Gallimard, 1968), pp. 32 ff., 56. For Foucault, analogy is only one of four basic modes of "resemblance" common in Renaissance thought. The process of analogy as a link between nature and spirit is nicely realized by Duncan when he follows the poem quoted below with one linking the tree metaphor to theosophical tradition and its tree of life. That second poem is one form of the inner life to which one is "transported" by a sense of affinity with the physical tree.

20. Some of Duncan's best metaphors link natural desire, human action, and scientific codes; see for example: *RB*, pp. 8, 12, 50–52; *BB*, p. 59. See also *OF*, p. 81 as the most medieval of his analogical poems, where letters are literally part of the world's text.

21. At the center of Duncan's poetic structures is his vision of love: "When I imagine not overcoming but including, loving takes place in the place of desiring. (*Der*, p. 41). Like Snyder's, his poetry is not dialectical, seeking to resolve opposites, but cumulative, seeking to hold them in a dance where the parts enrich one another. This process of cumulative structure, Jerry Rothenberg, *Technicians of the Sacred* (New York: Anchor Books, 1969), p. 399 ff., sees as the basic rhetorical form in primitive poetry (see also *OF*, p. 69, on Pindar).

22. Martin Heidegger, *Introduction to Metaphysics*, trans. Ralph Mannheim (New York: Anchor, 1959), pp. 105–13. I quote from p. 110.

23. Alfred North Whitehead, *Process and Reality* (New York: Macmillan, 1969), pp. 405–13. I quote successively from pp. 405, 406, 407. Duncan often refers to Whitehead, but alters his idea of God's primordial phase from Whitehead's abstract, mathematically inspired "eternal objects" to a more theosophical Jungian notion of eternal perfect man seeking realization.

24. Charles Altieri, "The Book of the World: Robert Duncan's Poetics of Presence," *Sun and Moon* 1 (1976): 80–86.

25. Duncan's attack on the ego is unrelenting: poetry is inspiration by forces beyond the self in which the self participates. In fact, poetry in this respect is once again an ontological model for the way every subject is first of all an object of forces that transcend him. See *PP*, p. 141; *TL*, p. 59; and *NG*.

26. Duncan's vision takes practical form in *BB*, where he is the only contemporary poet successfully to include the sufferings of the war in Vietnam within his myth. He does so first of all by defining his pretext or "Form of Forms" as Eros. Eros is a better figure for the poetic word than Logos because it expresses the word's union with breath and bodily desire and because it seeks to gather experience into a loving union. Moreover, Eros links the poetic word with an ethical model—the ideal of community that enables Duncan to judge the war and attribute it to American individualism (see *BB*, pp. 71, 81–83). Finally, Eros can be linked with Heraclitean strife; it is the contained tension of the bow that creates its power (a power linked to poetry if one considers Apollo). Combining Heraclitus's view of experience as based on strife, with the erotic urge to incorporate strife into community, Duncan can envision the war as a productive darkness. Underwritten beneath the war and the exiles it has created is the myth of Christmas and natural myths of dying and redeeming gods. See "Earth's Winter Song" and

"Stage Directions" (*BB*, pp. 93–94, 128–32) for his best renderings of this vision, although the myth also informs the volume as a unit.

27. I take this distinction and the one below between the kinds of faith needed to participate in different types of poems as matters of degree, not as clear and distinct oppositions.

28. L. S. Dembo, in *Conceptions of Reality in Modern American Poetry* (Berkeley, Calif.: University of California Press, 1966), pp. 217–19, is one example of those refusing the leap of faith. He makes Duncan an exemplar of the mystifications about language inherent in the Romantic tradition.

29. For Duncan's closest similarity to Brown, see his meditation on the true life of poetry as the life of a saint or a God unwilling to compromise with the contradictory pulls of reality in *Parable, Myth and Language*, ed. Tony Stoneburner (Cambridge, Mass.: Church Society for College Work, 1967), pp. 14, 17–18.

30. John Ashbery, *The Tennis Court Oath* (Middletown, Conn.: Wesleyan University Press, 1962), p. 51, abbreviated for future reference in the text *TCO*. Other abbreviations used for Ashbery's work are: *The Double Dream of Spring* (New York: Dutton, 1970), *DDS*; and *The Heroes* in *Artist's Theatre in New York: Four Plays*, ed. Herbert Machiz (New York: Grove, 1960), *AT*.

31. The contrasting Romantic and contemporary perspectives on erasing, I take from a lecture "The Art of Erasure" given by Richard Howard. His discussion of Ashbery in *Alone with America* (New York: Atheneum, 1971) nicely illustrates the poet's total lack of anxiety and the self-contained quality of his texts (see especially pp. 34–35). Also helpful on Ashbery is Roland Barthes's idea (taking Sartre one step further) that the reader can be free only when the text has no plot, no insistence on particular readings, but offers instead a ground for freely combining and recombining elements. See his "The Death of the Author" in *The Discontinuous Universe*, ed. Sallie Sears and Georgianna Lord (New York: Basic Books, 1972), pp. 7–12. Finally, I am indebted to Vic Cabas who in an excellent paper for me showed how Ashbery works to de-realize the world into a two-dimensional space of language.

32. In Paul Carroll, *The Poem in Its Skin* (Chicago: Follet, 1968), see pp. 14–15 for Carroll's discussion of allusion and pp. 17 ff. for materials illustrating the reader's freedom. Below, I quote from p. 21. In the discussion I doctor Carroll's ideas with medicine derived from Barthes and Jacques Derrida.

5

The Struggle with Absence:
Robert Creeley and W. S. Merwin

i

The poetry of Snyder and Duncan presents in relatively extreme terms the changes in sensibility that characterizes the shift from modernist to postmodern poetics. But all self-consciously postmodern poetry is not so optimistic about reconciling subject and object or a sense of process with a celebration of plenitude. The work of Robert Creeley and W. S. Merwin, for example, demonstrates how fully postmodernist poetry can take account of the tragic and problematic implications of their postmodern ideals without falling into outworn tragic or existentialist poses.

If one takes their skeptical explorations abstractly, Creeley and Merwin seem to repeat a familiar group of modern dilemmas—dilemmas of identity, self-consciousness, the intractability and inconstancy of language, and finally the need for the subject to feel "grounded" in a variety of relationships not dependent solely on fictions created by the individual consciousness. But what makes them particularly interesting for me is that they encounter these problems precisely because they seek the ideals of plenitude in immanence that the other poets have found ways to accept. In pursuing experiences of intense presence, both poets find themselves confronted continually with ironic possibilities and with a torturous sense that the very presence they pursue leaves them only with a deeper and deeper realization of how much they need that is absent in the moment. Yet they do not give up their quest, and at times they articulate moments of satisfied presence more profound and more dramatically engaging than those offered by their peers.

Creeley, for example, seeks from the beginning a way of knowing how human and natural energies might coalesce in a single momentary "field," but the more intense and full that moment becomes, the more problems it creates. The poet is left on an emotional peak, from which he seems isolated both from the banal realities of ordinary life and from the past and future identities he must assume in that reality. Moreover, that intensity grows inseparable from the fear that its only source is his own nervous energy, and hence intensity itself threatens to become a form of solipsism. No sense of presence can suffice for him unless it assures the self of a ground beyond consciousness and provides a framework defining and giving value to the experience of absence. His poetic career is the continual testing of possible means for satisfying this need.

In Merwin's case, at least in the poems written in his later style, which are the ones I am primarily interested in, the problem with presence takes two basic forms. He sees first of all that openness to flux is no guarantee of a satisfying sense of presence. Flux after all is appearance, and finding its value requires that one undergo all the pains of interpretation registered by hermeneutic thinkers. Moreover, the presence felt in natural experience mocks one as much as it soothes, for it is a presence of what is continually dying. Appearance must be destroyed or, more properly, de-created, if one desires to overcome the recurrent experience of loss and come to know a presence or being that abides. But de-creation itself, that favorite principle of modern poetry, constitutes the second problem. De-creation can appear to be the only absolute presence, for it seems that consciousness might never find a source outside itself that can satisfy the demands for value it dictates. Consciousness seems insatiable in its dissatisfied tearing away of appearances beneath appearances. Man's one valid absolute may be this continual act of negation. Negation may, in fact, be the one absolute in a universe where the destructions by consciousness are complemented by the possibility that death and change are the only constants and thus, in the traditional terms of metaphysics, the only gods.

Other poets, of course, could be chosen to illustrate similar tensions, James Wright for example, but I find Creeley and Merwin the most exciting—both poetically and intellectually—of those who meditate on the problems involved in secularizing a poetic faith that sometimes seems inherently religious and in opposition to the ordinary concerns of secular life. In addition, Creeley and Merwin stand poles apart—despite their shared concerns—and thus they again provide visions and stylistic experiments that represent basic directions within the poetry of the sixties. Creeley's tense and colloquial short lines typify strategies for dissecting the minute particulars of psychic life, while Merwin's elaborate metaphors, biblical rhythms, and depersonalized imaginative landscapes reflect the enterprise of those seeking to come to terms with the undefinable anxieties of contemporary consciousness by exploring more generalized, impersonal, and unconscious dimensions of psychic experience. Creeley derives from the tradition of Williams and Olson and creates new possibilities for that tradition, while Merwin, like Bly, experiments with

European surrealist traditions for evoking the deep and permanent stuctures of conscious and unconscious life.

ii

Robert Creeley's poetry is an interesting attempt to integrate the confessional, radically subjective lyric with Olson's objectivist poetic. When it succeeds it provides a significant new development of the tradition Williams initiated in American poetry. Other contemporaries close to Williams, like Olson and Denise Levertov, pursue a sense of radiant presence through rapt attention to essentially objective concrete events. Conceiving the evils of absence as caused by abstractions, by the desire to interpret experiences or relate them to universals, they feel that they can make affirmations only by renouncing the claims of the individual ego and by subordinating the mind's tendencies toward reflection to the rigorous discipline imposed by the need to see particular phenomena in fresh and vital ways. Creeley, on the other hand, cannot renounce the ego because, like Lowell, his central need is to feel a subjective sense of vitality and purpose. To Creeley, attention means an acute self-consciousness, for he sees the threat of absence primarily in psychological rather than in ontological terms. His central fear is of the absence of the self to consciousness, of the mind spinning fictions that have no vital relationship to the total self. His work returns again and again to the theme "All I Knew or know/Began with this—/emptiness."[1]

Yet his way of restoring a sense of full selfhood is radically different from Lowell's pursuit of extreme emotional states. Creeley seeks his identity in the same field of experience explored by other objectivist poets—in those immediate and familiar experiences which occupy so much of daily life, but which one rarely attends to. Attend Creeley does, but in a much more reflective, philosophical fashion than one finds in poets more concerned with perception. It is no easy task, however, to shift Olson's poetic from perceptive to essentially psychological and reflective experiences. One can distinguish two basic problems that beset a poet who attempts this enterprise, problems intensified by tensions inherent in Creeley's nervous and peripatetic personality. First of all, Creeley's need to establish his personal identity through the objectivist lyric fosters the potentially alienating self-consciousness that the poetics of energy fields is intended to overcome. With Olson, he distinguishes sharply between a poetry of description in which there is an unbridgeable gap between the self who makes statements about the world and that world he refers to and a poetry of action that expresses the energies of life *within* the world (see *QG*, pp. 182–83). But Creeley usually wants the impossible union of feeling the self within the world and of having some insight into a stable identity that persists in these experiences. He is not content to take as his principle of plenitude the continuity and harmony of natural processes, but he wants that principle to be connected somehow with a sense of his own personal needs and desires. He thus must try to take up a position at once within the flux of experience and outside reflecting upon its relationship to his own personality.

This helps explain why Creeley is a more self-consciously philosophical poet than most objectivist poets; he wants not only to present experiences but also to dramatize his attempts to reflect upon, interpret, and understand the experiences and whatever "grounds" they can provide. This philosophical orientation creates the second problem, because it never allows him to escape the pressures inherent in the modern fear that reflective thoughts are merely subjective fictions. Creeley's poetic subject is ultimately not consciousness in the world, but Robert Creeley trying to make sense of the world. So he can never rest content that the dynamic energies made present in his poems result from an essential harmony between the world and consciousness. The field of the poem, instead, always threatens to show that its energies are only those of a particular self-consciousness reflecting on itself and creating the ground it wishes to find outside itself. In a similar way Creeley cannot find for the subjective self the kind of plenitude others experience in seeing their particular experiences of intense presence as illuminations of a deeper, abiding order. Because his intense experiences may be self-generated, each of them offers moments of vitality that are only evanescent and that threaten upon dissolving to leave only greater needs and a more nagging sense of how divided a self he is in his ordinary life. Full identity seems to disappear the moment one reaches for it and tries to make it stable, leaving only the need for more intense moments of presence, which in their turn will only exacerbate the feelings of emptiness. Creeley's frequent use of the word *want* summarizes this particular version of an old Romantic problem: *want* expresses both the constant pressure of desires seeking their resolution or "rest" and the basic void or lack that generates and is generated by this quest. Yet he does not despair, for the quest itself continues to provide possible solutions and the materials for a continual poetic dialogue of the mind with itself and with its wants.

For Love, his collected early poems, derives much of its energy from the recurrent threat of the void, or emptiness of a desiring mind. The volume begins, for example, with Creeley identifying with Hart Crane, who is separated from his home and friend, "stuttering,/by the edge/of

the street, one foot still/on the sidewalk, and the other/in the gutter
. . ." (*FL*, p. 15) like a passive stuffed bird incapable of real movement.
It proceeds to elaborate this initial condition primarily by exploring a
series of gaps—between people, between image and reality, between the
memory of failure and the dream of an open future—culminating in
Creeley's reflections on the psychic processes involved in his literal
divorce from his first wife. Resolving these problems depends in large
part on finding a language capable of bridging "hart" and head, inner
reality and outer event, so that meaningful action might be possible.
However, such a language will not come easily, especially when it must
carry so heavy a burden of self-reflexive honesty. As Creeley's poetic
line never lets the reader forget, the threatening void is not just a metaphor but a condition of self-consciousness. The abruptness and the tor-
tuous pausing demanded by the short line, evoke the sense that one is
dangling at the edge of an abyss. From this impending annihilation, the
poet strives to restore the possibility that human language can gain control over the silences that threaten it.[2] Yet even within the line, voids
continually emerge as Creeley's irony and ambiguity undermine the secure
world ordered by language and embody the difficulty of making connections. His description of Kenneth Patchen applies also to himself: "the
punning, the discontinuous sequence, etc.—he is not the first man to call
attention to horror, to the horror now on us, by the use of its own
methods. It is that things don't 'follow' . . ." (*QG*, p. 235).

Many of the poems in *For Love* try to survey the underlying conditions that create the explicit voids and the torments embodied in the
style. As the style indicates, language itself is one of the primary villains,
for it promises a wholeness it cannot fulfill. Language in ideal form
promises to make the self objectified and communicable to another, yet
its reality entraps us in webs of meanings which we do not intend. The
words stand emptied of us and we face them turning once more on a self
we can neither fix nor possess. "I Know a Man" contains Creeley's most
fundamental dramatic statement on the problem of language and its
relation to the void:

> As I sd to my
> friend, because I am
> always talking,—John, I
>
> sd, which was not his
> name, the darkness sur-
> rounds us, what
>
> can we do against
> it, or else, shall we &
> why not, buy a goddamn big car,

drive, he sd, for
christ's sake, look
out where yr going.

(FL, p. 38)

The speaker's generalized angst here actually intensifies the horror of
the void. His vague speech gives nothing concrete to hold on to; instead
it further broadens the gap between human subjectivity and the world
with which it must come to terms. Drunkenness becomes the poem's
metaphor for inauthentic speech that deepens the darkness evoking the
speech in the first place. Drunken speech stems not from perception,
but from the need to fill voids, to put off silence. Unlike speech that
is devoted to some referential order, speech that strives to communicate
a feeling or perception, drunken speech takes off from its own momentum.
Each succeeding statement is born from some associative speech pattern,
not from any referential logic.[3] The protagonist becomes the passive and
helpless victim of his own powers of speech, and his failure is most
clearly portrayed when he utters an octosyllabic line (l. 9). To Creeley
the long line courts the void by not defending itself, by trying simply
to cover the emptiness, and by suggesting possible coherence and orders
it cannot really manage. The only reply is the one John gives—keep
your eye on experience; live in it and avoid the purely verbal universe.

But even the perceptual universe will not solve the desire for coherence. In "The Rhyme" Creeley asks how one can look where he is going
when there are no privileged positions for observation and no landmarks:

There is the sign of
the flower—
to borrow the theme.

But what or where to recover
what is not love
too simply.

I saw her
and behind her there were
flowers, and behind them
nothing.

(FL, p. 23)

The tension here results from the ambiguities of a present world in which
everything is named, so that one sees signs and not the things themselves.
This world of signs is a sight world, a world without depth. When one
tries to go beneath the signs, to recover "what is not love [read "Love"]/
too simply," he discovers a void ("behind them/nothing") that mocks his
desire. The gap exists between sign and some kind of experienced vitality,
some sense that things are embedded in a context that gives them value.

There is, in short, no underlying "ground" (as religious thinkers like Kierkegaard put it) that can unite words as elements in abstract sign systems with the qualities of emotional experience ideally the source and content of language.[4] And until one can capture these qualities, one is doomed to feel a nothingness precisely in those areas where self-hood and love might be possible.

Creeley's epistemological failure to find a secure ground is mirrored in a set of psychological problems emerging from the same conditions. Not only words but all mental images are basically phenomena, not part of a monumental world, and thus possess subjective but not absolute truth. From this emerges the problem that the self can trust as valid neither his image of the other (see *FL*, pp. 134, 140, 91, 87, 50, 56–57) nor the other's image of him. The fundamental danger in this condition is solipsism, the sense that one's isolation is a necessary condition and that only the sure, rather than the "unsure/egoist," can be "good for himself" (see "The Immoral Proposition," *FL*, p. 31).[5] The second alternative, the possibility that the self cannot be known by someone else, leads to another experience of absence—this time of the self to itself. As the self sees that it is known only through images or "faces" that do not express its reality, the real self tends to grow more and more unstable the more frantically one tries to find and hold it. Often one comes to doubt whether there remains any real self at all. Consider "The Sign Board":

> A face that is no face
> but the features, of a face, pasted
>
> on a face until that face
> is faceless, answers by
>
> a being nothing there
> where there was a man.

(FL, p. 129)[6]

Even when a man resists the definitions of himself posed by others, he must still integrate into a seamless whole the disparate experiences in which he finds himself engaged. "The Flower" beautifully illustrates the fragmented self who, in his very desire to experience himself as a self-conscious unity, generates only aestheticized fragments that mock the desire that spawned them:

> I think I grow tensions
> like flowers
> in a wood where
> nobody goes.

Each wound is perfect,
encloses itself in a tiny
imperceptible blossom
making pain.

Pain is a flower like that one,
like this one,
like that one,
like this one.

(*FL*, p. 96)

The poem is problematic for any interpreter because he must project onto it psychological explanations for the processes described. Nonetheless it seems reasonable to suppose that the speaker in the first stanza, already bothered by the uncertainties of self-consciousness ("I think I grow"), grows tensions in order to create some kind of life or inner vitality in his essentially empty and lonely self (hence the tensions are "flowers/in a wood where/nobody goes"). To produce the desired vitality, however, the pain from the tensions must become the object of consciousness; but consciousness tends to set off the particular experience it focuses on, to turn the dynamics of life into the static isolation of the work of art. The resulting condition is presented in the last stanza, primarily through the tone, which is quiet and sensitive, yet barely capable of restraining its despair. The primary experience is one of increasing distance, of a consciousness that is withdrawing from any dynamic interchange with experience. As the speaker alternates from "this one" to "that one," the reader gets a terrifying glimpse of the way the mind can move from participation to pointing and cataloging. And cataloging is fragmenting: the repeated "ones" both mock the speaker's desire for a single unified consciousness and remind the reader that consciousness cannot create its own unity. Without some kind of dialectic with others or with experience, consciousness is left turning each of its objects into unique aesthetic phenomena. The quest for unity leaves only the ironic fact of the unbridgeable distance between separate beings.

Perhaps the sure "egoist," the self-satisfied solipsist, can be so confident of his own unity that he neither recognizes the gulf between himself and other people nor creates gaps between himself and the world by continually desiring realities that transcend his present condition. But Creeley is by nature a man of intense energy always overflowing the boundaries of his selfhood and asking some response in the world beyond himself:

I think that a lot of my first wife's understandable bitterness about our relationship was the intensity she was having to deal with. I mean

everything was so intense and involved always with tension. My way
to experience emotion was to tighten it up as much as possible . . .
I can't let anybody sleep because I don't want to miss anything. I
want it all, and so I tend at times, understandably, to exhaust my
friends—keep pushing, pushing, pushing . . . I do so love the intensity
of people that I can't let anything stop until it's literally exhaustion.
[*PR*, p. 162]

If such continual thrusting into the void is to be acceptable, Creeley must
find some reconciliation with it, some ground or goal for the energy. In
For Love he moves toward two possible solutions.

   There is, first, the possibility that all words need not be empty
signifiers; there might be a mode of speech for articulating the dynamic
life of the person and objectifying it in such a way that it can be shared:

> that for each
> man is a speech
> describes him, makes
> the day grow white
> and sure, a quietness of water
> in the mind,
> lets hand, descriptive
> as a risk, something
> for which he cannot find
> a means or time.
>
> ("The Pool," *FL*, p. 141)[7]

The way of realizing this speech is most fully presented in "The Dishonest
Mailmen":

> They are taking all my letters, and they
> put them into a fire.
>
>   I see the flames, etc.
> But do not care, etc.
>
> They burn everything I have, or what little
> I have. I don't care, etc.
>
> The poem supreme, addressed to
> emptiness—this is the courage
>
> necessary. This is something
> quite different.
>
> (*FL*, p. 29)

The first six lines here summarize the problems of ordinary language or what Heidegger calls "idle talk."[8] The speech of one's "letters" is not demanding; formulas seem adequate to the message, so one need only mention the first few words and "etc." suffices for the rest. But within this public and formulaic language (whose words are the dishonest mailmen), there is room only for the lowest common denominator of the self, the self about which one really does not "care." There remains, however, another self-desiring expression, and between him and the spoken self a gulf begins to open—a gulf created in the poem by the speaker's self-contempt and by the separation of a hostile "they" and an inadequate defensive "I." The last four lines, then, oppose the ideal to this condition. The poem, authentic speech, requires the courage to confront two kinds of emptiness—the void between self and other and the void between conventional self and the new particular experiences it encounters. In the face of this nothingness, authentic speech creates "something," a concrete real object in the world instead of the vague "etc." of "idle talk." And in the successful speech, the tension between "I" and "They" is eliminated: the last stanzas present only the recurrent "this," which insists that here is a particular "occasion" in which all the opposing energies can find common ground.

One can best understand many of Creeley's typical poetic strategies as attempts to wrench the formulas of "idle talk" into authentic speech in order to wrench speech back into the world of action. Creeley's use of a very limited vocabulary and set of images is an attempt to create a personal speech. He wants to break through the merely phenomenal images provided in language by restating his essential experiences in a variety of closely related ways. Eventually the range of perspectives will allow the reader himself to penetrate the sense of the words as merely signs and allow some intuition into the essential reality of the man and his energies behind them. A complementary effect is created by Creeley's persistent ambiguity, especially by his habit of allowing many possible modifiers or referents for crucial words in his poems. The ambiguity in effect calls into question the formulas of ordinary language; it asserts that this order is too static and conventional to allow reality to emerge: "the American writer has constantly to refind, and, equally, to redefine wherein lies the value of the words he uses" (QG, p. 318). Redefinition can take place because, when the linguistic order crumbles, the dramatic situation (or the ontological rather than the verbal context) becomes the only valid "definer of words" (QG, p. 312). (For example, in the line "what or where to recover/what is not love/too simply" [FL, p. 23] there is no linguistic indication of what "too simply" modifies; only repeated experiences of the poem as context can lead one to interpret the lines.) Situation, or place, or ground, comes to inform the words and thus makes possible the particular, vital, personal language Creeley postulates in "The Dishonest Mailmen."

Personal speech, even when achieved, however, cannot by itself be a satisfying solution: to express pain is only partially to resolve it, especially when one has not yet discovered his ideal audience for that speech. Speech can define the individual but does not guarantee that definition being accepted; for this Creeley needs to find an adequate relation with another person. The structure of *For Love* as a volume establishes the terms by which such a relation can be formed: the volume begins with the various kinds of alienation expressed in "Hart Crane," runs through the dissolution of Creeley's first marriage, and comes eventually around to the resolution provided by his second wife, Bobbie: "Into the company of love/it all returns" (*FL*, p. 160). Her naturalness, openness, and refusal of abstraction allow him "to live at last" (*QG*, p. 323), grounded ultimately by the three powerful stresses of the final line:

> The night is a pleasure to us,
> I think sleeping, and what warmth secures
> me you bring,
> giving at last freely of yourself.
>
> Myself was old, was confused, was wanting—
> to sing of an old song,
> through the last echo of hurting,
> brought now home.
>
> ("The Snow," *FL*, p. 155)

"In her tired mind's keeping" (*FL*, p. 158), the poet finds his "place to come home to" (*FL*, p. 149) and thus resists the terrifying sense of voids that had lurked on the horizon of all his experiences. Creeley enters the volume stumbling ("Preface") and leaves it free to move within the ordered patterns of the informing and sustaining dance:

> For friendship
> make a chain that holds,
> to be bound to
> others, two by two,
>
> a walk, a garland,
> handed by hands
> that cannot move
> unless they hold.
>
> (*FL*, p. 157)

In some of the love poems, Creeley cleverly uses puns to reinforce the idea of Bobbie as existential ground for his otherwise diaphanous self. Instead of the ambiguities of those poems dealing with the problems of empty signifiers and his own confusions, these love poems confidently and lightly play on the rich multiplicities of language available when one is placed in a clear existential context:

> If it falls flat
> I'm used to it. Yet
> cannot grow when
> I can't begin again.
>
> Nowise to secure
> what's left to others. They
> forget.
> But I remember.
>
> How carelessly ease falls
> around me! All the trees
> have it, the leaves
> all green!
>
> I want to grow in ground too,
> want it to come true
> what they said about if you planted
> the acorn the tree would grow.
>> ("The Kid," *FL*, p. 112; see also *FL*, p. 128)

The puns here present at once a kind of abstract statement of psychological desires ("come true," "ease," "fall flat") and concrete reference to specific sexual activities so that the two reinforce one another. The psychological can be satisfied precisely because its desires are rooted in and sustained by a physical place and process. Given a place in experience, then, nothingness can become sexual (see *W*, p. 113), and loss becomes rest and peace. For Creeley there is no exaggeration when he dedicates *For Love* "for Bobbie—who makes all things possible"; she provides the foundation wherein empty signs and dangerously empty people find a form.

In *Words*, however, Creeley's general resolution has begun to crumble. Holding hands does not so much resolve the problem of nothingness as cover it over and deny that it really exists so long as one finds love. More important, at the end of *For Love*, Creeley had given Bobbie too much power. She became the only active agent whereas she should be part, not all, of the solution; Creeley must find a basis within himself as well as in his relationship with his wife: "You cannot sit in a woman's lap, however comfortable. And, despite the humiliation, the door must be shut of necessity—until you can bang it down or open it" (*QG*, p. 115). Finally, Creeley had conceived of Bobbie and the home she made possible as a permanent peace outside the flux of time, but he soon realized that real peace must be found within, not beyond, the flux:

> People try with an increasing despair to live, and to come to some-thing, some place, or person. They want an island in which the world will be at last a place circumscribed by visible horizons. They want to love free of a continuity of roads, and other places. This island is, finally, not real, however tangible it once seemed to me. I have found that time, even if it will not offer much more than a place to die in, nonetheless carries one on, away from this or any other island. [*QG*, p. 7]

The central task of *Words* is to elaborate the ideal of ground or place so that it can be reconciled with the flux. One can, in fact, best appreciate the theme of "place" in *Words* by seeing how Creeley further adapts to his own secular purposes the metaphor of Ground of Being. First, Creeley's ground must be a dynamic relationship that allows a perpetual change and reformulation, while nonetheless providing a sense of security, a sense that he belongs in a world from which he has become more and more alienated: "I'm really speaking of my own sense of place. Where 'the heart finds rest,' as Robert Duncan would say. I mean that place where one is open, where a sense of defensiveness or insecurity and all the other complexes of response to place can be finally dropped. Where one feels an intimate association with the ground under foot" (*PR*, p. 157). Second, "place" must be concrete, must allow one to ex-perience himself, not "as some egocentric center, but to experience one-self as in the world" (*QG*, p. 64; see pp. 63–68). All possibility for relationship depends on making contact, on getting out of one's head to a state where "the weather/occurs, the mind/is not its only witness" (*W*, p. 98).[9]

To transcend the gap between words or concepts and things, to find place or, more properly, to put place into the processes of time, one must redefine his relationship to desire. So long as a person retains the concept that man is a creature whose essence is his infinite freedom, he will perpetually live beyond his existing self in the quest for new identities. Creeley, on the other hand, wants to limit the sense of possibility, to posit a biological *telos* or limit that will contain and define the gaps between the desired image and reality. In other words, "choice is signifi-cantly the act of recognition" (*QG*, p. 71), not the power to define identity but to realize it. In his later writing, this reflection on valid and invalid definitions of freedom has provided Creeley with terms by which he could formulate his earlier fear of the void:

Freedom has always been for me a difficult experience in that, when younger, I felt it had to propose senses of experience and of the world I was necessarily not in possession of—something in that way one might escape to. I mistook, I think, the meaning of "freely to write what one chooses" . . . because I took "freely" to mean "without significant limit" and "chooses" to be an act of will. I therefore was slow in realizing the nature of Olson's proposal, that "Limits/are what any of us/are inside of," just that I had taken such "limits" to be a frustration of possibility rather than the literal possibility they in fact must provoke. [QG, pp. 70–71; see also I, p. 112; P, p. 79]

"For W. C. W." goes a step further. Not only must freedom be redefined to recognize limits, but one must come to accept the eternal gap between desire and act. Total self-definition, or any total coincidence between a desiring agent and the goal of desire, is impossible. The two are in perpetual oscillation, driving one another on like mature lovers, or like the process by which the desire for self-knowledge breeds an infinite series of poems all trying to satisfy the wants unfulfilled by the previous act:

> The rhyme is after
> all the repeated
> insistence.
>
> There, you say, and
> there, and there,
> and and becomes
>
> just so. And
> what one wants is
> what one wants,
>
> yet complexly
> as you
> say.
>
> Let's
> let it go.
> I want—
>
> Then there is—
> and,
> I want.

(W, p. 27)

The poem is based on the contrast between two ways of apprehending the world—one based on a rage for order and the other on a commitment to the flux ("let's/let it go"). Rhyme is an attempt to impose a fictive order on the world; time ("and") and space ("there") must correspond to the orders of speech. Realizing such a correspondence would satisfy man's deepest desire—to attain coincidence between desire and result, but the two possible ways of reading "what one wants is/what one wants" qualify that satisfaction. If the reader stresses the copula, he is asserting that desire and act can coincide, yet the repetition is also a kind of tautology, a solution preordained in the fictive order one remains within. Rhyme satisfies the desire for coincidence by merely restating the world in another way whose correspondence is preordained by the poet, despite the rhythms of the existential world. Real desire, though, is not cyclic but durational and hence linear or spiral; it moves toward change, not repetition. Consequently, its inability to be satisfied completely, its tendency to generate new desires, must be accepted in the larger form created by one's awareness of the flux.

Creeley carefully reinforces his contraries here by setting the impersonal and unspecific pronouns "one" and "you" of the first half of the poem against the "I," the active agent of desire who really exists only when the world is allowed its own rhythms. (In the rhymed world, "I" is only a part of the fictive universe, and its identity is dictated by whatever pattern is governing the repetition—much as the subject is merely a grammatical or mythical role in the structuralist description of reality.) Creeley also opposes two perspectives on the word "there," a word which defines the world outside the self. "There" is only a fictional creation ("there, you say") in the hermetic world of the rhymed universe, but when desire confronts objects that it does not already control, the self discovers a real world beyond his ego, "then there is." ("There" is a demonstrative adverb stressing the existential world that complements but is not exhausted by "I want," and also is itself an object of consciousness, that is, a state of being, the state of "thereness.")

By accepting the gap between desire and fulfillment, Creeley makes it possible to see these voids as essential and even productive elements in the dialectic of experience. The silence or absence now exists within a form or rhythm and becomes an "interval" (W, pp. 129, 137–38). Analogously, silence becomes a vital aspect of poetry's communicative power: "A quiet is left to say more than can the violence" of exaggerated rhetorical speech (QG, p. 272). Creeley even integrates "nothing" into the experience of value by stressing its active power as "nothing." Thus he uses the traditional terms of negation that underlie a good deal of mysticism to define both love (FL, p. 84) and truth (W, p. 87). It is only when the world becomes in part "no thing" that one can see value emerge from its demonic facticity; "no thing" allows the possibility that the world of things can lose its mere objectivity and take on the dimension of vitality that is basic to the experience of value.[10]

"Joy" correlates the new willingness to accept nothingness with the predominant theme of "place":

> I could look at
> an empty hole for hours
> thinking it will
> get something in it,
>
> will collect
> things. There is
> an infinite emptiness
> placed there.

(*W*, p. 113)

When emptiness can be grounded by its existence within a recognized form and "placed" in the sexual orifice, it becomes possibility instead of threat. The empty hole appeals because the world is no longer all filled up, harshly opaque, and horizontal; rather it is open to, even demands, the active engagement in it of another if it is to be fulfilled. "There" is no longer the place of the hostile other, but the necessary complement to oneself that calls to and promises ground for the isolated consciousness.

Creeley dramatizes the way interpersonal relations can make a value of nothingness in "The Language," where the punning technique of the love poems in *For Love* emphasizes that nothingness is at the same time metaphysical abstraction and concrete fact:

> Locate I
> love you some—
> where in
>
> teeth and
> eyes, bite
> it but
>
> take care not
> to hurt, you
> want so
>
> much so
> little. Words
> say everything,
>
> I
> love you
> again,
>
> then what
> is emptiness
> for? To

fill, fill.
I heard words
and words full

of holes
aching. Speech
is a mouth.

(W, p. 37)

The speaker here tells the woman that the words "I love you" must be rooted in physical acts; words by themselves "say everything" and hence nothing. But she is dissatisfied with the reduction of "I love you" to sheer physical response, so the words are repeated and the man then questions the role of the emptiness between physical act and word. He comes to realize that words are statements of a desire that complements yet goes beyond the physical interplay. By saying "I love you," the woman asks that both physical and psychological voids be filled, and in so doing she creates for the man a new possibility he can reach out to satisfy. The rich duality in the last lines ("Speech/is a mouth") then explains how the two levels, physical and psychological, are complementary. Speech is a mouth because it is a hole made productive as a physical activity that, on the analogy of the lover's mouth, brings peaceful relief to the openings created by the woman's desires.

Creeley's quest for a secure place, however, has yet to be satisfied. In *Words* he saw a way to accept and find value in the flux and recognized that "place" can never be an island but must be found within a series of shifting accommodations to the other and to one's environment; in other words he learns to say "Here." There remains as the task for *Pieces* the problem of locating that "here"—not only in momentary reconciliations but in some larger system or locality that defines it and its possibilities. As Creeley reconciled himself in *Words* with one form of nothingness, in *Pieces* he must admit another kind of void or absence —one not so much in the rhythm of one's life as in the actual condition or absent system that defines the terms of that rhythm. In the most simple terms, "here" requires a whole system of language for its meaning, especially for its opposite term "there," just as the person needs to reconcile himself to the social and psychological forms that define his own particular apprehension of place:

Here now you are—
by what means?
And who to know it?

(P, p. 60)

> Where we are there must
> be something to place us.
> Look around. What do you see
> that you can recognize?

(*P*, p. 64–65)[11]

"Here" for Creeley states an ideal of pure presence, of a relationship between subject and world where each is transparent to and completely adequate for the other. Nothing is lacking, just as the field of vision allows a certain kind of completeness, a sense that one is totally aware of his environment. However, that unity is destroyed as soon as one tries either to act on or speak about what is seen, for then exterior purposes and systems come into play and alienation sets in. The ideal of "presence" then necessarily involves a harmony with natural rhythms—in fact to a dualist or humanist it approximates the nonreflective existence of animals. Human subjectivity introduces other factors into the world not easily reconciled with pure presence; man for example can, and perhaps at certain stages of development must, become conscious of the essentially absent codes that inform his arrangement of the world in words or numbers or define his sense of being a member of various collectivities like his family, class, or nation. "Here" is primarily a solipsistic demand, "We break things in pieces . . . hearing them fall just to hear it" (*W*, p. 82), and requires the complementary consciousness of "there," if a man is to find a secure "place." Ultimately "here" and "there" must form a kind of dialectic (albeit an unstable one, especially for Creeley) in which permanence and flux, absence and presence inform one another:

> There might be
> an imaginary
> place to be—
> there might be.
>
> . . . . . .
>
> What have I seen,
> now see? There were
> times before
> I look now.

(*P*, pp. 58–59)

The rest of the poem elaborates the dialectic, but later in the volume it is stated more forcefully:

> Make time
> of irritations,
> looking for the
> recurrence—

> waiting, waiting,
> on the edge of its
> to be there
> where it was, waiting.
>
> Moving in the mind's
> patterns, recognized
> because there is where
> they happen.
>
> (*P*, p. 70)

In *Pieces* Creeley uses the rich word *ways* as a basic means for embodying the "here-there" dialectic; the word evokes traditional religious associations while pointing to a necessary interplay between defined objective structures (paths and accepted modes for acting) and the subjective consciousness that must realize or use these structures. Moreover, "ways" picks up the metaphor of driving, which in Creeley's prose had become a favorite means for stating his vision of the ideal relationship between man and world. Driving embodies the ideal union of unself-conscious human control with the feeling that one is moving in and with the natural world. "Everything is, in effect, falling into place. You're not intentionally putting it there, but you're recognizing the feeling of its occurring there" (*CP*, p. 8) because the " 'articulate' driver . . . can follow the road with precisely the right response to each condition before him" (*PR*, p. 179; see also *QG*, p. 58). Creeley, like most important recent American poets, is trying to resolve the dualisms of man and nature, subject and object, and embody their harmonious interrelationships in his poems. But he also shares with these poets a solution that tends to be solipsistic; it accounts only for the interactions of a single consciousness with its immediate environment and does not take into account either the rest of the traffic or the codes by which harmony is achieved, both between car and road or car and the other cars.

Claude Levi-Strauss uses the same metaphor in *The Savage Mind*, but with an appreciation of the traffic patterns that helps explain what Creeley is trying to attain in *Pieces*. Levi-Strauss asks if there is any modern analogue for the primitive's feeling of unity with his conditions, for that incredible awareness of the subtlest nuance in his environment which makes him appear a part of the forest. Levi-Strauss really wants to know if one can recapture this form of primitive consciousness without necessarily returning to the accompanying conditions. He finds his answer in the incredible yet un-self-conscious intricacy of present-day traffic systems: the driver recognizes and naturally responds to all the signals of the other moving cars, yet at the same time he realizes that he is not a subjective observer outside the flow but is himself an object within the dynamic exchange of signals—active agent, yet defined and limited, he is both expressing himself and being expressed by the dance of which he is a part.[12]

The goal, then, is to see the self at the same time as both subject and object, container and contained. Creeley most fully approximates the possibility for such a resolution in the series of number poems that explore the ways in which "the power to tell/is glory" (*P*, p. 10). The poems each move from the unique context of the poet's associative response to the stimulus of a particular number painting (by Robert Indiana) out to the consciousness that all the associations inhere within the form of a single number and then that all the numbers are informed by the pattern of the number system itself:

> move forward, backward,
> then, and the same
> numbers will occur.
>
> What law
> or
> mystery
>
> is involved
> protects
> itself.

("Nine," *P*, p. 33)[13]

The mediation on numbers takes up from the "Fragments" that concludes *Words* and explains how "pieces" can become "peaces." Number, like language, absorbs into itself the gap between individual and universal. In commonsense terms, at least, numbers and words refer to specific events; yet they also incorporate these particulars into communal forms, for both numbers and language, perhaps even the human presence they help define, are essentially relational systems with each particular defined by the absent system of which it is a part. Creeley has always considered himself essentially a poet of relationships, and in *Pieces* he is moving beyond particular relationships to their underlying forms, which provide the secure base that had always been the goal of his efforts.[14]

"Zero," the poem following the lines quoted above, explains how the "law or mystery" enters human experience. The poem expresses Creeley's acceptance of this new sense of absence; zero is the absence needed to ground and generate the form of the relational system of numbers:

> Where are you—who
> > by not being here
> are here, but here
> > by not being here?
>
> . . . .
>
> [You] walk the years in a
> > nothing, a no
> place I know as well as
> > the last breath
>
> I took, blowing the smoke
> > out of a mouth
> will also go nowhere,
> > having found its way.
>
> Reading that primitive systems
> seem to have natural cause for
> the return to one, after ten—
> but this is not ten—out of
> nothing, one, to return to that—
>
> . . . .
>
> What
> by being not
> is—is not
> by being.
>
> When holes taste good
> we'll put them in our bread.
>
> > > > (*P,* pp. 33–34)

To see what Creeley is after here, one needs for a moment to retrace Gottlob Frege's abstractions on the nature of zero. Zero, first of all, cannot refer to any object: there is no way of imaging "O" visible stars. Zero, in fact, cannot even be identical to itself, for then it would have an object and be "one." Yet "one" or identity cannot logically exist without zero, because the possibility of there being a progression of numbers depends upon some lack of identity, some zero relation, between the progression and some generating source. This source in turn cannot have a definable identity or else it would correspond to the number system and one would enter the vicious circle of using a system not identical with its foundation to describe that foundation. In Creeley's psychological terms, the initial absence or lack of identity is what prevents man from being a god, or at least a solipsist, which is a secular version of playing god, for both god and the solipsist may be defined as those whose being is everywhere identical to itself.[15] Because man is not identical to himself, he is subject to all the terrors of the void, but that very same involvement in absence leaves room by which he can participate in forms that surpass and contain him. The relation between zero and one is a perpetual dialectic by which each creates and defines the other, while both at the same time generate the number system that contains them. In the same way, the poet, his emptiness with the desires it causes, and the forms he generates exist in perpetual interpenetration —containing and defining his existence. When holes are accepted, the daily bread can be transformed into the ritual center of a communal feast.

Some of the basic elements in Creeley's later style strive to embody this interpenetration of particularity with the universal forms that shape it. Speaking of "A Piece," one of his first experiments with numbers, Creeley says, "For me it was central to all possibilities of statement. One might think of 'counting sheep.' . . . To count, or give account, tell or tally; continuingly seems to me the occasion" (*CP*, pp. 16–17).[16] The numbers work at the limit of possibility because they are at the same time utterly concrete and completely abstract (that is, numbers are basic to unique experiences and yet are capable of being applied to a whole range of particulars). In the same vein, Creeley focuses on absolutely common terms like *here, there, the, one,* for they are so obviously elements of man's particular perception of the world; yet when taken as objects of reference, they also describe universal experiences in which the particular words incorporate numerous possible experiences. Every poet desires a unique dramatic context that becomes at the same time an occasion for others; every poet tries to make his "here" also a "there" in which others can participate. Normally though, this objectification demands the selection of particular details or metaphors that Creeley feels tend to "displace" the original force of the emotion (*P*, p. 49). Objects do, of course, present some bases for shared feeling, but more immediate to both poet and his audience are the words by which they tally and adjust their position in relation to whatever objects may be at hand.

On the metaphysical level, Creeley wants by the use of these relational terms "to get the sense of 'I' into Zukofsky's 'eye'—a/locus of experience, not a presumption of expected value" (*P*, p. 68). In other words, he is trying in his use of terms like *here* and *the* to project the actual dynamic moment of apprehension, the field of energy exchange where self and world meet, before the encounter is translated into the irreconcilable terms of subject and object (the names of objects already imply the division of self and world). Such terms make it possible to retain for consciousness the energies that underlie perception and in so doing to capture those moments which precede subjectivity while defining its conditions.[17]

In the center of this moment, Creeley has discovered the presence of an absence that, while it forces man to admit that even in his limited place he cannot be God, nonetheless provides the conditions for his accepting, finding a place for, and even rejoicing in the presence of the other. "They," one of Creeley's finest lyrics, presents just this realization:

> What could
> they give me I
> hadn't myself
> discovered—
>
> The world,—that
> I'd fallen upon
> in some
> distracted drunkenness—
>
> Or that the rules
> were wrong, an
> observation they
> as well as I
> knew now—
>
> They were imagination
> also. If they
> would be as the
> mind could see them,
>
> then it all was
> true and the
> mind followed and
> I also.

(P, p. 47)

"I" here is both Creeley himself and the abstract condition of becoming a subject—a condition of which one can only become conscious through the presence of another, for only when there are two can men really speak of one. Moreover, the two contraries "they" and "I" must share some form; their minds must "follow" if either is to be able to define himself in any meaningful way. With "Followed," Creeley's poetic questionings arrive at the recurrent contemporary metaphor of redeemed experience seen as a dance. His use of the metaphor is both distinctive and indicative of a major difference between the contemporaries and the early moderns. Creeley's dance is radically simple: it conceives a satisfying view of Presence as accepting the dynamic and ordered (because true to the laws of natural process) interchange of self and world, here and there. Moreover, the sense of dance depends on neither a grounding myth nor elaborate metaphor. The dance is available to all because of the simplicity of its elements, both in reality and in the figures of the poem. Creeley achieves universality for his dance by preserving the abstract and inclusive dimensions of the most simple relational elements of language. There is no question of belief, no need for doctrine to support what is in fact basic to all experiences of connection. Poetry has come a long way from Yeats and his fellows for whom the dance was usually a transcendent state reached only by the artist or sensitive spectator in rare moments of vision achieved with great difficulty and sacrifice. The dance remains in an ideal world out there while we can only be the dissatisfied spectators here longing to cross the unbridgeable chasm between the two worlds. For Creeley, for the postmodern poet in general, the task has become to imagine and create the possibility that all men can integrate note and interval, dancer and the dance.

iii

It is easy, and perhaps ultimately even correct, to condemn W. S. Merwin's recent poetry as excessively difficult, impersonal, abstract, and disembodied. But the condemnation gets one nowhere until one comes to terms with the enormous task Merwin has set himself since rejecting his earlier style. Merwin's problem was a typical modern one—great poetic talent without very much to say. To test the limits of that talent and to map his own thematic and imagistic landscape, Merwin has been forced outside the usual realms of English and American poetry. His quest, embodied in the stylistic shift as well as in the contents of the poems, is to find out "what do I have that is my own," "what is essential to me" that can "sustain me for my time in the desert."[18] This desert is familiar: it is the sense of alienation and absence created by a separation from community, a lack of faith in both traditional beliefs and the possibility of trusting in any general explanations of phenomena, a sense of the gulf between desires and actions or desires and interpretations of desire, and a divorce between a sense of private identity and the shallowness of public roles. In Merwin's terms: in the beginning is the desert, and its abiding deity is "Division, the mother of Pain" (*MT*, p. 53).

Merwin's poems enter that desert and carry on their quest in two basic forms. There are first of all fairly simple coherent lyrics asserting a desired unity or crying out in despair. It is easy, even ennobling, to identify with the powerful statements of pain in poems like "Lemuel's Blessing," "Acclimatization," and "Psalm: Our Fathers." And because the poems are fairly clear, one is free also to enjoy Merwin's tremendous facility with language and the witty precision of his surreal images. In its more recondite moments, however, the quest becomes difficult and metaphysical. There a reader finds himself disoriented and groping for secure ground: whose is this disembodied impersonal voice, and what does it seek in those regions of the mind it asks one to enter where the self-consciously allegorical imagination merges with a surrealistic one bringing images from the depths of the unconscious? Difficult as these dislocations are, Merwin's verbal authority and the powerful questions he is asking convince one to follow him into this difficult terrain.

In America's literary traditions, with the controversial exception of the late Eliot whom Merwin often echoes, selfhood is an affair of presence. One can feel oneself integral when, like Creeley, one achieves harmony with the place where he stands and with the desires and objects also occupying or impinging on that place. The dream is Whitman's, although its manifestations vary: if one can gather and accept all that touches his consciousness in a given moment—either by a particularizing catalog or through some symbolic or mythical field—he has overcome division and found at least a momentary home. For Merwin, however, the gross particulars usually mock any potential sense of essential reality. They are doomed to pass away and change, as are the moods and feelings they generate. This illusory present is more insubstantial than the darkness or painful sense of absence it replaces. Moreover, the language one uses to fix those particulars, or even to comfort oneself by lamenting their passing, eventually mocks one with its inadequacies and its absences ("My words are the garment of what I shall never be/Like the tucked sleeve of a one-armed boy" [L, p. 62]). Compare with Creeley's sense of place, Merwin's "The Cold Before the Moonrise":

> It is too simple to turn to the sound
> Of frost stirring among its
> Stars like an animal asleep
> In the winter night
> And say I was born far from home
> If there is a place where this is the language may
> It be my country

> (L, p. 46)

The poem does not even consider the possibility of being at one with the natural scene (in part because the title indicates the speaker's awareness of an imminent change). It seeks instead, as the only possible harmony, a language capable of expressing his grief and division. But one cannot live in so simple a language, for language is as distant from him as he is from the particulars of the scene. Language will not allow him the consolation of defining absence in a specific form and therefore of controlling it. Instead language doubles the initial loss by making him conscious that he must define it through the problematic mediations of words and thus further divides the speaker from any home at all. He remains a disembodied consciousness that cannot be articulated.

Nonetheless, Merwin refuses to be only a poet of despair:

> Absolute despair has no art. I imagine the writing of a poem, in whatever mode, still betrays the existence of hope, which is why poetry is more and more chary of the conscious mind, in our age. And what the poem manages to find hope for may be part of what it keeps trying to say. [*DV*, p. 272]

Like Olson, he seeks to find out what is on the other side of despair, but this means more than asserting new solutions. It entails entering and inhabiting despair in the hope that he might eventually pass through its boundaries. The goal is to uncover a kind of secular absolute—some presence that endures beneath change and that might provide "metaphysical solace," if not ethical direction. To realize what endures the poet must find ways of articulating a present not bound to specific particulars. The first task then is to de-create romantic expectations about presence and desires for the pregnant moment by placing the reader in a kind of absence. Like the mystic, Merwin's first step is to withdraw from the world as it is known and to intensify the despair about the value of the methods or the inclusive fictions that lie at one's disposal. This is the reason for Merwin's "apartness" or "suspended regard" (*PJF*). A cold impersonal distance prevents one from touching, from becoming too intimate with, the things and moods that pass away. One might conceive Merwin's voice in the terms of the common modern distinction between fear and anxiety—fear being uneasiness about specific objects or goals and anxiety a more generalized discomfort whose specific cause or even resolution seems impossible to define. With Kafka, Merwin senses that metaphysical poetry can begin only from the perspective of anxiety. Moreover, while fears tend to be personal, anxiety stems often from the breakdown of collective myth and represents collective problems. It is thus only from the perspective of anxiety that the poet might achieve public solutions for common problems. As Heidegger puts it, one must "experience in Nothing the vastness of that which gives every being the warrant to be. That is Being itself."[19] One can only glimpse a Being that endures within change after he has cast off his *Drunk in the Furnace* (New York: Macmillan, 1960): "The focusing on one place in that way was deliberate, and it led me to see how limited the possibilities of that were, for me, then. Something else would be needed" (*PM*, p. 7). To realize this "something else," which Merwin links with "the true source" (*PM*, p. 7), the poet must be abstract. This need not mean that poetry must deal overtly with ideas; abstraction is a condition of vision, a way of pursuing informing principles that ultimately might be the simplest, most concrete properties of being. Mathematics, for example, is radically abstract, yet as is seen in Creeley's *Pieces*, it seeks the simplest, most fundamental relationships. Merwin's poetry seeks to be a mathematics of the imagination:

> First you must know that the whole of the physical world floats in each of the senses at the same time. Each of them reveals to us a different aspect of the kingdom of change. But none of them reveals the unnameable stillness that unites them. At the heart of change it lies unseeing, unhearing, unfeeling, unchanging, holding within itself the beginning and the end. It is ours. It is our only possession. Yet we cannot take it into our hands, which change, nor see it with our eyes, which change. . . . None of the senses can come to it. Except backwards. . . .
>
> Somewhere on the other side of that a voice is coming. We are the voice. But we are each of those others. Yet the voice is coming to us. That is what we are doing here. It has to pass through us in order to reach us. It has to go through us without pausing in order to be clear to us. Only in the senses can we pause because only in the senses can we move. The stillness is not in the senses but through them and the voice must come through the stillness. Each in turn we must become transparent. [*MPC*, pp. 56–57]

Plenitude must be approached "backwards," and the normal functioning of the senses must be disturbed if one is to know the stillness they participate in. The model is mystical—the *via negativa*—and not the affirmative intensity of visionary poets like Blake and Yeats. Conceptually, mysticism has been allied with many Romantic and post-Romantic ideas of poetry, especially with surrealism (witness Bly), but no American except Eliot (and he with a doctrine to support him) has risked as much emptiness as Merwin in pursuit of plenitude. Indeed Merwin is so disturbing in large measure because his roots are European —in poets like Rilke and Follain who have developed numerous variations on the *via negativa* as the way to an enduring presence.

Merwin begins to explore the productive role of absence toward the end of *The Moving Target*, when he starts to reflect on ways the new style developed in the volume can provide the "something else" that could not be found in *The Drunk in the Furnace*. To read these poems with much appreciation, however, one needs briefly to survey the landscape of division drawn by the first two-thirds of the volume. The first third has as its dramatic center "Lemuel's Blessing," with its portrayal of Lemuel's pathetic, yet curiously noble quest to find "what is essential" to him. Lemuel seeks desperately to hold to some form of inner self, although he is so reduced by society's uses of him that he imagines himself a dog (what might have been at first only a metaphor collapses into literalness, as it does in schizophrenia) whose only vision of a free, self-dependent spirit is the wolf he prays to. Surrounding this poem are numerous others dramatizing alienated selves: "Home For Thanksgiving," for example, expresses a selfhood so tenuous it can be preserved only by sewing "himself in like money" and avoiding all contact with others, while "Noah's Raven" presents a speaker so self-contained that he renounces all society for a future "always beyond them." Others like "Sire," "The Nails," and "Acclimatization" render a condition of absence from the essential self so profound it makes even problematic selfhood seem almost a luxury. In "The Nails" the speaker seeks a central self he can offer in love, but the refrain "it isn't as simple as that" renders an oppressive self-reflexiveness, only euphemistically called *self*-consciousness. "Alone like a key in a lock/Without what it takes to turn," the lover cannot respond to the necessities of the moment:

> Winter will think back to your lit harvest
> For which there is no help, and the seed
> Of eloquence will open its wings
> When you are gone.
> But at this moment
> When the nails are kissing the fingers good-bye
> And my only
> Chance is bleeding from me,
> When my one chance is bleeding,
> For speaking either truth or comfort
> I have no more tongue than a wound
>
> (*MT*, p. 19)

If he had no mouth, he would have no desire to speak and he would be free; there would be no nagging absence trying to complete the moment. But instead there remains a sense of potential that intensifies the unfulfilled desire. For a man, having a mouth implies having something to say, but that logic only metamorphoses the mouth into a wound —paradoxically deepened by its desire to be healed. With the dream of identity generating primarily this wound of tormented absence, Merwin turns in the volume's second third to the hope that what is essential might be found outside the self, in contact with a vital present. However, the speakers usually cannot break through the categories of their own psyches to make contact with the fluctuating present. Division becomes a problem of knowledge, not of action as it had been in the first poems. The persona can remember "another time/When our hands met and the clocks struck/And we lived on the point of a needle, like angels" (*MT*, p. 34), but now one finds it impossible even to remember what was known, for he is so far from "the days":

> It's the old story,
> Every morning something different is real.
> This place is no more than the nephew of itself,
> With these cats, this traffic, these
> Departures
> To which I have kept returning,
> Having tasted the apple of my eye,
> Saying perennially
> Here it is, the one and only,
> The beginning and the end.
> This time the dials have come with the hands and
> Suddenly I was never here before.
> Oh dust, oh dust, progress
> Is being made
>
> (*MT*, p. 43)

Man is the object, not the subject, of progress, and he is perplexed by Eliot's memory and desire:

> Coming late, as always,
> I try to remember what I almost heard.
> The light avoids my eye.
>
> How many times have I heard the locks close
> And the lark take the keys
> And hang them in heaven.
>
> (*MT*, p. 41)

The speaker "almost" hears what he desires. Its proximity makes him act. Yet he actually hears only symbolic reminders that what he desires remains absent from him. The speaker is tempted by the potential in the moment as another speaker was by having a tongue, but he fares no better. He ends up only with another wound, a fictive unknowable heaven that continues to generate desire ("how many times") but not to satisfy it. He is doomed to the shadowy absences created by fictive images— blocked by his own being (his faulty eye) from the fullness of "the light," "More and more/I get like shadows; I find out/how they hate" (*MT*, p. 37).

In that hatred, however, the shadow plays an important dialectical role—defining the quality of the light and the forms of relationship light has to the landscape. Because its existence depends on an object that stands between it and the source of the light, the shadow testifies to the presence of a true source, even if it is condemned never to participate directly in that presence. And shadows create contrasts that make dramatically evident the many variations the light takes in its encounters with the landscape. Without shadow, as, on an analogical plane, without consciousness, there would be only a single unqualified and unappreciated mode of being. In addition, the shadow, like Snyder's mirror, offers a backward transparent image of one's own place within and without natural experience, and it possesses a kind of "unnameable stillness." The shadow is one basic place Merwin's personnae try to occupy in order to recognize what creates their condition. It is the embodiment in landscape of the "suspended regard"—a function performed in the mind by memory and silence.

Memory, then, will play a crucial role in helping one to glimpse that heaven where the keys are hidden. Memory is not captive within the present; in fact, as Augustine insists in his meditation on memory in the tenth book of *Confessions*, it exists nowhere. Yet memory allows one to call from the past what matters, what has an essential relation to the self—who also exists nowhere yet is manifest as a desire for coherence and recurrence. Memory enters Merwin's world to bridge the gap so often evoked in the I/eye pun. The I is divided because it cannot trust the eye that links man to the world of process, and the world of process is unknowable because the I's consciousness distorts what the eye sees. Memory preserves what recurs and hence seems important to both eye and I. Moreover, memory is impersonal, not only because it occupies no place but more important because in many ways it follows its own laws and does not serve the will. It is perhaps governed by the eye as much as by the I, and perhaps governed beyond them by a single power. Finally, memory is impersonal because, like the shadow, it is both particular and abstract: as a shadow changes form yet remains essentially the same when the direction of light changes, the memory recalls particular images, yet seems also to leave traces of basic recurrent patterns in its operation. (In another vocabulary, the memory is the place of the unconscious.) For Merwin, as for Augustine, memory is a vital key to "the singing beyond" (*MT*, p. 64) since it allows access to a realm of being where the limited self and the contingent present merge into the grander transpersonal union:

In this passage, and in much of Follain's prose, as well as in his poems, the regard is suspended, whether deliberately or helplessly and the complexity of its circumstance as the bearer of memory is clear. Who is the "I" who is thinking those exact things about the puddles and the shadows; and who recognizes that the shutter fastenings in the shape of busts of little people were wearing Renaissance feather bonnets? Is it the child of eleven or so, or the man who left when that war was over and has gone to Paris and the legal profession and the literary world? It is more than both: it is the suspended regard which they share; and the evocation of this "impersonal," receptive, but essentially unchanging gaze often occupies, in Follain's work, the place of the first person.

It does so because memory has a special role in his writing. It is not simply a link between past and present, life and poetry. Memory, as distinct from the past it draws on, is what makes the past a key to the mystery that stays with us and does not change: the present.

Follain is deeply concerned with the mystery of the present—the mystery which gives the recalled concrete details their form, at once luminous and removed, when they are seen at last in their places, as they seem to be in the best of his poems. This is their value "in themselves." At the same time it is what gives them the authority of parts of a rite, of an unchanging ceremony heralding some inexorable splendor, over a ground of silence. And for Jean Follain it is a fulfillment not only of a need for ceremony but of a fondness for the ceremonies, in which each detail, seen as itself, is an evocation of the processions of an immeasurable continuum.

And both the passage of time and the sense of the unchanging show the details to be unique. Follain never regarded them otherwise—that is the child whom he did not betray. [*PJF*, p. 77]

Merwin's description of Jean Follain might serve as the best description extant of Merwin's own sense of value. Memory is evoked in the "suspended regard," whereby the impersonal occupies the place of the I/eye, and in turn memory brings to the horizon of the present a ground of silence or shadow that both allows particulars to stand out and encloses them in a sense of "the immeasurable continuum" that endures. "Daybreak" concludes *The Moving Target* with a sense of what Merwin can "find hope for" by dramatizing just such a perspective:

> Again this procession of the speechless
> Bringing me their words
> The future woke me with its silence
> I join the procession
> An open doorway
> Speaks for me
> Again

(*MT*, p. 97)

The particulars here emerge only indirectly, since the poem takes place within a consciousness reflecting on a scene. It might be the last stanza of a meditative Romantic lyric. Merwin is deliberately making the reader come to realize that the speechless bring words, for as one tries to fill out the poem and imagine how daybreak might justify claims that it is a "procession" and an "open doorway," one finds himself re-creating the scene from memory and working his way out of the poem's reflective distance from what it describes. In effect, the reader is asked to fill the empty space created by a poem beginning in a displaced consciousness, and from that absence (both thematic and, in the reader, psychological) he comes gradually to recognize a set of enduring relationships. Daybreak is a threshold moment where conflicting forces are tenuously balanced and where all the natural elements have important psychological and symbolic analogues. Daybreak is that moment of very pale, bare, and almost absent light (seeming to appear without a source for the sun is not yet visible) where light and darkness seem absolutely essential to one another. At daybreak the departing darkness literally creates the stark "procession" ritual in which the details of the present gradually become separate and emerge into their separate beings. But at daybreak, the particulars appear less as entities than as parts of the single pale light. Daybreak is a mode of natural speech whereby the "silence" of the future retains its mystery and yet seems to call the speaker forth into its still plenitude. This union of speech and silence provides the analogue in consciousness to the merger of light and darkness; it makes possible one's "singing" "between the two deserts" (*MT*, p. 50). Moreover, daybreak is a recurrent phenomena; it complements, evokes, and sustains memory's function of securing one's confidence in duration. Waking can be a terribly frightening experience without the kind of cyclic consciousness echoed in the poem's own structural repetitions of "again." The final "again" seems the volume's response to Lemuel's prayer: what is essential is what can be accepted in its duration. The necessity of daybreak, like the necessity driving Merwin's speakers to their alienation, can be comforting because it makes one feel at one with those deepest rhythms of invisible being. And it is the traces of that invisible being, called up by one's sense of recurrence, which gives intellectual resonance to the sense of the scene as a "procession." A procession is a ritual, religious form—here for natural experience—and a procession allows the individual to be himself and also to participate in a collective ritual force. The poem's structure enchances this meaning, for in the central line of the poem's seven-line cyclical form (balanced by the "agains") the speaker takes up the burden and joins his subjective self to the actions of the entire scene. He realizes here what Merwin has defined as the essential condition of poetry—that it be "experience" not "action," not something that is "communal" and "may be shared with machines" but a moment of being "personal and inseparable from the whole" (*DV*, p. 270). Experience is the doorway to complete Being.

"Daybreak" provides the moment of the open doorway where process and recurrence, self and whole, are reconciled, but it neither adequately dramatizes the scene nor explores the conditions and meaning of that reconciliation. Rather it echoes and fulfills other poems toward the end of *The Moving Target* that explore more fully why and how this moment of union with essential process can be satisfying. Recurrent process is the embodiment in nature of the fact of necessity, and necessity in turn is the concept by which memory restores man to his home in process. Necessity is the authentic force in man and nature underlying the illusory phenomena: "May I bow to necessity, not/to her hirelings" (*L*, p. 25). So long as "Hope and grief are still our wings/ . . . we cannot fly" (*L*, p. 4) because they provide illusions of freedom that mask the need to bow to necessity and the consequent possibility one may find the open doorway. The fictive world of human hopes and fears occupies consciousness without grounding it; man seeks human reasons or aims explaining events in a world where "everything that does not need you is real" (*L*, p. 35).

Two poems best summarize how one comes to recognize necessity and how that recognition helps one to find selfhood within the fundamental rhythms of natural being. "The Way to the River" is the easier and less successful because it ultimately relies on love—a phenomenon simply asserted by Merwin and hard to reconcile with most of his landscape. Conceptually, love seems too easy, too traditionally an emblem of the union of the personal and the whole (since love is potentially universal) to resolve displacements as disturbing as Merwin's despairing poems. Nonetheless, the poem connects love and necessity in some interesting ways. The goal of the poem is to achieve the contemporary version of paradise, to be able to say and to accept the words "be here":

> Be here the flies from the house of the mapmaker
> Walk on our letters I can tell
> And the days hang medals between us
> I have lit our room with a glove of yours be
> Here I turn
> To your name and the hour remembers
> Its one word
> Now
>
> Be here what can we
> Do for the dead the footsteps full of money
> I offer you what I have my
> Poverty

To the city of wires I have brought home a handful
Of water I walk slowly
In front of me they are building the empty
Ages I see them reflected not for long
Be here I am no longer ashamed of time it is too brief
    its hands
Have no names
I have passed it I know

    Oh Necessity you with the face you with
    All the faces

This is written on the back of everything

But we
Will read it together

                            (*MT*, p. 77)[20]

To say "be here," one must reach the river, the reality of the present, and he must be willing to let it be, not to act upon it and transform it to satisfy his desires. Two attitudes make this possible. The first is "love," for love in Merwin is the opposite of desire; love accepts and dwells with. It brings no intentions to what it experiences and thus dwells with silence, not with names ("We say goodbye distance we are here/We can say it quietly who else is there/We can say it with silence our native tongue" [*MT*, p. 79]). The corrollary of love, then, is the act of accepting one's poverty, an act that frees one from imposing desires on the present to make it fit certain dreams and thus allows one to see not how he differs from the river but what he shares with it. In this poem to accept one's poverty is to accept time ("I am no longer ashamed of time") and to recognize in a fresh way that "a great disorder is an order" and that change is the one condition of permanence.[21] As awareness of one's poverty makes one relax his hold on any specific fiction, he can begin to see how change is the one permanent feature of necessity. And change, like love, is both particular and universal; the hour's one word is "Now" because all time shares the qualities of presence and dissolution. So change as necessity can be seen as an absolute condition of being; that is, it becomes a kind of God informing a different kind of analogical book of nature. Those reduced by poverty to recognize that absolute can recognize as well how fully they share and, even more, participate in the absolute condition of being. Merwin's poetry often borders on theology in both tone and theme precisely because he pursues such fundamental issues and seeks analogical religious solutions. Perhaps most important in this specific solution is its open-endedness; a sense of recurrence and continuity makes possible for the lovers a realistic dream of an open-ended yet structured future. Few religions can do more; without this vision of necessity and the concommitant sense of selfhood, Merwin's actors usually face a far more problematic sense of the void to come:

> I am the son of the future but she shows me only her
>   mourning veil
> I am the son of the future but my own father.
>
> *(CL,* p. 92)

"For Now" presents a more extreme religious model for experiencing necessity; it dramatizes an Eliotic process of negative mysticism as the way to achieve a "poverty" beyond even love. The title's dual meanings suggest the poem's basic strategy; "For Now" is a dedication to the reality of the moment, but it is also a provisional statement of a strategy for acting within the flux to uncover more permanent qualities of that moment. To "come to myself" in an abiding present one must perform a provisional stripping of the self; he must reverse Whitman's self-expanding catalogs and say "goodbye" to all those mere "guests" of himself "expecting hosts" until he has achieved that poverty where he can recognize necessity. The abiding self, if there is one, is not in its possessions but in that consciousness of what remains when all those possessions have been stripped away. (This is a secondary meaning of the poem's statement "Tell me what you see vanishing and I/will tell you who you are.") By its conclusion this negative "Song of Myself" demands the surrender of Merwin's and the speaker's most intimate and most often affirmed qualities, and there occurs a glimpse of what remains:

> Goodbye distance from whom I
> Borrow my eyes goodbye my voice
> In the monument of strangers goodbye to the sun
> Among the wings nailed to the windows goodbye
> My love
>
> You that return to me through the mountain of flags
> With my raven on your wrist
> You with the same breath
>
> Between death's republic and his kingdom
>
> *(MT,* p. 95)

The "you" who returns here is richly ambiguous: the pronoun is left undefined because the "you" sought throughout the poem ("You are not here will the earth last till you come") is essentially an ineffable presence knowable only when names are left behind, but it probably includes "my love," the reader (since he comes back through the empty signifiers of the "mountain of flags"), and the speaker's essential self.

All three in fact are now inseparable from that selfhood which on the level of necessity is a collective and unnameable one. This objectified mystery returns wearing on its wrist not a watch to measure time but a raven, a symbol of time experienced as the painful sum of the series of "goodbyes." With this bodily knowledge of time, the speaker now literally shares the same breath with the collective "you." Breath here suggests the achievement of ineffable knowledge, the speech beyond speech, and links that knowledge with the central force that is at once energy of life and experience of death. Breathing is one of the deepest bodily experiences of what it means to exist in time; each inhalation necessary for life must be followed by an exhalation that is its own death.[22] The ancient equation of breath and spirit is a profound one. Breath mediates between death's "kingdom," which is the universal mastery of death over all life, and his "republic" where one dies as he lived—each alone. Death's kingdom, though, is the stronger force; thus the poem's concluding image. At this nadir of selfhood, one recognizes how death, like change, is an absolute condition of being and hence a God one can know and participate in, without the mediation of fictive myths. And within this absolute, man is in a way reborn, for, as Merwin often reminds his readers, to be dying is to be immortal, to be united with a force that permeates all life (see *L*, p. 48).

It is not a very large jump from the ineffable presence of the "you" realized in poverty to the dramatic sense of darkness as source of true presence in "Finally," but the shift nonetheless sows the seeds for more complex and occasionally quite different meditations in *The Lice*:

> My dread, my ignorance, my
> Self, it is time. Your imminence
> Prowls the palms of my hands like sweat.
> Do not now, if I rise to welcome you,
> Make off like roads into the deep night.
> The dogs are dead at last, the locks toothless,
> The habits out of reach.
> I will not be false to you tonight.
>
> Come, no longer unthinkable. Let us share
> Understanding like a family name. Bring
> Integrity as a gift, something
> Which I had lost, which you found on the way.
> I will lay it beside us, the old knife,
> While we reach our conclusions.
>
> Come. As a man who hears a sound at the gate
> Opens the window and puts out the light
> The better to see out into the dark,
> Look, I put it out.
>
> (*MT*, p. 22)

The true self is his dread and his ignorance because it is incompatible with the easy habits and superficial qualities of the active life in time and in society. The true self calls from the darkness, and to come to it one must share that darkness. In putting out the light, the practical self no longer creates a shadow by standing between the light and the ground, but merges completely with the shadow and the kingdom of darkness that includes it. In effect, the speaker avoids the problem of finding the source of light by making absolute its antagonistic opposite. In the darkness, where the shadow need no longer hate, one finds a completeness impossible for the rational consciousness that is condemned to the tensions and oppositions of the daylight. Darkness here is the ontological analogue of the unconscious and of the furnace where the drunk finds the spirits necessary if he is to continue his song.

"Finally" provides a dramatic basis for my returning once more to the topic of Merwin's style, in its pursuit of "something else" beyond what the poetry of the local in *The Drunk in the Furnace* could provide. The essence of that style is its negation of the light of ordinary experience. The rejection of punctuation is only a small part of its de-creating qualities, for at every opportunity that style breaks down expected connections—by exploding verbal clichés, by continually refusing normal continuities of logical, chronological, or dramatic development, and by rearranging the ordinary landscape into a psychological, surreal one. In effect, Merwin, like Creeley, cannot trust ordinary language; easy speech belongs to the world of drunks and presidents, census-takers, and wavers of flags. Ordinary language can rarely survive dislocation, because its function is to cover over emptiness, not to lead beyond itself into the mysteries of silence.[23] A student of mine summarized Merwin's style with the observation that a miner's children should be pale. But since Merwin, unlike Creeley, will not trust a poetics of place, one must ask further what one can learn from remaining pale, from denying roots in any place or even in dramatic contexts, and from retaining the "suspended regard." I have shown how absence, like the shadow, helps define the enduring present, but one needs now to see how that absence also provides access to realities only dimly suggested by absolute conditions of natural being. The "something else" Merwin pursues is "the true source" (*PM*, p. 7) whose home is what Merwin has called "the Great Language" that poetry is always trying to speak:

The demand is often for a substitute, a translation, and is regularly made by those who are poorly acquainted, or uncomfortable, with the original idiom. But the original seems more and more frequently to be, not a particular mode of poetry, but the great language itself, the vernacular of the imagination, that at one time was common to men.

It is a tongue that is loosed in the service of immediate recognitions, and that in itself would make it foreign in our period. For it conveys something of the unsoundable quality of experience and the hearing of it is a private matter, in an age in which the person and his senses are being lost in the consumer, who does not know what he sees, hears, wants, or is afraid of, until the voice of the institution has told him. [*DV*, pp. 269–70]

Merwin's most complete poetic meditation on this "true source" may be found in an earlier poem, "The Annunciation," which beautifully explores the complex dimensions of the term *conception*. Mary's moment of conception, the moment both literal and figurative of the spirit becoming flesh, is a sense of the present so full that she can only image it in terms of an absence beyond the limited perceptions of the ordinary ego and the practical names Joseph taught her for dealing with the world:

> But grew
> Clouding between my eyes and the light
> And rushing upon me, the way the shadow
> Of a cloud will rush over the sunned fields
> In a time of wind; and the black coming down
> In its greatness, between my eyes and the light,
> Was like wings growing, and the blackness
> Of their shadow growing as they came down
> Whirring and beating, cold and like thunder, until
> All the light was gone, and only that noise
> And terrible darkness, making everything shake
> Like the end of it was come, and there was
> No word for it, and I thought Lord, Lord, and thought
> How if I had not gone out on the light
> And been hidden away on the vanished light
> So that myself I was empty and nothing
> I would surely have died, because the thing
> That the darkness was, and the wings and the shaking
> That there was no word for it, was a thing that in myself
> I could not have borne and lived. And still came
> Nearer and darker, beating, and there was
> Like a whisper in the feathers there, in the wings'
> Great wind, like a whirring of words, but I could not
> Say the shape of them, and it came to me
> They were like a man, but none has yet come to me,
> And I could not say how. Only, in the place
> Where, myself, I was nothing, there was suddenly
> A great burning under the darkness, a fire
> Like fighting up into the wings' lash and the beating
> Blackness, and flames like the tearing of teeth,
> With noise like rocks rending, such that no word

Can call it as it was there, and for fire only,
Without the darkness beating and the wind, had I
Been there, had I not been far on the hiding light
I could not have borne it and lived. And then the stillness:

(*GB*, p. 35)

This stillness is wordless, yet seems to contain within it a Word, a form profoundly human but mocked by the human forms of active life. Within this Word the darkness and the light look into one another (as in "Daybreak"), and the shadow merges with the light:

Though in itself it was like a word, and it was
Like no man and no word that ever was known,
Come where I was; and because I was nothing
It could be there. It was a word for
The way the light and the things in the light
Were looking into the darkness, and the darkness
And the things of the darkness were looking into the light
In the fullness, and the way the silence
Was hearing, like it was hearing a great song
And the song was hearing the silence forever
And forever and ever. And I knew the name for it;
There in the place where I was nothing in
The fullness, I knew it, and held it and knew
The way of it, and the word for how it was one,
I held it, and the word for why, Or almost,
Or believed I knew it, believed, like an echo
That when it comes you believe you know
The word, while it rings, but when it is gone
You had not learned it, and cannot find it, even
Though the sound still breathes in your ear. Because
Then the light looked away from the darkness
Again, and the song slid into the silence
And was lost again, and the fullness rose, going,
And the sound of its going was the sound of wings
Rushing away in darkness, and the sound
That came after them was the stillness hushing
Again, and time sudden and hard to believe,
And forever was emptiness again, where time fell,
And I was standing there in myself, in the light,
With only the shape of the word that is wonder.

(*GB*, pp. 36–37)

Such intense vision cannot last; the self can surrender to it for only so long and eventually must come back to its own isolation, now facing an ordinary silence even more hostile and barren than before. The only way back is through memory and the re-creative act of poet and Holy Spirit making the word with one's breath:

> Only
> If I could remember, if I could only remember
> The way that word was, and the sound of it. Because
> There is that in me still that draws all that I am
> Backwards, as weeds are drawn down when the water
> Flows away; and if I could only shape
> And hear again that word and the way of it—
> But you must grow forward, and I know
> That I cannot. And yet it is there in me:
> As though if I could only remember
> The word, if I could make it with my breath
> It would be with me forever as it was
> Then in the beginning, when it was
> The end and the beginning, and the way
> They were one; and time and the things of falling
> Would not fall into emptiness but into
> The light, and the word tell the way of their falling
> Into the light forever, if I could remember
>   And make the word with my breath.
>   (*GB*, p. 39)

"The Annunciation" presents the characteristic rhythms of Merwin's imagination at its most intense, but the poem's resolution remained viable only within his earlier self-consciously aesthetic style. In the later mode it is too simple to trust in the power of the limited word and the human breath. The poet can no longer make the adequate word with his breath, nor so readily imagine the darkness redeemed in a spiritual light; he can only put out the false words of limited consciousness and point beyond them to an absence he evokes but does not describe. The poet now has "no more tongue than a wound" and must seek salvation in and through that wound ("the beginning/Is broken/No wonder the addresses are torn" [*L*, p. 24]). Incarnational poetics gives way to the poetics of absence so well described by Martin Heidegger in his essay on Trakl.[24] The essay is a meditation on Trakl's line "Something strange is the soul on earth." What, Heidegger asks, are the implications of this condition for the poet? His task is to accept his "apartness" as stranger and make of it the true site of poetry. By maintaining his distance from the world the poet preserves what is unborn in the nature of mortal man—a sense of being, quieter and more "stilling" than those who are at home in the world can know. The soul in its apartness also keeps alive a sense of pain and melancholy that is at once a tearing away from the things of the world and the way to acceptance. For pain is the "animator," the discontent that drives man to bring being out of concealment (Heidegger defines truth as *a-letheia*, out of forgetfulness) into the light shared by the soul, itself on fire in its pain. Heidegger's effulgent and evocative prose is difficult to summarize, but the following sentences should give some idea of the tone and themes of the piece:

> The language of the poetry whose site is in apartness answers to the home-coming of unborn mankind into the quiet beginning of its stiller nature. . . .
> Because the language of this poetry speaks from the journey of apartness, it will always speak also of what it leaves behind in parting, and of that to which the departure submits. . . .
> The ambiguous tone of Trakl's poetry arises out of a gathering, that is out of a unison which, meant for itself alone, always remains unsayable. The ambiguity of this poetic saying is not lax imprecision, but rather the rigor of him who leaves what is as it is, who has entered into the "righteous vision" and now submits to it.

This concept of apartness as the fidelity of the stranger to his necessary alienation and ultimately as the site in which being can be gathered is basic to understanding Merwin's style with its impersonal "suspended regard." "That Biblical waif, ill at ease in time, the spirit" (*DV*, p. 270) can be known only in a silence or darkness echoed by poetic language. Merwin's later work denies the self-referential, autotelic qualities of language to pursue what he calls a kind of transparence in which the words are "in the way as little as possible" (*RAR*, p. 36) and seemed used up by the real. Yet this transparence is an ambiguous one for he wants language also to become "itself something you cannot catch hold of." These diaphanous words point beyond their vanishing to a silence only reached through transparence. Thus the language keeps pushing one out of time to the apartness where the apparently disembodied speaker dwells. There he can function as the shadow does in "The Last One" or darkness in "Finally"; he keeps alive a hope of the spirit ill at ease in time and allows a glimpse into the source or silence. The voice retains a cold dignity—justly proud of refusing to depend on things or "activity" and faithful to the Great Language.[25]

The voice of apartness exists somewhere between the echoes of speech in time and its absent source. And Merwin's work seen as a whole sustains this relationship by creating an elaborate system of echoes, so that the reader gradually feels his own apartness from each specific act of naming. Merwin's recurrent use of a basic vocabulary of images— knives, shadows, gloves, salt, ash, and so on—forces on the reader a sense that no specific instance of an image contains its complete meaning. If one compares Merwin's system of images with that of a poet like Yeats, the way they reinforce absence becomes clearer. Yeats, especially in his *Vision* years, wants the images to absorb the world, to reflect how style and personality can transform the flux and hold reality and justice in a single thought. In Yeats the repeated images function like a theological system, metaphorically reinforcing a universe of analogies. Merwin on the other hand, uses repeated images not to systematize the world, but to tempt the reader with the possibility of system and of a single informing principle sustaining that system. He leads the reader beyond particulars, but leaves him lost in this new mental space. The system is never realized; the images are echoes of one another uttered by a biblical waif stranded in time and not the tools of a Promethean imagination reconstituting the real. Nonetheless, and this is the major point, the echoes perform a kind of religious function because as they thrust one into apartness, into an absence beyond the immediate referential reality one expects from a poem, they make evident how much men are creatures of absence by the very fact that they can be taken in. If all men enter apartness, they in effect grant the claims upon them of that absence which is the central reality for consciousness in our time. Salvation must lie in whatever formed silence can be realized in that apartness.

With *The Lice*, however, when Merwin becomes fully self-conscious about the implications in the apartness of his style, Heideggerean optimism comes to seem too simple a perspective. The faith that within apartness one holds and gathers a numinous Being need perhaps not be rejected, but it must be tested and called into question. The epigraph to the volume is a cue to a different, more problematic landscape:

> All men are deceived by the appearances of things, even Homer himself, who was the wisest man in Greece; for he was deceived by boys catching lice: they said to him, "What we have caught and what we have killed we have left behind, but what has escaped us we bring with us."

While a moving target is a teleological image—a goal of desire difficult but not impossible to hit, the epigraph to *The Lice* suggests that even the desire to know is a privative state, a disturbance by lice of some primordial stillness. And more problematic yet grows the value of what one can know, for to know is to define that informing darkness and thus to "mis-take" its mystery. How simple I have been to overlook the possibility that the darkness invoked at the end of "Finally" might not be a positive essential self in tune with an active source of being. The darkness is precisely that—a darkness—perhaps a source of light to one who can preserve apartness but perhaps also only prelude to the deeper darkness of nonbeing or the Void that might be the only true stillness. Absence may not be the means to a suprahuman fullness, but may be itself the only absolute worth pursuing:

I

Encouragement meant nothing

Inside it
The miners would continue to
Crawl out of their dark bodies
Extending the darkness making
It hollow
And how could they be rightly paid

Darkness gathered on the money
It lived in the dies the miners pursued it what
Was their reward

Some might bring flowers saying Nothing can last
Some anyway
Held out their whole lives in their glass hands

Sweeter than men till past the time
Some with a pure light burned but over
Their heads even theirs
Soot wrote on the ceiling
An unknown word

Shutting your eyes from the spectacle you
Saw not darkness but
Nothing

On which doors were opening.

. . . .

III

At one stroke out of the ruin
All the watches went out and
The eyes disappeared like martins into their nests

I woke to the slamming of doors and got up naked
The old wind vanished and vanished but was still there
Everyone but the cold was gone for good

And the carol of the miners had just ended

(*L*, pp. 20, 22)

The Moving Target sought to encounter "nothing that is not there," but
The Lice, with its pervading concern for the reality of death and the
implications of that reality for human consciousness seeks to question

"the nothing that is." The ultimate question in *The Lice* is whether death can be seen as an absolute condition within and enclosed by life and process or whether life is merely inadequate prelude to the ultimate void beyond all the songs of human miners and only figured by death's occurrences in time.

To appreciate the tensions of *The Lice* one must oppose to the Heideggerean voice it seeks to keep alive another, darker vision by E. M. Cioran, a thinker indebted to Heidegger and sharing his humorless portentous tone.[26] Like Heidegger, Cioran sees apartness, pain, and division as the indispensable means to a final homecoming, but for Cioran one comes home only by entering a more radical apartness. He must renounce all desire and enter the plenitude of a void that is "nothingness stripped of its negative aspects, nothingness transfigured." There is no return from nothingness to a deeper sense of the Being that abides; the more apart one grows the more he recognizes how all being— material objects and the thoughts and desires these objects engender in man—is sheer appearance doomed to vanish. The only freedom is to create vanishing rather than be subject to it:

> To undo our bonds, we must, in the future, refrain from adhering to anything whatever, anything but the nothing of freedom.

> Ideally, we would be able to lose, without regrets all taste for beings and things, each day honoring some creature or object by renouncing it; thus making the rounds of appearances and dismissing each in turn, we would achieve a state of unremitting withdrawal, which is the very secret of joy.

> To evade the intolerable, let us resort to distraction, to flight, let us seek a region in which no sensation deigns to assume a name, and no appetite to incarnate itself, let us win back the primordial repose, let us abolish, along with the past, odious memory but especially awareness, our immemorial enemy whose mission it is to leave us destitute, to wear us down.

The clearest analogue to Cioran's vision in *The Lice* is the poem "Divinities," an attempt by Merwin to return once more to theology and reimagine how man can conceive the absolute conditions of being:

> Having crowded once onto the threshold of mortality
> And not been chosen
> There is no freedom such as theirs
> That have no beginning

> The air itself is their memory
> A domain they cannot inhabit
> But from which they are never absent

What are you they say that simply exist
And the heavens and the earth bow to them
Looking up from their choices
Perishing

All day and all night
Everything that is mistaken worships them
Even the dead sing them an unending hymn

(*L*, p. 59)

The pure nonbeing of those without beginnings embodies a stillness and
a necessity more profound than any to be found within process (Keats's
dying and obscure gods are replaced by those never born). The dead
sing a hymn to these divinities in reverence for an absolute self-sufficiency
and eternity of loss that the dead only approximate. For the dead had
a beginning, and thus suffered death and even after death were not
free from the processes of decay and memory. Yet it is only by imaginatively entering death, as Merwin does so often in the volume, that one
can even approach the knowledge of the void. Death is something man
carries with him and can never catch, yet once he begins to imagine it
as a condition of being it is life that becomes the shadow always es-
caping his grasp. "Looking East at Night" beautifully renders this
perspective:

Death
White hand
The moths fly at in the darkness

I took you for the moon rising

Whose light then
Do you reflect

As though it came out of the roots of things
This harvest pallor in which

I have no shadow but myself

(*L*, p. 36)

The poem is almost the direct opposite of "Daybreak": here the dusk
is an open doorway out of life with its pale, expansive stillness quietly
mocking the glories of the sunset. The eastern sky evokes death because
its light seems at home in the encroaching darkness, and because like
death and the moon it shines with reflected light. But whose light does
death reflect? The simplest answer is that death is a reflection of one's

consciousness of his individuality (see *L*, p. 70), and this answer helps explain why selfhood becomes mind's shadow in the last line. Selfhood blocks the mind from that lunar light. On a deeper level, though, death is also a dim reflection of an absolute nonbeing at "the roots of things," which uses death to harvest being unto itself. The self then is shadow not only because its characteristic activities block the light, but because that light provides a radically new perspective on how insubstantial the self and its body really are. The more one holds to the necessities of the world the wider and deeper the shadow.

The omnipresence of death and the power of void need not remain metaphysical abstractions. One of Merwin's more terrifying visions is his realization of how intensely modern life both participates in and actively pursues that void. What is language, for example, but a way of continually generating partial absences that separate man from being, "My words are the garment of what I shall never be/like the tucked sleeve of a one-armed boy" (*L*, p. 62). Man keeps projecting words to capture a reality, yet he finds in the end only more words and deeper doubts about his ability to capture experience. For language is no longer referential, but, as Jacques Derrida puts it, a process of "supplementation."[27] Because "the beginning is broken," "the addresses are torn" (*L*, p. 24), everything one can describe in order to know, one can only know by a further description. Language tries to make things present, but it leaves only an absence requiring more words, ad infinitum. And even when words do seem to catch hold of a reality, the epigraph of *The Lice* is a reminder that they kill it. In "Fly" (*L*, p. 73) Merwin employs a standard Romantic idea that having "believed too much in words" he killed the bird he tried to train, but he also adds the further ironic fear that he killed whatever part of himself ("so that is what I am") might have been united with the bird's natural sense of being.

If man only killed with words, however, nonbeing would still be essentially a metaphor and life more acceptable. The tragic irony, though, is that modern man, in his quest to make everything present and knowable on his terms, is in fact killing what there is to hold him to life. Hope in life must confront not only the abortive "why not" logic of rationalist activism (see "The Last One," *L*, p. 10) but the actual fact of a war destroying a nation, its countryside, and perhaps the future of all mankind (see the sequence of poems culminating in "For a Coming Extinction.") Yet the very concreteness of the situations creating despair here require a shift in tone. In attacking society and even in relating destruction to his themes of absolute despair, Merwin introduces a rage for moral order that qualifies and redirects any ultimate surrender to the void. "If I were not human/I would not be ashamed of anything" (*L*, p. 71) is on one level just another statement of a consciousness desiring to erase itself into nonbeing. Nonetheless it returns the reader and Merwin to a mode of necessity evident in other despairing moments. Being human condemns men not just to shameful deeds but to a desire to criticize and correct those deeds. A void sought in despair is an impossible paradox, for the very conditions generating despair keep alive also a sense of moral possibilities and a dream of fuller being. Not only does Merwin resist unjust war and the destruction of nature, but he makes poems of that resistance. The poems, of course, may only attach one to a dying planet and actually increase the number and beauty of things that must die, but they also suggest the possibility of an abiding permanence—capable of providing an alternative to the void. It would be an exaggeration to claim that in *The Lice* Heidegger's vision of apartness ultimately prevails over Cioran's, but Heidegger's at least continues to survive. Language, for example, need not be only a process of supplementation: in the silence within the overlapping words trying to define and judge experience, an informing presence might be taking shape:

> This silence coming at intervals out of the shell of names
> It must be all one person really coming at
> Different hours for the same thing
> If I could learn the word for yes it could teach me questions
> I would see that it was itself every time and I would
> Remember to say take it up like a hand
> And go with it this is at last
> Yourself
>
> The child that will lead you

(L, p. 38)

And even death itself not only calls one to the void but gives one a vantage point from which to reflect upon the processes that worship it:

> I think all this is somewhere in myself
> The cold room unlit before dawn
> Containing a stillness such as attends death
> And from a corner the sounds of a small bird trying
> From time to time to fly a few beats in the dark
> You would say it was dying it is immortal

(L, p. 48)

The bird in this interior landscape affirms an immortality based on its doomed resistance to its doom.

The conflicting perspectives culminate in "Looking For Mushrooms At Sunrise," the volume's final poem. What hope Merwin can derive from the volume's journey is embodied here, but it remains qualified by the appeals of death and the void:

When it is not yet day
I am walking on centuries of dead chestnut leaves
In a place without grief
Though the oriole
Out of another life warns me
That I am awake

In the dark while the rain fell
The gold chanterelles pushed through a sleep that was not mine
Waking me
So that I came up the mountain to find them

Where they appear it seems I have been before
I recognize their haunts as though remembering
Another life

Where else am I walking even now
Looking for me

(L, p. 80)

The poem's final question casts the reader back to other questions raised along its way. What is it that calls him to the mushrooms—is it some common life process they share that the morning wakes in him, or is it a deep participation in the blankness of death only imaged in "a sleep that was not mine"? What is the other life he remembers—an instinctive childlike sharing in natural growth or a state of nonbeing before life? Do the mushrooms live in or live off the darkness and the decaying chestnut leaves in which they thrive? Finally, does the final question suggest that the speaker envisions those incomplete and fragmented parts of himself participating in a natural process by which the living feed off the dead, or do these fragments seek the complete identity of nonbeing?

Merwin's next volume, *The Carrier of Ladders*, tries to journey beyond these questions to a resolution like that of *The Moving Target* in which the speaker can celebrate a moment of plenitude realized within process. One can find out where he is walking only by concentrating on what he can share with the present rather than on what escapes it. It is impossible to assert that Merwin overcomes the appeal of the void; he merely recognizes how the pursuit of an ultimate absence only furthers the division he seeks to master and renders absurd any moral vision so needed in political crises. Merwin returns, then, in many of the poems, to a mode of vision closer to that of *The Moving Target,* but the poetry is less nervous and desperate. The lines become shorter and more confident than in the preceding books, and the language grows less surreal and epigrammatic, more concrete and rooted in dramatic contexts. If there is any progress it lies in the more firmly articulated landscape (apartness can be realized by a more controlled surrealism and dislocation) and in the ways Merwin learns to link the imaginative forms of the Great Language with the rhythms of process. The goal of many poems in the volume is to reach that moment when the bearer of the dead and the carrier of ladders (the characters in the epigraph) share the same essential starting point, a point within process where necessity grounds and supports the poet's ladders: "And what is wisdom if it is not/now/in the loss that has not left this place" (*CL,* p. 8).

It is possible to submit the *Carrier of Ladders* as a volume to the same kind of analysis I applied to Merwin's other works, but the volume's final and probably best poem, "In the Time of the Blossoms," should suffice here to illustrate his new way of integrating loss and presence. Emptiness need not be imaged as another place, a space of pure imagination; rather, emptiness too can be "here," available both to the attentive mind and to the memories evoked by the full participation attention creates:

> Ash tree
> sacred to her who sails in
> from the one sea
> all over you leaf skeletons
> fine as sparrow bones
> stream out motionless
> on white heaven
> staves of one
> unbreathed music
> Sing to me

(*CL,* p. 138)

The scene, with its repeated "ones," presents a natural moment that reconciles many of those divisions which permeate Merwin's work. The "leaf skeletons fine as sparrow bones" of the ash tree in bloom remind one of how deeply death participates even in the fullest moments of natural blossoming. And like Yeats's chestnut tree, the ash reconciles flux and stasis as the blossoms balance in the wind and seem to multiply in their composed plenitude. Moreover, the ash tree evokes a kind of "mythological present," reenacting that moment preserved within the memory of the Great Language when the tree was conceived as a sacred, mythic phenomenon. The landscape not only speaks as an open doorway but preserves those dimensions of imaginative speech invested in it by generations of men. The goddess here "who sails in from the one sea" is Nemesis: "The ash tree was one of the goddesses' seasonal disguises, and an important one to her pastoral devotees, because of its association with thunderstorms and with the lambing month, the third of the sacral year."[28] The tree is symbol of fertility, but also of the dangers of fertility. The ash tree was thought to draw lightning, and thus was associated with the Furies (who are Ash-nymphs) in their dual roles as figures of divine judgment and as bringers of rain. The fullness of life is never far from the realities of death and judgment, but it is precisely this fact that makes worship authentic and "awe-full" and that allows man's religious imagination to appreciate so fully these moments when life balances and transcends the death it carries with it. The tree's motionless motion and balance of life and death allow one to see its participation in a cosmic music—now unbreathed because it transcends the life-and-death rhythm of breathing and far surpasses in its gathering power the mere words one makes out of that breathing. The speaker is no longer maker, tormented by his own inadequate breath, but once again in an open doorway accepting his role as mediator of that music into consciousness. The last line of the poem is the first to mention the poet, for he is at once peripheral to the scene's fullness and the necessary completion of it if that fullness is to be known. The poet is once again objectified, but not in the terrifying objectifications of the self-consciousness in the volume's opening poem. His objectification is now the condition of his homecoming, at one with necessity and plenitude.

This triumphant moment, however, remains only a moment within flux. There is no assurance even within the poem that the poet can translate his passive receptiveness into a principle of recurrent activity. The unbreathed music can sing to him, but his own songs require breath and the problematic division between living and dying each breath entails. Merwin's triumph here is less a solution than a successful mode of dissolution that can ground and comfort the terror of the way. It establishes the chance of a momentary harmony that justifies a quest one cannot begin by justifying. In retrospect, "In a Time of Blossoms" allows one to see what has been involved in the moments of stasis experienced through light and through darkness. The silences of The Lice can, at least at times, merge into the creative silence of a unity with natural being. Even the more despondent poems in seasons other than spring (like "Psalm: September Vision," "Late Night in Autumn," "February," and "Banishment in Winter") achieve a kind of harmony with that process, precisely in and through the despondency they share with the landscape:

I am the son of untruth but I have seen the children in Paradise
    walking in pairs each hand in hand with himself . . .
I am the son of ruins already among us but at moments I have
    found hope beyond doubt beyond desert beyond reason and
    such that I have prayed O wounds come back from death
    and be healed. . . .
I am the son of love for which parent the blood gropes in dread
    as though it were naked and for which cause the sun hangs
    in a cage of light
    and we are his pains

(CL, p. 96)

Notes to Chapter 5

1. Robert Creeley, *Pieces* (New York: Scribner's, 1969), p. 58. The following abbreviations will be employed for Creeley's writings: *Pieces, P; For Love* (New York: Scribner's, 1962), *FL; Words* (New York: Scribner's, 1967), *W; A Quick Graph* (San Francisco, Calif.: Four Seasons Foundation, 1970), *QG; The Island* (New York: Scribner's, 1963), *I;* "Contexts of Poetry," issued as *Audit* 5, No. 1 (Spring 1968), *CP;* "Interview," *Paris Review,* no. 44 (1968), pp. 155–87, *PR.*

2. Joel Oppenheimer appropriately titles an essay on Creeley "The Inner Tightrope," *Lillabulero,* no. 8 (Winter 1970), pp. 51–52. (The issue also contains a review of *Pieces* by Russell Banks, which is the best essay I have seen on Creeley.) For Creeley's own sense of the void evoked by his line, see his interview with David Ossman in *The Sullen Art,* ed. Ossman (New York: Corinth, 1963), pp. 59–60. John Logan has described the experience of hearing Creeley read as listening to a voice with a tear in it.

3. Maurice Blanchot in "La Parole Vaine," an epilogue to René des Forêts, *Le Bavard* (Paris: Union Generale d'Editions, 1963), pp. 170 ff., fully develops the connections between drunken speech and a language that is really a shadow language, "un reflet d'un reflet dans un miroir de parole . . . ou tout risque de se perdre" (pp. 172–73).

4. Whitehead is Creeley's philosophical model, although, as I shall demonstrate, Creeley's theory of language and sense of Being are similar to Heidegger's. Creeley's frequent play between an empty and full use of the copula renders dramatically Heidegger's distinction between Being as *essent* and Being as *esse,* Being as a mere property of things and Being as a force in itself. See, for example, "A Birthday" (*W,* p. 138), which repeats "so we are" so that the reader recognizes the difference between "are" and "Are," between Being as a descriptive state and Being as something actively realized. But I must add that for Creeley neotheological concepts like "Being" only add a level of abstraction to the important aspects of presence—the particulars of the poem's dramatic situation.

5. See also *FL,* p. 100: "Being unsure, there is the fate/of doing nothing right," where "nothing" is both pronoun and noun, where it stands for something else and

itself describes a state of being. If in *For Love* only the sure egoist can survive, there recurs a complementary desire for violence, a desire to reduce everything to the vision of the individual (see, for example, "The Crow," *FL*, p. 30).

6. R. D. Laing, *The Divided Self* (Baltimore, Md.: Pelican, 1965), explains the processes involved. Creeley often finds himself becoming the passive object of the other. In "The End" (*FL*, p. 39), for example, he carefully makes the syntax express the emotion: "A feeling like being choked/enters my throat." See also the self-objectification involved in the form of the pronoun in "For A Friend" (*FL*, p. 91): "Himself alone is dominant/in a world of no one else."

7. "In release from despair. The poem begins here. In time, if you want, and also in place. Its locus is that effect, of itself, on that corpus of the particular, the world in detail. What effect can be made is in the poem—not then alien, or strange to its locality. Our language is more uniquely ourselves than any other act, it is our marriage" (*QG*, p. 101).

8. Heidegger's distinction in *Being and Time,* trans. John Macquarrie and Edward Robinson (New York: Harper, 1962), pp. 203–14, between "idle talk" and "authentic speech" is very suggestive for Creeley. "Idle talk" is speech without a "ground" (Heidegger's term, pp. 212–14), the process of speaking without really expressing the nature of one's encounter with Being. "Idle talk is the speech of empty signs." "Authentic speech," on the other hand, is the speech of Being in the world, of consciousness as it forms for itself its participation in Being; it is "disclosure" of Being. Authentic speech is man's participation in "Logos," in the power to draw together or gather Being. Heidegger's, I should add, is simply a powerful version of a standard Romantic distinction now under sharp attack from Derrida.

9. See also "A Place" (*W*, p. 85). The distance between Creeley and the early modern humanists is never so evident as when Creeley reacts against the much worshipped "shaping power of imagination": "When contact is broken, becomes the touch of the mind, then hell becomes particular, and not at all a place where bad people go, etc. When the imagination projects for itself a world more real than that which it literally experiences, this is hell, a forfeit, as Dante said, of the goods of the intellect" (*QG*, p. 209).

10. Again Whitehead and Heidegger are relevant. The difference between "thing" and "no thing" is the difference between the world perceived as "misplaced concreteness" and the world perceived as event. In Heidegger's terms the difference is between appearance and Being. One can also see the importance of "no thing" if one remembers the Hegelian dictum that desire manifests itself in the world as negation.

11. See also pp. 54, 58–59, 70, and the following from *P*, p. 31: "Like a mirror/ it returns here/by being there." The mirror is an important metaphor because it defines the means and possibility for self-consciousness and intersubjective harmony: "What had broken was only a mirror, and a very unreal one, but it was all they saw themselves in. They had made it, both of them, with what care they possessed. You here, me here, together there. . . . The mirror broke because she was no longer to be reflected there, as she had even agreed to be. Each thing he now did, right or wrong, could not be placed in that reflection any longer" (*I*, p. 100). (So long as the reflecting mirror depends on the subjective will and not some form, Creeley is doomed to anxiety.)

12. Claude Levi-Strauss, *The Savage Mind* (Chicago: University of Chicago Press, 1966), p. 222. His conclusion deserves to be quoted in full: "It is neither

men nor natural laws which are brought exactly face to face but systems of natural forces humanized by driver's intentions and men transformed into natural forces by the physical energy of which they make themselves the mediators. It is no longer a case of the operation of an agent on an inert object, nor of the return action of an object, promoted to the role of an agent, on a subject dispossessing itself in its favour without demanding anything of it in return; in other words, it is no longer situations involving a certain amount of passiveness on one side or the other which are in question. The beings confront each other face to face as subjects and objects at the same time." Italo Calvino, T_0 (New York: Harcourt, 1969), p. 136, uses the same metaphor but is more willing than Creeley to surrender subjectivity entirely and allow the signs of the traffic to be the only reality. Ashbery is the contemporary American poet who might subscribe to Calvino's model.

13. The sequence ends with the following quotation, which links the form of numbers to other recurrent forms like "the form of days" (P, p. 53): "The edge which opens on the depth has no terror; it is as if angels were waiting to uphold him, if it came about that he leaped from the height. . . . The sun, which shines behind him, knows whence he came, whither he is going, and how he will return by another path after many days . . ." (P, p. 35).

14. Gottlob Frege, *The Foundations of Arithmetic*, trans. J. L. Austin (Oxford: Blackwell, 1968). In proposing the basic thesis that number is essentially a relational system, Frege points out one interesting way in which the absent system provides a security impossible in concrete experience: "Even so concrete a thing as the Earth we are unable to imagine as we know it to be: instead we content ourselves with a ball of moderate size, which serves us as a symbol for the earth. . . . Thus although our idea often fails entirely to coincide with what we want, we still make judgements about an object such as the earth with considerable certainty. . . . Time and time again we are lead by our thought beyond the scope of our imagination, without thereby forfeiting the support we need for our inferences" (p. 71).

15. Ibid., p. 58; pp. 87–88 on zero; pp. 89–90 on zero as the ground of one. See also Jacques Derrida, "La Differance" in *Tel Quel: Theorie d'ensemble* (Paris: Edition de Seuil, 1968). Creeley plays on the equation of God and the solipsist by exploding the cliche "God Knows" at the end of "The Immoral Proposition" (*FL*, p. 31) and setting it against the "unsure egoist." One might also note how Creeley's definition of zero quoted above is analagous to Merwin's use of Heraclitus's parable of the lice.

16. The next sentence, "But again I had found myself limited by the nature of the adding machine I had unwittingly forced upon myself," indicates how unstable any reconciliation Creeley makes with specific forms must be because his first fidelity is to the demands of his own energies. For an example of the way Creeley tries to make his sense of "there" particular to the demands of his own life, see "How that fact of" (*P*, p. 71). There are possibilities of practical resolution here, even if they do not completely satisfy him. Thus the volume ends with four unanswerable questions, yet they are not punctuated as questions. I think Creeley wants to suggest that he has accepted these questions as indicative facts necessary for any human life still in process. The persistence of doubts in Creeley (and in poststructuralist criticism) have made me aware too late of the limits of my dialectical critical approach here and in my ensuing discussion of Merwin. I am convinced that it makes some sense to speak of development and tentative solutions to problems that in turn create further problems. But it is equally important to

stress, as I have not, the way a poet's particular set of themes and styles creates a kind of differential field in which there is no progress, only a series of permutations and oppositions that sustain one another. This differential model is a further development of what it means to shift from vertical to horizontal models of discourse. Still the very fact that neither the poets (except for Ashbery) nor their critics realized this aspect of horizontality for a long time suggests that readers still need to speak of concepts like development.

17. Creeley's task here is similar to William James's interest in the meaning of nonreferential "transitional" words like *if* and *by*. Also like James and especially like Maurice Merleau-Ponty, Creeley is trying to describe a state where knowledge is not merely response to stimuli but the result in part of some active intention on the part of the beholder.

18. W. S. Merwin, *The Moving Target* (New York: Atheneum, 1969), pp. 16, 8. For Merwin's work I use the following abbreviations in the text: *The Moving Target, MT*; *The Lice* (New York: Atheneum, 1968), *L*; *The Carrier of Ladders* (New York: Atheneum, 1970), *CL*; *Green With Beasts* (New York: Knopf, 1956), *GB*; *The Miner's Pale Children* (New York: Atheneum, 1970), *MPC*; "Statement" *The Distinctive Voice*, ed. William Martz (Glencoe, Ill.: Macmillan Free Press, 1966), pp. 268–72, *DV*; "Poems by Jean Follain," *Atlantic Monthly* 226 (1970): 77–79, *PJF*; "Interview" in *Road Apple Review* 1 (1969): 35–36, *RAR*; and an essay interview, Frank McShane, "A Portrait of W. S. Merwin," *Shenandoah* 21 (Winter 1970): 3–17, *PM*.

19. Martin Heidegger, "What is Metaphysics," in *Existence and Being*, ed. Werner Brock (Chicago: Gateway, 1949), p. 353.

20. For what love means to Merwin see also *MT*, pp. 78–79, 36–38; *L*, p. 62; and the closing groups of poems in each of his three earliest volumes.

21. The idea of change as necessity is central to Richard Howard's fine discussion of Merwin in *Alone With America: Essays on the Art of Poetry in the United States Since 1950* (New York: Atheneum, 1971).

22. For this sense of breathing I am indebted to Howard's lecture "The Art of Erasure" (Lecture at SUNY/Buffalo, 1974).

23. Heidegger's distinction between "idle talk" and authentic speech is again relevant here, though Merwin always wonders if silence is not the only authentic speech. To be more exact, one might define Merwin's sense of authentic speech as a focused silence created by language on the verge of disappearing. Sheer silence is a surrender to the blindness of the Gods or the temptation to passivity demonically offered by "things" (*MT*, p. 12).

24. Martin Heidegger, "Language in the Poem," in *The Way to Language*, trans. Peter Hertz (New York: Harper and Row, 1971), pp. 159–98. The discussion here is based primarily on pp. 180–95, and I quote below, pp. 191, 191–92, 192.

25. Merwin's use of startling metaphors or *conceits* is a powerful way of forcing readers to recognize both the "apartness" of language and the way its freedom from the logic of particulars allows it to penetrate the silences where Being lies. A similar and suggestive effect is created in "The Wave" (*L*, pp. 25–26) where Merwin shifts from a repeated past tense ("I inhabited") used to describe his memory of experiences passing away to a present when he turns to language. See also "Things" (*MT*, p. 12) and "Watchers" (*L*, p. 77) for the horror attendant on his fears that one might lose the absence of "apartness" and surrender to the materiality of things or to a landscape cleared of hiding places for eyes to watch one out of the darkness.

26. I use here E. M. Cioran's essay "Encounter With the Void" in *Hudson Review* 23 (1970) : 37–49. I quote below pp. 43, 39, 41.

27.   For the clearest discussions of this concept, first worked out in Derrida's *De La Grammatologie* (Paris: Les Editions de Minuit, 1967), see Francois Wahl, "La Philosophie entre l'avant et l'aprés du Structuralisme," in *Qu'est-ce que Le Structuralisme* (Paris: Éditions de Seuil, 1968), esp. pp. 423–30, and J. Hillis Miller, "The Still Heart: Poetic Form in Wordsworth," *New Literary History* 2 (1971) : 297–310.

28. Robert Graves, *The Greek Myths* (New York: Braziller, 1957), pp. 126–27. I also use his discussion on p. 38. It is important to notice here how Merwin's themes and scene are essentially the same as in "Daybreak," but he includes the scene within the poem (it is a more trustworthy presence than the processes of mind) and, more important, includes the "Great Language."

6

Denise Levertov and the Limits of the Aesthetics of Presence

My major concern so far has been to illustrate what I consider significant achievements by postmodern poets in the sixties. It seems fair now to claim that the poets studied are all accomplished craftsmen, able to make language and structure dramatize and intensify their imaginative explorations of immanent values. And, more important, in articulating these values, the poets manage to continue the Romantic enterprise of locating visionary and aesthetic aspects of imaginary activity firmly within basic existential concerns. In a time when many writers were tempted to rest content with claims for autotelic formal achievements or assertions about the imagination as a source for free play or disorder in a repressive culture, these poets have managed to ally poetry with the work of philosophers altering the culture's perspectives on the nature of thinking itself. Instead of posing explanations for phenomena or elaborating abstract mythic or conceptual systems, they turn to constructing and reflecting upon the kinds of attitudes and stances that can place man in relationship to experience where old questions seem irrelevant and the power of basic ties to both culture and nature stands clear. The poets—especially O'Hara, Snyder, Creeley, and Merwin—each give resonance and imaginative life to Heideggerean claims that poetry is the taking up of sites in which being, or the numinous familiar. discloses itself and testifies to the powers of the attentive mind.

If, however, I attend only to craft or to the power of particular imaginative stances, I run the risk of oversimplifying the poetry and the poetics of postmodernism. The craft and the attitudes ultimately derive from specific philosophical assumptions, and one can fully understand the poetry only if one recognizes the problems and the possibilities inherent in these assumptions. Poetry does not usually present and defend ideas in a way amenable to assessing their truth, but one can, perhaps must, nonetheless, discuss the *adequacy* of its philosophical assumptions. If one is to take poets seriously, both as representatives of their culture and as participants in a dialogue about what it means to be fully human at a given time, one must ask how completely and complexly their assumptions register and account for perennial and specific problems. One must discuss whether their perspectives can respond to the multiple tensions between mind and world, individual and society, and the person and his own desires, which are constant features of both cultural heritage and daily existence.

When one puts pressure on postmodern poetics by asking questions about philosophical adequacy, one immediately confronts a powerful contradiction: considered as metaphysical or religious meditation, the poetry of the sixties seems to me highly sophisticated; it takes into account all the obvious secular objections to traditional religious thought and actually continues and extends the inquiries of philosophers as diverse as Heidegger, Whitehead, and Wittgenstein. This very success, however, makes it disappointing that the poetry fails so miserably in handling social and ethical issues. One cannot avoid asking why this is the case, and when he does he finds that at least one poet, Denise Levertov, has preceded his questions. (In this respect, at least, poets continue to be Pound's "antennae of the race.") Miss Levertov has been one of the major voices of the new poetry in the 1960s, and while not very original, she is often quite a good poet devoted to developing concrete moments in which the numinous emerges out of the quotidian. Yet what interests me most about her work, what I shall now develop, is her experience of the inadequacy of the aesthetics of presence when in *The Sorrow Dance* (1966) and subsequent volumes she tries to adapt her poetic to pressing social concerns caused by the war in Vietnam. Miss Levertov presents a very compelling critique of that aesthetic, but even more telling is her own lack of poetic power and authority when she tries to adapt the principles that had shaped her work to social questions. In effect, her later work testifies to the most basic intellectual weaknesses of the contemporary aesthetic and presents a challenge that I hope will be met by poets in the seventies.

Let me first briefly sketch her earlier objectivist celebrations of presence as plenitude. As she summarizes her poetic career, the informing myth or "plot behind the plot" is the desire to combine and reconcile "the spirit of Here and Now" learned from Williams "with the Romantic spirit of quest, of longing to wander towards other worlds" inherited from her father's interest in traditions of mystical thought:

I find my main theme again in the title poem of *Overland to the Islands*: "Lets go," it begins, "much as that dog goes/intently haphazard"; and ends, "there's nothing/the dog disdains on his way,/

nevertheless he/keeps moving, changing pace and approach but/not direction—every step an/arrival." The last phrase, "every step an arrival," is quoted from Rilke, and here, unconsciously, I was evidently trying to unify for myself my sense of the pilgrim way with my new American, objectivist influenced, pragmatic and sensuous longing for the Here and Now; a living-in-the-present that I would later find further incitement to in Thoreau's notebooks.[1]

To unify these strands in her work Miss Levertov gathers into her poetry elements of all three approaches to presence explored in chapter 2. From Olson, and more directly from Duncan and Creeley, she takes her objectivist ideals: verse must capture the energies of the attentive consciousness open to the event of arriving each step along the way. But like Creeley, her tone and dramatic context differ radically from Olson's bardic voice and generalizing perspective. Both poets keep the less hero-oriented dimensions of Olson's aesthetic, but use them in specific domestic contests that share O'Hara's emphases on the local, the casual, and the contingent. Finally, in her desire to correlate objectivist ideals with the mystical attitudes that sustain the "pilgrim's way," her pursuit of presence leads to meditations on the deep image[2] and the development of techniques to render a "slip inward," or in her case a slip beyond, to a sense of the infinite depth and mystery at the horizon of what is sharply seen.

Her most characteristic image for reconciling the sense of continual arrival in a satisfying present with the "pilgrim way" is the image of ripeness, as exemplified by the last stanza of "Under the Tree":

> let the oranges
>
> ripen, ripen above you
>
> you are living too, one
>
> among the dark multitude

(*WEBH*, p. 42)

Presence as plenitude here is very different from Olson's energy of spring or Snyder's "Communionism," or even his movement into the "back country of the mind." Rather this stanza concentrates a slow process of satisfaction (the repeated "ripen") blending into a sense of transcendent union. The poem dwells lovingly on "one," a word at once requiring a strong pause and, because it is enjambed, a quick transition into the "dark multitude." Ripeness then functions in several ways. As a physical image it renders a sense of the scene as self-contained plenitude. But ripeness is of its very nature a transitional state; it testifies to the fact that individual perfection is not essentially an end in itself but a means for becoming a functioning and satisfying element in the total process. The tree puts forth fruit in order to nourish the seed and create new life. Moreover, from man's perspective the ripe fruit calls out to be eaten, and thus is another way to sustain life. Psychologically a similar ripening process takes place for the speaker. The stanza's initial imperative, "let," summarizes the poem's moral movement. The speaker is willing to accept process as process and to dwell with attention on the fullness of the "Here and Now." Like the fruit, she is at once fully there and gradually preparing for a new relationship to the total life process, a relationship embodied in the shift in attention from the trees to herself and then to the climatic sense of oneness. (In many of Miss Levertov's poems this movement from ripeness to union takes explicit sexual form.) Finally the sense of oneness leads in the last line to the "slip beyond" into a metaphysical vision of shared process at a deeper level of awareness. "Dark multitude" is unfortunately vague and abstract, but in a sense these qualities are necessary to get the intended feeling of the whole physical scene being carried into a level of experience where the mind itself sees its place in an all-embracing process.

How different from this satisfying enclosed space and relaxed accepting attitude is the opening poem of *Relearning the Alphabet*:

> Dreamed the thong of my sandal broke.
> Nothing to hold it to my foot.
> How shall I walk?
>   Barefoot?
> The sharp stones, the dirt. I would
> hobble.
> And—
> Where was I going?
> Where was I going I can't
> go to now, unless hurting?
> Where am I standing, if I'm
> to stand still now?

(RLA, p. 3)

Every step is no longer an arrival as she replaces confident assertion with a series of questions that set the dominant tone of the volume. This poet of place and attention now can neither stand peacefully nor follow a purposive path. Moreover, accustomed to merging her ego into a field of actions, she now feels that field breaking up into a public self merely playing roles and a genuine "I" that grows so deeply private one must fear for its continued presence:

Between chores—
hulling strawberries,
answering letters—
or between poems,

returning to the mirror
to see if I'm there.

(*RLA*, p. 59)

Even touching and tasting, two of her most recurrent acts of celebration, now only alienate the sensitive spirit from the things of this world:

At any moment the heart
breaks for nothing—

poor folk got up in their best,
rich ones trying, trying to please—

each touch and a new fissure appears,
such a network, I think of an old

china pie-plate
left too long in the oven.

(*RLA*, p. 19)

Black beans, white sunlight.
These have sufficed.

Approval of mothers, of brothers,
of strangers—a plunge of the hands
in sifted flour, over the wrists.
It gives pleasure. . . .

But hunger: a hunger there is
refuses. Refuses. Refuses the earth.

(*RLA*, p. 51)

No orange will compensate for the fact that the present moment is now inextricable from the continual awareness of the senseless suffering and death created by the war in Vietnam. The psychological counterpart to this hunger is the doubt about her previous poetic stance that permeates *Relearning the Alphabet*:

What do I know?
          Swing of the
          birch catkins,
          drift of
          watergrass,
          tufts of
          green on the
          trees,
          (flowers, not leaves,
          bearing intricately
          little winged seeds
          to fly in fall)
          and whoever
          I meet now,
          on the path.
It's not enough.

(*RLA*, pp. 5–6)

What she knows can no longer suffice because she is now confronted with two problems her aesthetics of presence cannot handle. With the war so dominant a fact of experience, especially for the poet whose sensitivity now becomes a kind of curse, she perceives in the present at least as many inescapable reminders of suffering and pain as causes for awe and religious acceptance. Second, the war brings home the poet's helplessness. What mystery she does perceive in the present is too personal and too particular to help her either judge or transform the suffering. The "dark multitude" has shown itself as a mass of isolated individuals who share only confusion. In "The Cold Spring" she seeks to renew her sense of the numinous sources or origins that can sustain the way of poetic affirmation, but she finds instead that at the source of the spring feeding poetic inspiration, the life-giving waters are reddened and muddied by human violence. The eye now is only a physical instrument recording ambiguities and can give no direction, no structure, to the I: "Reduced to an eye/I forget what/I/was" (*RLA*, p. 9).

"Advent 1966" is Levertov's most powerful statement of the changed landscape where the sensitive eye, which once served to unite the "I" with the numinous scene, now sees only a demonic version of incarnation. And this reversal of traditional possibilities for satisfying mythic transformations is paralleled by the fact that now the intense literal reality of the flames from napalm no longer allows the shift to mythic dimensions of fire so easily and movingly rendered in "Eros at Temple Stream" (*OTS*, p. 55):

. . . because of this my strong sight,
my clear caressive sight, my poet's sight I was given
that it might stir me to song,
is blurred.
        There is a cataract filming over
my inner eyes. Or else a monstrous insect
has entered my head, and looks out
from my sockets with multiple vision,
seeing not the unique Holy Infant
burning sublimely, an imagination of redemption,
furnace in which souls are wrought into new life,
but, as off a beltline, more, more senseless figures aflame.

And this insect (who is not there—
it is my own eyes do my seeing, (the insect
is not there, what I see is there)
will not permit me to look elsewhere,

or if I look, to see except dulled and unfocused
the delicate, firm, whole flesh of the still unburned.

                                         (*RLA*, p. 4)

Relearning the Alphabet has a place in the modern tradition of volumes of poetry revaluing a whole poetic career and tentatively exploring new directions. Like Yeats, Eliot, and Stevens before her, she knows what she has to do, but she has considerably less at her disposal to help her realize the new goals. Her task is twofold—to awaken the sensitivity of those supporting the war so they might see its evils (see *RLA*, pp. 13, 27), and to formulate an ethic and an aesthetic that might help restructure the consciousness of society. The poetry of numinous presence must grow more discursive in order to propound values at once more explicitly ethical than those of immanence and more general than those bound to the now muddied objective contexts of specific moments of perception. The poetics of presence must be complemented by models allowing society "to equate human with humane" (*RLA*, p. 104) in order to help people accept the "task" of becoming " 'more ourselves' in the making" (*SD*, p. 82).

Where, however, is she to find within her sense of poetry and the poet's role, style and themes adequate to the task she sees as necessary? Where will she find an ethical basis for creating models of humane behavior? To what value structures can the poet turn when for most of her life she has rejected humanism and the early moderns' use of tradition and creative imagination as the basis of her ideals? While she recognizes that the aesthetics of presence no longer suffices, she has only its implicit ethical ideals to work with. That aesthetic is built on visions of immanence whose only ethical corollary is the command to let be *Heid* and to recognize the fullness of what lies before one. Such an ideal might provide the goal for a transformed society, but it will not give much help in determining or propounding the means for creating such a society. Moreover, that aesthetic is intensely antisymbolist (see *SD*, p. 40) and can provide little guidance when the poet feels that she must deal with symbolic generalizations and must transform moments of vision into the basis of discursively presented structures of value. With so much cut away in order to reach the numinous present, what has the contemporary poet left with which to build an ethical vision based on his insights?

I am now entering aspects of the crisis presented in *Relearning the Alphabet* that are no longer under Miss Levertov's self-conscious control. She wants to raise questions in order to provide at least tentative answers, but the poems giving answers only make one realize that the crisis is a deeper one than she seems to think. She tries to work out a solution by turning to the notebook form, for here she can remain faithful to the now confused present while replacing the dramatic poem of sharply realized perceptions with one loose enough to allow moral reflections. In this form she can discuss moral issues (without pretending to a structured moral vision) and can allow moments of moral conviction to emerge from her intense suffering and inner contradictions. If the poet cannot adequately judge her age intellectually, she can provide personal witness of what it is doing to its sensitive and reflective spirits. Moreover, unwilling and perhaps unable to construct heroic models of resistance that may be mere fictions, she can in the notebook form capture as models of humane behavior whatever acts strike her, without endangering the power of the acts themselves by either interpreting them or excessively dramatizing them. Personal example is perhaps the only ethical model for social action that makes coherent sense within an aesthetics of presence because it simply shifts attention from the numinous qualities of natural scenes to the qualities of human actors in social situations.

In theory, then, the notebook form makes a certain amount of sense, given Miss Levertov's plight. But it simply does not work, and perhaps could not work to achieve what she desires. The notebook style at best can serve as a historical document dramatizing the problems of a sensitive consciousness at given moments. But it has little reconstructive value because it provides no checks—either formal or in demands for lyric intensity—against the temptations—so strong when one is driven by moral outrage—to easy rhetoric and slack generalizations. Moreover, the form exerts very little authority: it seems only the cries of a passive victim. Here perhaps the "wise passiveness" cultivated by the poetics of presence shows its ultimate weakness. It is, of course, not easy for the poet, so lacking in real social power, to assert authority, but there are, if she will ally herself with them, (moral and artistic traditions that demand and support resistance to the kind of forces oppressing Levertov. But before I get into theoretical questions about the limitations of all modern political poetry, I shall look closely at the undeniable weaknesses in Miss Levertov's efforts. Then one can hardly doubt that there are better philosophical and aesthetic foundations for public poetry, and one can see how deeply her own work is victimized by the very problems she describes in the aesthetics of presence.] (That description, I might add, is a considerable achievement.)

The following lines are the climactic narrative section of Miss Levertov's "From a Notebook: October '68–May '69":

> O happiness
> in the sun! Is it
> that simple, then,
> to live?
> —crazy rhythm of
> scooping up barehanded
> (all the shovels already in use)
> careless of filth and broken glass
> —scooping up garbage together
> poets and dreamers studying
> job together, clearing
> refuse off the neglected, newly recognized,
> humbly waiting ground, place, locus, of what could be our
> New World even now, our revolution, one and one and
> one and one together, black children swinging, green
> guitars, that energy, that music, no one
> telling anyone what to do,
> everyone doing,
>
> each leaf of
> the new grass near us
> a new testament . : .
>
> Out to the dump:
> acres of garbage glitter and stink in wild sunlight, gulls
> float and scream in the brilliant sky,
> polluted waters bob and dazzle, we laugh, our arms ache,
> we work together
> shoving and kicking and scraping to empty our truckload
> over the bank
> even though we know
> the irony of adding to the Bay fill, the System has us there—
> but we love each other and return to the Park.

Thursday, May 15th
At 6 a.m. the ominous zooming, war-sound, of helicopters
breaks into our sleep.

To the Park:
ringed with police.
Bulldozers have moved in.
Barely awake, the people—
those who had made for each other
a green place—
begin to gather at the corners.

Their tears fall on sidewalk cement.
The fence goes up, twice a man's height.
Everyone knows (yet no one yet
believes it) what all shall know
this day, and the days that follow:
now the clubs, the gas,
bayonets, bullets. The War
comes home to us. . . .

(RLA, pp. 106–7)

The details are flat, often sentimental, asserting rather than manifesting value (for example, "black children swinging, green/guitars, [what other colors could they be?] that energy, that music" or the sentimental polarity of tears and cement). And loose propagandistic phrases like "the people" and "The War/comes home to us" neither create fresh insights nor bear up under intellectual analysis. More telling is the pathetic quest to make assertions of value in generalizations that seem simplistic. "Happiness/in the sun" might be a simple moment of life, but it is not an adequate model for basing so general a conclusion as, "Is it that simple, then,/to live." No, for our culture it is not, whether one accepts its vision of authentic life or whether one wants to change it in any meaningful way. And the symbolic equation of the grass revealed in its freshness when the garbage is removed with "a new testament" has a certain momentary validity, but it is too slight an event on which to hang so portentous and inclusive a symbolic referent.[3] Here human action restores a simple natural dynamism, but that is a far cry from receiving the vision, structure, and ground of a new law as implied by the metaphor. No wonder she does not develop this but quickly changes her perspective. Where she arrives, though, is even more problematic. Miss Levertov has a quick mind; she recognizes the irony of removing garbage only to add to the Bay-fill destroying the San Francisco harbor, and she records this both to dramatize the self-irony a revolutionary can maintain and to stave off her critics. But her clever way of dismissing the irony will not do.

In fact, it makes childish and questionable the love she is trying to celebrate. It is precisely that easy praise of human virtues and the tendency to assert it in order to cover up political contradictions that has made the new calls to revolution suspect and undermined the authority of those poets celebrating it.

What bothers me most in this passage, though, is the way it exemplifies problems I suspect are endemic to a poetics of immanence. That aesthetic, in the pursuit of an unmediated sense of Being and in its attempts to make ontologically real harmonies perceived between aesthetic and natural processes, tends in social questions to confuse art and life and to misuse poetic categories of thought. Miss Levertov, as I have shown, explicitly denies a symbolic way of thinking in her pursuit of objects; numinous experiences require primarily attentive participation and not artificial interpretive acts of the reflective mind. Not terribly conscious or analytic, then, about what symbols she does use, she is likely to misuse the poet's synthesizing power by constructing problematic analogies like that between the uncovered grass and the New Testament. After encountering repeated instances of this kind of faulty thinking, the reader is likely to grow skeptical, and to replace a sympathetic openness to her work with an analytic attitude—scrutinizing language he should trust the poet has scrutinized so that he can simply respond to it.

A more elaborate misuse of aesthetic categories takes place here when she facilely extends the particular experience of cooperation at People's Park into a universal model for the new society to be created by the revolution. It takes very little skepticism to note that this group is politically homogeneous and gathered together for a short time to achieve a particular purpose that has obvious mythical values underlying it. Such a model is far removed from the problems encountered in creating or maintaining a political society, particularly in cultures that value freedom and difference. A political society must unify groups with a variety of sensibilities, interests, and priorities, and it must do so with structures capable of enduring through time and of defining laws and modes of compromise. The poetic imagination is mythic and tends to confuse imaginative visions of shared ends and unified societies with complex social conditions requiring that, since it is almost impossible to have people agree on ends, people come up with ways of getting them at least to share certain rules of behavior in the pursuit of individual ends.[4]

This social denial of the complexity and differences constitutive of modern societies is reinforced by a characteristic postmodern view of the nature of evil. The aesthetics of presence is essentially monistic, conceiving evil as basically only a privation, a failure to perceive correctly or to align one's consciousness with the latent harmonious orders of a given scene. The dream is that proper action will follow naturally from a correct understanding or, more radically, a correct positioning in which the understanding receives its "sentences" from the situation. But however appealing the metaphysics of this vision might be, the realm of politics is largely constituted by the need to correlate different visions and priorities. When faced with practical choices, one can hardly escape the fundamental dualist conceptions of the differences between people's perceptions and, when perceptions agree, differences between the priorities accorded to what is perceived. Poetry, one might say, is primarily a meditative mode of consciousness that seeks to bring minds into accord with one another by dramatizing a given perspective. But politics is a mode of action, where the distribution of goods and powers requires reconciling different perspectives. It is not enough to see how others might see; people need to find forms of agreement that do not require sharing the same particular perspectives and priorities. Poetry unifies perspectives within provisional dramatic points of view; society must seek abstract agreements acceptable to dramatic positions widely separated in time, space, and quality.[5]

Given these conditions, one must recognize the fact that no poetry is likely to have much direct impact on the social order. Still, as high modernism makes clear, in style if not in content, political poetry need not be embarrassingly simplistic. This form of poetry can profoundly engage one's sympathies, if not political allegiances. To do so, however, political poetry, and perhaps the more general category of ethical as opposed to perceptual poetry, must first of all recognize the enormous gulf between values found in meditating on nature and those explicitly developed by reflection on public themes and problems. With respect to public poetry, then, modernism is far more effective than the postmodern alternative because of the modernist reliance on tradition and the mythmaking or reconstructive imagination. First, tradition provides both a set of recurrent public and ethical problems that have been central to political debate and a series of roles and allusions that can give dignity and depth to the poet's social stance. Indeed the more fully one includes history in his work, as Yeats does for example in "Nineteen Hundred and Nineteen" and "Meditations in Time of Civil War," the more he perforce admits the complexity of political questions and achieves for himself a stance that can claim authority and universality for both its suffering and its ideals. Second, the very tension between ideals and the recalcitrance of history forces the poet to recognize the complexity of human motives and the enormous gulf, in both society and in the self, between the imagination and empirical reality.

Ideals make dualists of us all, but they need not force us to despair.

The third advantage of the modernist poetic, in fact, stems directly from this gulf. For in order to reconcile desires bred by the traditions of imaginative literature with the realities societies produce in the name of these ideals, poets had to distinguish between social values and a deeper ground for values carried by the tradition but never realized.[6] This social condition generates in turn an ethical distinction between empirical or social and ideal or best selves, and it gives the poets a powerful set of analogies between remaking the self imaginatively and reconstituting social order. In the poetry, then, social conflicts need not remain abstract nor invite self-righteous judgment. Social order becomes the parallel to the poet's remaking himself in terms of ideal images, and his struggles to establish poetic orders at once repeat and give authority to his pursuit of social order—an order dependent on correlating psychological and social materials. By making the self an analogue for redeemed society, these poets were easily tempted by elitist and authoritarian models of order, and they had their own problems in successfully distinguishing between art and politics. But because they were so aware of the ideal (not necessarily "fictive") status of their visions, their poetry maintained a sense of the difficulties and possible self-delusions involved in relating art and life, poetic tradition and political realities. And, more important, because they distinguished between perception and making or reconstructing viable social myths and images, their public poetry retained a sense of drama and conflict. They could create personae who could do more than pathetically record their hopes and confusions in the form of private notebooks. They felt that they could speak to society, not simply be overheard by it lamenting impersonal, demonic forces, and hence they articulated dignified forms of public speech as a last noble, if hopeless, model for the poet's active relationship to his society.

More than Levertov's work is at stake in this contrast, and the problems in developing an adequate postmodern public poetry are largely symptoms of psychological problems inherent in the aesthetics of presence. The quest for immanent plenitude, for example, leads readily toward quiescent passivity. Snyder and Levertov make it clear that too strong a sense of evil as mere privation and too much reliance on strategies of perception or imaginative stances as the mode for overcoming that privation leave the self helpless or pathetic in relation to social forces. Moreover, by locating most or all significant values in moments of vision, the poet has great difficulty constructing specific ethical values or moral images that are more applicable and more general than specific epistemological poses. The pursuit of immanence simply does not bring into play important rational faculties of the mind, nor does it focus the poet's attention on historical and traditional forces that might both define the

contemporary situation and provide (values and images from the past)
one can use to judge and transcend it.

The postmodern ideal is that the poet's sense of cosmic order and
his awakened sensitivity will play the role once played by tradition and   *hum.*
by moral universals.) However, both moments of vision and individual
sensitivity can be terribly evanescent. One can see, for example, in the
work of Creeley and O'Hara that as soon as one requires specific personal and secular meanings from this poetic, he finds himself tormented
by pressures to have each moment of experience provide in intensity
what it cannot give on the level of ideas or principles. (There is simply
no conceptual level to the experiences the poets cultivate capable of
providing them with a sense of consistent identity.) In addition, it is
difficult to avoid fears of solipsism if one's sense of objective orders in
reality and one's ties to other consciousnesses depend upon a series of
intense moments of numinous awareness. Finally, this stress on the present
makes the poets painfully frustrated by those dead moments in which
the energies of place and psyche are not manifest. Merwin's two basic
fears—that what offers itself as presence may be mere illusion and that
negation may be the only valid plenitude—offer in abstract form the
logical alternatives to Snyder's and Duncan's plenitude—an alternative
constantly possible within the vision of value as presence free of moral
and social contents.

It will not suffice, however, to dwell on these possible problems inherent in the aesthetics of presence. Critics should probably be aware of the
spiritual tensions a poetic can create for poets, and even for the literate
culture that adopts their values, but they should also remember that,
for the modern mind at least, tensions and problems are the stuff poetic
dreams are made of. The critic must remain open to the power of poems
rendering these problems, and he must recognize that the poets themselves are not only aware of them but working to transcend them in their
poetry. Indeed the primary value of reflecting upon the limits of a general
poetic may well be the focus it provides on what that poetic has helped
the poets achieve. For without the constant pressures I have been describing, the many varieties of presence as plenitude and the general
project of rethinking the contemporary metaphysical situation would
seem quite trivial and unnecessary. The poems gain in authority and
power from the tensions in theme, psyche, and culture the poet manages
to articulate as their ground.

One ought finally to keep in mind that if the constrast with modernism serves to clarify the limits of the poetry of the sixties, it also helps
in another way to illustrate the significance of its achievement.[7] For in
their attempts to articulate the creative powers of the imagination, even

the greatest of the modernists blinded themselves to two primary needs in any society. They were unable to imagine culture except in ideal and mythic terms, and most of them could provide alternatives to what they saw as a vulgar positivist and philistine society only by returning to what now seem outmoded and indefensible forms of (organicist) social and metaphysical thought. The postmoderns would have performed a significant cultural role if they merely tried to right the balance. I hope I have shown that they have given their readers considerably more than that.

Whatever they have given cannot be enough. This is simply the fact of the spiritual condition in which we find ourselves. But they have made it possible for us to view our own experiences from the position that R. D. Laing calls *ontological security*. If they do not either reconcile us to society or lead us to want or to see how to change it, they do help reconcile us to the more general and perhaps more significant situations in which it is man's constant task to find ways of affirming his own existence. Postmodern poetry builds a temple out of nature, not a city, but that can be a considerable achievement even for those whose ultimate dream is some version of a redeemed society. History shows that man's efforts to build temples have little effect on the specific practices characterizing life in the city. Yet history also shows that without the temple, however it may be constructed, life in the city seems at best vulgar and callous, at worst a demonic force driving man back on the woeful inadequacy of endless introspection. When Lowell left Rome for Paris, the archetypal secular city, he found only the second alternative—forcing him to a more and more enervated self-consciousness and a desperate quest to locate all value in domestic experience. The other alternative, implicit in many poets and working for adequate expression in Miss Levertov's "Relearning the Alphabet," requires that one first seek ontological security and then gradually try to extend the terms of that security as the elements of a moral alphabet that one can begin applying to social issues.[8] Once identity has a fixed base, it is possible to endure the contradictions, restraints, and tentative projection of ideals that constitute the public moral life. As Hegel put it, the temple must exist before men can create in it the statue or image of the ideal man that will serve as the center for communal self-definition. Only then, he argues, can the subjective arts emerge to express the many ways that image can be reflected in the political and social organization of the community. While the other contemporary arts, in the throes of what John Barth has called "Exhaustion," continue to reinterpret the subjective aspects of a dying social order, the best postmodern poets are at work articulating the shape of a new temple that may provide the locus for a new image of man.

Notes to Chapter 6

1. The three quotations here are from Miss Levertov's "A Personal Approach," in *Parable, Myth, and Language* ed. Tony Stoneburner (Cambridge, Mass.: Church Society For College Work, 1967), pp. 19, 28, 23. In the text I use the following abbreviations for her work: "A Personal Approach," *PA*; "The Origins of a Poem," *Michigan Quarterly Review* 7 (1968): 233, 238, *OP*; "An Argument," *Floating Bear* 2 (1961) [no pagination], *FB*; *With Eyes at the Back of our Heads* (New York: New Directions, 1959), *WEBH*; *The Jacob's Ladder*, (New York: New Directions, 1961), *JL*; *O Taste and See* (New York: New Directions, 1964), *OTS*; *The Sorrow Dance* (New York: New Directions, 1966), *SD*; *Relearning the Alphabet* (New York: New Directions, 1970), *RLA*; *To Stay Alive* (New York: New Directions, 1971), *SA*. For a fuller treatment of her application of the aesthetics of presence, see Thomas A. Duddy, "To Celebrate: A Reading of Denise Levertov," *Criticism* 10 (1968): 138–52.

2. Her essay in *Floating Bear* (see n. 1) argues with Robert Kelley's definition of the *deep image* and proposes Miss Levertov's own view of the way to mystery in poetry. See also *OP*.

3. It is interesting to read Miss Levertov's poems on People's Park in the light of Northrop Frye's mythic reading of that event on the archetype of the expulsion from Eden. See Frye's "The Critical Path: An Essay on the Social Context of Literary Criticism," *Daedalus* 99 (1970): 336–37. Where Levertov participates in the myth, Frye sees beyond it, at least to the extent of understanding why the event appeals so to the imagination. Miss Levertov rarely asks why she responds the way she does. This is one indication of the intellectual shortcomings in her work.

4. I am here summarizing the argument of Alasdair MacIntyre, *Secularization and Moral Change* (New York: Oxford University Press, 1967), pp. 24–35.

5. Miss Levertov's discussion of evil is typical of contemporary poets, most of whom believe evil is not a fact of experience but a condition created by faulty ways of perceiving reality:

> What I have up to now been suggesting as the task of the poet may seem of an Emersonian idealism (though perhaps Emerson has been misread on this point) that refuses to look man's capacity for evil square in the eyes. Now as perhaps never before, when we are so acutely conscious of being ruled by evil men, and that in our time man's inhumanity to man has swollen to proportions of perhaps unexampled monstrosity, such a refusal would be no less than idiotic. . . . But Young's final injunction, in the passage just quoted, is what, for me, holds the clue to what must make the poet's humanity humane. Reverence thyself is necessarily an aspect of Schweitzer's doctrine of Reverence for Life, the recognition of oneself as life that wants to live among other forms of life that want to live. This recognition is indissoluble, reciprocal, and dual. There can be no self respect without respect for others, no love and reverence for others without love and reverence for oneself; and no recognition of others is possible without the imagination. The imagination of what it is to be those other forms of life that want to live is the only way to recognition; and it is that imaginative recognition that brings compassion to birth. Man's capacity for evil, then, is less a positive capacity, for all its horrendous activity, than a failure to develop man's most human function, the imagination, to its fullness, and consequently a failure to develop compassion. [*OP*, p. 237]

6. I have worked out the ethical vision of literature involved here in my essay "Northrop Frye and the Problem of Spiritual Authority," *PMLA* 87 (1972): 964–75.

7. Quentin Anderson, *The Imperial Self: An Essay in American Literary and Cultural History* (New York: Knopf, 1971), has attacked the contemporaries for continuing certain spiritual traits first pronounced in Emerson and Whitman, particularly their negation of history, their desire to link the individual ego to the cosmos by expanding consciousness, and their negating fixed communal and social roles or demands for action in favor of the quest to "incorporate" the universal into the self. My criticism obviously shares certain themes of his, but he falls into the trap I am trying to avoid: for him if literature is not social and devoted to reconciling the individual to society it is meretricious. Such emphases not only deny the importance of ontological questions, they even rule out the mediating role literature can play in shaping the ideals that lead one to work for social changes, even if the specific working out of these ideals in theory and practice is better accomplished in nonliterary ways.

8. Let me offer here in note form what probably should be an appendix on one important ethical scheme only implicit in most of the poetry but articulated in Miss Levertov's poem "Relearning the Alphabet" as one possible response to the crisis the volume presents. (Since she has not followed it up, it apparently did not satisfy her.) I refer to the possibility of basing ethical values not on myths or images of heroic perfection but on principles inherent in the language and in the prereflexive aspects of culture that man lives in as he does in nature. Philosophers influenced by Wittgenstein and J. L. Austin, like Stuart Hampshire and Stanley Cavell, are working on the problem, but Levertov's poem is especially significant for me because it typifies how in my case it was the poets and not the philosophers who marked out this line of inquiry.

One best approaches this possible ethical ideal by returning to the contrast between symbolist and immanentist models. One of the impulses giving authority to philosophies of immanence is a sense that neither cultural traditions nor humanistic theories of imaginative models of human excellence to be imitated have had any effect in altering the increasing insensitivity and inhumanity of society. The temptation, then, for Wordsworth and Nietzsche as well as for the contemporaries, is to turn away entirely from the idea of morality as based on self-conscious attempts to justify behavior in relation to rational, traditional, or ideal grounds. If change is to be possible it will come not from cultural forces but from natural ones capable of defining and influencing humane behavior. Nature, however, is a set of phenomena at once too general and too specific to ground discussions of ethical value—too general because it encompasses every form of behavior and cannot without submitting itself once again to rational argument define behavior adequate for man's specific form of life, and too specific because each moment of natural experience is different and requires intellectual structures if the moments are to be sorted and transformed into principles.

This helps explain, I think, why Miss Levertov's critique of her own aesthetics of presence is so compelling and why that aesthetic cannot be extended, as she tries, to ethical principles. But one is left with the question of whether there are no alternatives between ideal cultural models and amorphous natural ones. George Lukacs, in *Theory of the Novel*, trans. Anna Bostock (London: Merlin Press, 1971), pp. 63–64, 144–53, makes the key distinction that allows for a middle term between these extremes. In discussing Tolstoi's attempt to resist the problems of subjectivity and of the radical deformation of his culture by seeking a ground of values in natural laws and processes, he distinguishes this too amorphous nature from a second nature. This second nature is not the high culture but the complex of social meanings that the ordinary man relies on to define, without self-conscious reflection, the meaning of his fundamental actions and the rules he follows in moral actions. I am slightly transforming Lukacs into the perspective of the philosophers mentioned above, but their point is also his—that a morality can be self-consciously based not on imaginative ideals but on what is called "the constitutive rules" implicit in the basic institutions underlying virtually any social life. (See here in particular John Searle, *Speech Acts* [Cambridge: At the University Press, 1969], pp. 131–49, 175–98.) This second nature is in effect the broader and more specific ground needed: it locates within the familiar and the natural (at least in so much as the prereflexive and humanly universal can be treated as "natural") widely accepted yet not actualized moral principles.

Now to "Relearning the Alphabet." In the midst of the volume's erring ways, Miss Levertov sees at moments one possible alternative to her feeling that nature as she has known it only intensifies her present confusions:

> O language, virtue
> of man, touchstone
> worn down by what
> gross fiction
>
> O language, mother of thought,
> are you rejecting us as we reject you?

(RLA, p. 22)

> Without a terrain in which, to which, I belong,
> language itself is my one home, my Jerusalem.

(RLA, p. 97)

Language can provide the sense of origins and the secure basis for defining virtue no longer to be realized in the objectivist vision, for ordinary language is not created by the fictive imagination but has developed as a moral "touchstone" through mankind's continual arbitration of good and evil. Language is the repository of fundamental moral instincts, marking and valuing those distinctions and qualities which the culture has found basic to its fundamental human interests as it tries to define its experiences. The poem "Relearning the Alphabet" dramatizes how man can return to those simple moral terms as the ground of a new view of natural, antisymbolist morality. The alphabet is a syntax of moral values and their possible relations with one another. The poem's opening lines exemplify the way this syntax functions and state the poem's intention:

> A
>
> Joy—a beginning.   Anguish, ardor.
> To relearn the ah! of knowing in unthinking
> joy: the beloved stranger lives.
> Sweep up anguish as with a wing-tip,
> brushing the ashes back to the fire's core.

(RLA, p. 110)

The simplicity of this alphabet is important—both because the revived morality must be a morality of the "people," not of heroic imaginative men, and because it is opposed to the technological sophistication and complex computational models that support the destruction of Vietnam's simple pastoral culture. Erotic fire can once again be redeemed, now as the desire for cleansing destruction and as the universal archetypal desire to restore Koré (the phrase "fire's core" is Duncan's) from Hell into the praise of radiant life.

Earlier poems in the volume, as shown above, provide the questions this poem tries to answer, and they also help define the importance of the alphabet structure in which its wisdom is embodied. The note of questioning and doubt requires for its resolution some kind of structure so that in the process of a poem the experience of wandering can be countered by the faith that there is a ground and basis of judgment to which one can return "to dig down, to reexamine" (*RLA*, p. 102). Lost in the structureless ephemera of her notebook form where one can only record doubts and desires, not satisfy them, Miss Levertov cries out, "A beginning/Where shall we/begin?/Can't go/further" (*RLA*, p. 105). Later the poem envisions the possibility of that beginning when it sees the conditions needed for change: "Change is now/change is now/things that seem to be solid are not" (*RLA*, p. 108). But to realize that change, one must see how "Maybe what seems/evanescent is solid" (*RLA*, p. 109). What is evanescent, I take it, is the recurrence of life (fire's core*)* and of the moral qualities that justify man's faith in that life. To make that faith solid one needs a structure. And the excellence of "Relearning the Alphabet" is that it not only provides an abstract structure but in its formal patterns forces one to experience the abstractions as the concrete structure of experience. Thus as one reads the poem, he finds himself occasionally lost or wandering, but once he recognizes that each section will end by returning to moral terms employing the particular letter of its title, he finds himself both continually satisfied by these returns and surprised by the cleverness of the poet and the plenitude of moral possibilities she uncovers by her fidelity to her form. The section on the letters I, J, for example, begins with a painful stumbling that recalls earlier poems but surprises the reader by the multiple terms of its resolution:

> Into the world of continuance, to find
> I-who-I-am again, who wanted
> to enter a life not mine,
>   to leap a wide, deep, swift river. . . .
>
>   I go stumbling
>   (head turned)
>   back to my origins:
> (if that's where I'm going)
>   to joy, my Jerusalem.
>   (*RLA*, p. 112*)*

In a similar way the poem's concluding section takes on the difficult task of finding moral terms and images using the *z* sound and surprises the reader with its range of terms—in the process further enkindling the blaze of moral vision and providing precisely that beginning again desired by *Notebook* if absence is to be transformed once more into presence:

> Sweep up
> anguish as with a wing-tip:
>
> the blaze addresses
> a different darkness:
> absence has not become
> the transformed presence the will
> looked for,
> but other: the present,
> that which was poised already in the ah! of praise.
>   (*RLA*, p. 120*)*

This blend of the aleatory with underlying structures is crucial here because it captures the qualities of moral life on this outwardly prereflexive level of experience. Man is not aware of the laws or of their secure ground. Yet when man needs them, they are there if only he can stop dreaming of other more romantic and potentially more merely fictive possibilities. Here perhaps, as one comes to reflect on the plenitude of simple principles capable of satisfying both formal and moral needs, one can find a place where he can reconcile optimism of will with optimism of intelligence. Growing confidence in the poem's form might also testify to a possible confidence in ordinary experience. Here, in the language in which that experience is expressed and carried out, is one possible source for keeping the humane in humanity. Socially this entails making people conscious of how much of their lives are defined in simple communal terms, albeit abstract ones, and poetically it requires the specific strategies of contemporary poetics—the rejection of high tradition, the necessary angel, and the last Romantic hero in favor of careful intense attention to the natural and the familiar.

Bibliography: Works Cited

Primary Works

Ammons, A. R. *Corson's Inlet*. Ithaca, N.Y.: Cornell University Press, 1965.

Ashbery, John. *The Double Dream of Spring*. New York: Dutton, 1970.

――――. "The Heroes." In *Artist's Theatre in New York: Four Plays*, edited by Herbert Machiz. New York: Grove, 1960.

――――. *The Tennis Court Oath*. Middletown, Conn.: Wesleyan University Press, 1962.

Bly, Robert. "The Dead World and the Live World." *The Sixties* 8 (1966): 2–7.

――――. *The Light Around the Body*. New York: Harper & Row, 1967.

――――, ed. *Neruda and Vallejo: Selected Poems*. Boston: Beacon, 1971.

――――. "Prose vs. Poetry." *Choice* 2 (1962):65–80.

――――. "Review of Buckdancer's Choice." *The Sixties* 9 (1967):70–79.

――――. Review of Lowell's *For the Union Dead*." *The Sixties* 8 (1966): 93–96.

――――. "A Wrong Turning in American Poetry." *Choice* 3 (1963):33–47.

Coleridge, Samuel Taylor. *Biographia Literaria*. Edited by J. Shawcross. London: Oxford University Press, 1907.

――――. "On Poesy or Art." In *Biographia Literaria*.

Creeley, Robert. "Contexts of Poetry." *Audit* 5, no. 1 (Spring 1968): 3–18.

――――. *For Love*. New York: Scribner's, 1962.

――――. "Interview." In *Paris Review*, no. 44 (1968), pp. 155–87.

――――. *The Island*. New York: Scribner's, 1963.

――――. "Interview." In *The Sullen Art*, edited by David Ossman. New York: Corinth, 1963.

――――. *Pieces*. New York: Scribner's, 1969.

――――. *A Quick Graph*. San Francisco, Calif.: Four Seasons Foundation, 1970.

――――. *Words*. New York: Scribner's, 1963.

Dorn, Ed. *Gunslinger*. Los Angeles, Calif.: Black Sparrow, 1968, 1969.

Duncan, Robert. "Beginnings." *Coyotes Journal*, nos. 5–6 (1966), pp. 8–31.

————. *Bending the Bow*. New York: New Directions, 1968.

————. *Derivations: Selected Poems 1950–56*. London: Fulcrum Press, 1968.

————. "Notes on Grossinger's *Solar Journal*: Oecological Sections." Los Angeles, Calif.: Black Sparrow Press Broadside, 1970.

————. *The Opening of the Field*. New York: Grove, 1960.

————. *Roots and Branches*. New York: New Directions, 1964.

————. *The Sweetness and Greatness of Dante's "Divine Comedy."* San Francisco, Calif.: Open Spaces Press, 1965.

————. "Towards an Open Universe." In *Poets on Poetry*, edited by Howard Nemerov. New York: Basic Books, 1966.

————. *The Truth and Life of Myth*. New York: House of Books, 1968.

————. "Two Chapters from H.D." *Tri Quarterly*, no. 12 (Spring 1968), pp. 67–99.

————. *The Years as Catches First Poems*. Berkeley, Calif.: Oyez Press, 1966.

Levertov, Denise. "An Argument." *Floating Bear* 2 (1961), [no pagination].

————. *The Jacob's Ladder*. New York: New Directions, 1961.

————. "The Origins of a Poem." *Michigan Quarterly Review* 7 (1968): 232–38.

————. *O Taste and See*. New York: New Directions, 1964.

————. "A Personal Approach." In *Parable, Myth, and Language*, edited by Tony Stoneburner. Cambridge, Mass.: Church Society for College Work, 1967.

————. *Relearning the Alphabet*. New York: New Directions, 1970.

————. *The Sorrow Dance*. New York: New Directions, 1966.

————. *To Stay Alive*. New York: New Directions, 1970.

————. *With Eyes at the Back of Our Heads*. New York: New Directions, 1959.

Lowell, Robert. "Et in America Ego." Interview with V. S. Naipaul. Reprinted in *Profile of Robert Lowell*, edited by Jerome Mazzaro. Columbus, Ohio: Charles Merrill, 1971.

————. *For the Union Dead*. New York: Farrar, Straus and Giroux, 1964.

————. "I. A. Richards as Poet." *Encounter* 14 (February 1960):77–78.

————. "Interview." *Writers at Work: The Paris Review Interviews: Second Series*. New York: Viking, 1965.

————. *Life Studies*. New York: Farrar, Straus and Giroux, 1959.

————. *Lord Weary's Castle*. New York: Meridian, 1946.

————. *Near the Ocean*. New York: Farrar, Straus and Giroux, 1967.

———. *Notebook*. 3d ed. rev. and expanded. New York: Farrar, Straus and Giroux, 1970.

———. "Prose Genius in Verse." *Kenyon Review* 15 (1953) :619–25.

———. "Robert Lowell in Conversation with A. Alvarez." *The Review* 8 (August 1963) :36–40.

———. "Skunk Hour." In *The Contemporary Poet as Artist and Critic*, edited by Anthony Ostroff. Boston: Beacon, 1964.

———. "A Talk with Robert Lowell." *Encounter* 24 (1965) :39–43.

Merwin, W. S. *The Carrier of Ladders*. New York: Atheneum, 1976.

———. *Green with Beasts*. New York: Knopf, 1956.

———. "Interview." *Road Apple Review* 1 (1969) :35–36.

———. *The Miner's Pale Children*. New York: Atheneum, 1970.

———. *The Moving Target*. New York: Atheneum, [1963].

———. "Poems by Jean Follain." *Atlantic Monthly* 226 (1970) :77–79.

———. "A Portrait of W. S. Merwin." Interview with Frank McShane. *Shenandoah* 21 (Winter 1970) :3–17.

———. "Statement." In *The Distinctive Voice*, edited by William Martz. Glencoe, Ill.: Macmillan Free Press, 1966.

O'Hara, Frank. *The Collected Poems of Frank O'Hara*. Edited by Donald Allen. New York: Knopf, 1971.

———. *Robert Motherwell*. New York: The Museum of Modern Art, 1965.

———. "Try, Try." In *Artist's Theatre in New York: Four Plays*, edited by Herbert Machiz. New York, Grove Press, 1960.

Olson, Charles. *A Bibliography on America for Ed Dorn*. San Francisco, Calif.: Four Seasons Foundation, 1964.

———. *Causal Mythology*. San Francisco, Calif.: Four Seasons Foundation, 1969.

———. *The Distances*. New York: Grove, 1961.

———. *Human Universe and Other Essays*. Edited by Donald Allen. New York: Grove, 1967.

———. *Poetry and Truth*. San Francisco, Calif.: Four Seasons Foundation, 1971.

———. *Selected Writings*. Edited by Robert Creeley. New York: New Directions, 1966.

———. *A Special View of History*. Edited by Ann Charters. Berkeley, Calif.: Oyez Press, 1970.

———. "Syllabary for a Dancer." *Maps* 4 (1970) :3–18.

Snyder, Gary. *The Back Country*. New York: New Directions, 1968.

———. "Changes." In *Notes From the New Underground*, edited by Jesse Kornbluth. New York: Viking, 1968.

————. *Earth House Hold.* New York: New Directions, 1969.

————. "Interview." *Road Apple Review* 1, no. 4 (1969):59–68.

————. *Myths and Texts.* New York: Totem Press, 1960.

————. *Regarding Wave.* New York: New Directions, 1970.

————. *Riprap.* In *Collected Poems of Gary Snyder.* Edited by Stuart Montgomery. London: Fulcrum Press, 1966.

Wilbur, Richard. *The Poems of Richard Wilbur.* New York: Harcourt, Brace and World, 1963.

Wordsworth, William. *Lyrical Ballads.* Edited by R. L. Brett and A. R. Jones. London: University Paperbacks, 1963.

————. *The Prelude: A Parallel Text.* Edited by J. C. Maxwell. Baltimore, Md.: Penguin, 1971.

Secondary Works

Abrams, M. A. *The Mirror and the Lamp.* New York: Norton, 1958.

————. *Natural Supernaturalism.* New York: Norton, 1971.

Aiken, William. "Charles Olson: A Preface." *Massachusetts Review* 12 (1971):46–68.

Altieri, Charles. "The Book of the World: Robert Duncan's Poetics of Presence." *Sun and Moon* 1 (1976):66–94.

————. "From Symbolist Thought to Immanence: The Logic of Post-Modern Poetics." *Boundary 2* 1 (1973):605–41.

————. "Gary Snyder's *Turtle Island*: The Problem of Reconciling the Roles of Prophet and Seer." *Boundary 2* 4 (1976):761–77.

————. "Objective Image and Act of Mind in Modern Poetry." *Publications of the Modern Language Association* 91 (1976):101–14.

————. "The Poem as Act: A Way to reconcile Presentational and Mimetic Theories." *Iowa Review* 6 (1975):103–24.

————. "Poetry in a Prose World: Robert Lowell's *Life Studies.*" *Modern Poetry Studies* 2 (1970):182–98.

————. "Wittgenstein on Consciousness and Language: A Challenge to Derridean Theory." *Modern Language Notes,* 91 (1976):1397–1423.

————. "Wordsworth's Preface as Literary Theory." *Criticism* 18 (1976): 122–46.

————. "Wordsworth's Wavering Balance: The Thematic Rhythm of the *Prelude.*" *The Wordsworth Circle* 4 (1973):226–40.

Anderson, Quentin. *The Imperial Self: An Essay in American Literary and Cultural History.* New York: Knopf, 1971.

Austin, J. L. *Sense and Sensibilia*. New York: Oxford University Press, 1962.

Banks, Russell. "Notes on Creeley's Pieces." *Lillabularo*, no. 8 (Winter 1970), pp. 88–91.

Barthes, Roland. "The Death of the Author." In *The Discontinuous Universe*, edited by Sallie Sears and Georgianna Lord. New York: Basic Books, 1972.

———. *Writing Degree Zero*. Translated by Annette Lavers and Colin Smith. London: Jonathan Cape, 1967.

Bate, Walter Jackson. *From Classic to Romantic*. New York: Harper, 1961.

Berry, Wendell. "A Secular Pilgrimage." *Hudson Review* 23 (1970):401–24.

Blanchot, Maurice. "La Parole Vaine." In René de Forets, *Le Bavard*. Paris: Union Generale d'Editions, 1963.

Boyers, Robert. "A Mixed Bag." *Partisan Review* 36 (1969):306–15.

———. "On Robert Lowell." In *Profile of Robert Lowell*, edited by Mazzaro.

Brown, Norman O. *Life Against Death*. Middletown, Conn.: Wesleyan University Press, 1959.

Burnshaw, Stanley. *The Seamless Web*. New York: Braziller, 1970.

Carroll, Paul. *The Poem in Its Skin*. Chicago: Follet, 1968.

Cioran, E. M. "Encounter with the Void." *Hudson Review* 23 (1970): 37–49.

Cosgrave, Patrick. *The Public Poetry of Robert Lowell*. London: Victor Gollancz, 1970.

De Man, Paul. "Intentional Structure of the Romantic Image." In *Romanticism and Consciousness*, edited by Harold Bloom. New York: Norton, 1970.

———. "The Rhetoric of Temporality." In *On Interpretation: Theory and Practice*, edited by Charles Singleton. Baltimore: Johns Hopkins University Press, 1968.

Dembo, L. S. *Conceptions of Reality in Modern American Poetry*. Berkeley, Calif.: University of California Press, 1966.

Derrida, Jacques. *De la Grammatologie*. Paris: Les Editions Minuit, 1967.

———. "La Differance." In *Tel Quel: Theorie d'Ensemble*. Paris: Edition de Seuil, 1968.

———. "Structure, Sign, Play." In *The Languages of Criticism and the Sciences of Man*, edited by Richard Macksey and Eugenio Donato. Baltimore, Md.: Johns Hopkins University Press, 1970.

Donoghue, Denis. *The Ordinary Universe: Soundings in Modern Poetry*. New York: Oxford University Press, 1968.

Dorn, Ed. *What I See in the Maximus Poems*. Ventura, Calif.: A Migrant Press Pamphlet, 1966.

Duddy, Thomas. "To Celebrate: A Reading of Denise Levertov." *Criticism* 10 (1968):138–52.

Ehrenpreis, Irvin. "The Age of Lowell." In *Robert Lowell: A Collection of Critical Essays,* edited by Thomas Parkinson. Englewood Cliffs, N. J.: Prentice-Hall, 1968.

Eliot, T. S. *T. S. Eliot: Selected Essays*. Edited by Ezra Pound. New York: Harcourt Brace, 1950.

Ellmann, Richard. "The Two Faces of Edward." In *Backgrounds to Modern Literature,* edited by John Oliver Perry. San Francisco: Chandler, 1968.

Eshelman, Clayton. "Translating Cesar Vallejo: An Evolution." In *The Triquarterly Anthology of Contemporary Latin American Literature.* New York: Dutton, 1969.

Foucault, Michel. *Les Mots et Les Choses*. Paris: Gallimard, 1968.

Frege, Gottlob. *The Foundations of Arithmetic*. Translated by J. L. Austin. Oxford: Blackwell, 1968.

Frye, Northrop. "The Critical Path: An Essay on the Social Context of Literary Criticism." *Daedalus* 99 (1970):268–342.

———. *The Stubborn Structure*. Ithaca, N.Y.: Cornell University Press, 1971.

———. *A Study of English Romanticism*. New York: Random House, 1968.

———. "Towards Defining an Age of Sensibility." In *Eighteenth Century English Literature: Modern Essays in Criticism,* edited by James Clifford. New York: Oxford University Press, 1959.

Goodman, Paul. *Speaking and Language*. New York: Random House, 1972.

Graves, Robert. *The Greek Myths*. New York: Braziller, 1957.

Hall, Donald. *Contemporary American Poetry*. Baltimore, Md.: Penguin, 1962.

Hassan, Ihab. "POSTmodernISm." *New Literary History* 3 (1971):5–31.

Heidegger, Martin. *Being and Time*. Translated by John Macquarrie and Edward Robinson. New York: Harper, 1962.

———. *Introduction to Metaphysics*. Translated by Ralph Mannheim. New York: Anchor, 1959.

———. *On the Way to Language*. Translated by Peter Hertz. New York: Harper and Row, 1970.

———. "What is Metaphysics." In *Existence and Being,* edited by Werner Brock. Chicago: Gateway, 1949.

Howard, Richard. *Alone with America: Essays on the Art of Poetry in the United States Since 1950*. New York: Atheneum, 1971.

Kelly, Robert. "Notes on the Poetry of Deep Image." *Trobar* 2 (1961): 14–15.

Kenner, Hugh. *The Pound Era*. Berkeley, Calif.: University of California Press, 1971.

Kermode, Frank. *Continuities*. New York: Random House, 1968.

———. *The Romantic Image*. New York: Vintage, 1964.

———. *The Sense of an Ending: Studies in the Theory of Fiction*. New York: Oxford University Press, 1967.

Kierkegaard, Soren. *Sickness Unto Death*. New York: Anchor, 1954.

Krieger, Murray. *The New Apologists For Poetry*. Bloomington, Ind.: University of Indiana Press, 1963.

———. *The Tragic Vision*. Chicago: University of Chicago Press, 1960.

Laing, R. D. *The Divided Self*. Baltimore, Md.: Pelican, 1965.

Lawrence, D. H. *Apocalypse*. New York: Viking, 1966.

———. *Studies in Classic American Literature*. New York: Viking, 1961.

Lefèbre, Maurice. *L'Image Fascinante et le Surréel*. Paris: Librarie Plon, 1965.

Lévi-Strauss, Claude. *The Savage Mind*. Chicago: University of Chicago Press, 1966.

Lukacs, George. *History and Class Consciousness*. Cambridge, Mass.: MIT Press, 1969.

———. *Theory of the Novel*. Translated by Anna Bostock. London: Merlin Press, 1971.

McFarland, Thomas. *Coleridge and the Pantheist Tradition*. London: Oxford University Press, 1969

MacIntyre, Alasdair. *Secularization and Moral Change*. New York: Oxford University Press, 1967.

Martin, Jay. *Robert Lowell*. Minneapolis, Minn.: University of Minnesota Press, 1970.

Matthews, William. "Thinking About Robert Bly." *Tennessee Poetry Journal* 2 (Winter 1969):48–57.

Mazzaro, Jerome. *The Poetic Themes of Robert Lowell*. Ann Arbor, Mich.: University of Michigan Press, 1965.

———, ed. *Profile of Robert Lowell*. Columbus, Ohio: Charles Merrill, 1971.

Meiners, R. K. *Everything to be Endured: An Essay on Robert Lowell and Modern Poetry*. Columbia, Mo.: University of Missouri Press, 1970.

Merleau-Ponty, Maurice. *The Phenomenology of Perception*. Translated by Colin Smith. London: Routledge and Kegan Paul, 1962.

Miles, Josephine. *The Primary Language of Poetry in the 1940's*. Berkeley, Calif.: University of California Press, 1951.

Miller, J. Hillis. *The Form of Victorian Fiction*. South Bend, Ind.: Notre

Dame University Press, 1968.

———. *Poets of Reality*. Cambridge, Mass.: Harvard University Press, 1965.

———. "The Still Heart: Poetic Form in Wordsworth." *New Literary History* 2 (1971):297–310.

Mills, Ralph. *Creation's Very Self: On the Personal Element in Recent American Poetry*. Fort Worth, Tex.: Texas Christian University Press, 1969.

Moran, Ronald, and Lensing, George. "The Emotive Imagination: A New Departure in American Poetry." *Southern Review*, n.s. 3 (1967):51–67.

Oppenheimer, Joel. "The Inner Tightrope." *Lillabulero*, no. 8 (Winter 1970), pp. 51–52.

Parkinson, Thomas. "For the Union Dead." *Salamugundi*, no. 4 (1966–67); pp. 90–95.

———. "The Poetry of Gary Snyder." *Southern Review* 4 (1968):616–32.

Paul, Sherman. "From Lookout to Ashram: The Way of Gary Snyder." *Iowa Review* 1, nos. 3 and 4 (1970):76–89, 70–85.

Perloff, Marjorie. "Realism and the Confessional Mode of Robert Lowell." *Contemporary Literature* 11 (1970):470–87.

Ransom, John Crowe. *John Crowe Ransom: Poems and Essays*. New York: Vintage, 1955.

———. "Poetry: A Note on Ontology." In *Modern Criticism: Theory and Practice*, edited by Walter Sutton and Richard Foster. New York: Odyssey, 1963.

Reed, John. "Going Back: The Ironic Progress of Lowell's Poetry." In *Profile of Robert Lowell*, edited by Mazzaro.

Rexroth, Kenneth. *The Alternate Society*. New York: Herder and Herder, 1970.

———. *Assays*. Norfolk, Conn.: New Directions, 1961.

Richard, John Pierre. *Onze Etudes Sur La Poesie Moderne*. Paris: Editions Du Seuil, 1964.

Roethke, Theodore. *The Poet and His Craft*. Edited by Ralph Mills. Seattle, Wash.: University of Washington Press, 1965.

Rosenthal, M. L. "Dynamics of Form and Motive in Some Representative Twentieth Century Lyrics." *English Literary History* 37 (1970):136–51.

———. *The New Poets*. New York: Oxford University Press, 1967.

Rothenberg, Jerome, ed. *Technicians of the Sacred*. Garden City, N.Y.: Anchor, 1969.

Schneidau, Herbert. "The Age of Interpretation and the Moment of Immediacy: Contemporary Art vs History." *English Literary History* 37 (1970):287–313.

———. *Pound: The Image and the Real.* Baton Rouge, La.: Louisiana State University Press, 1969.

Scott, Nathan. *The Wild Prayer of Longing: Poetry and the Sacred.* New Haven, Conn.: Yale University Press, 1971.

Searle, John. *Speech Acts.* Cambridge: At the University Press, 1969.

Spears, Monroe. *Dionysius and the City: Modernism in Twentieth Century Poetry.* New York: Oxford University Press, 1970.

Staples, Hugh. *Robert Lowell: The First Twenty Years.* New York: Columbia University Press, 1962.

Tate, Allen. *Essays of Four Decades.* New York: William Morrow, 1970.

Wahl, Francois. "La Philosophie Entre L'avant et L'apres du Structuralisme." In *Qu'est-ce que Le Structuralisme.* Paris: Editions de Seuil, 1968.

Wasserman, Earl. *The Subtler Language.* Baltimore, Md.: Johns Hopkins University Press, 1954.

Wasson, Richard. "Notes on a New Sensibility." *Partisan Review* 36 (1969):460–77.

Watt, Ian. *Rise of the Novel: Studies in Defoe, Richardson, Fielding.* Berkeley, Calif.: University of California Press, 1957.

Whitehead, Alfred N. *Process and Reality.* New York: The Free Press, 1969.

———. *Science and the Modern World.* New York: Macmillan Free Press, 1967.

Willey, Basil. *The Seventeenth Century Background.* New York: Anchor, [1934].

Wimsatt, W. K. *The Verbal Icon.* New York: Noonday, 1958.

Index

Abrams, M. L., 50 n. 6
Aiken, William, 125 n. 20
Ammons, A. R., 40–41
Anderson, Quentin, 241 n. 7
Arendt, Hannah, 69
Ashbery, John, 44, 52 n. 18, 117, 119, 130–31, 163–65, 166 n. 8, 169, nn. 30–31, 223 n. 16; "Leaving the Atocha Station," 165
Augustine, 56–57, 155–56, 199
Austin, J. L., 241 n. 8

Banks, Russ, 220
Barth, John, 122, 239
Barthes, Roland, 52 n. 21, 169 n. 31
Bate, W. J., 51 n. 10
Berry, Wendell, 128
Berryman, John, 65, 68, 77 n. 14
Blanchot, Maurice, 220
Bly, Robert, 18, 32, 43, 46, 52 n. 20, 78, 80, 82–93, 97, 99, 100, 109, 110, 116, 123–24 n. 5; "Counting Small Boned Bodies," 86–87; "A Home In Dark Grass," 88–89; *The Light Around the Body*, 85, 86-90; "Looking Into a Face," 88; *Silence in the Snowy Fields*, 85
Boyers, Robert, 70, 150, 167 n. 17
Brooks, Cleanth, 125 n. 14
Brown, N. O., 163, 165, 167 n. 15
Burnshaw, Stanley, 52 n. 166 n. 2

Carroll, Paul, 119–22, 163, 169 n. 32
Cioran, E. M., 213, 216, 224 n. 26
Coleridge, S. T., 17, 30–40, 46, 50 n. 5, 51 nn. 7 and 9, 77 n. 13, 83
concrete universal, 41–43, 47–48, 51 n. 13, 95
confessional poetry, 17, 53, 60–69, 82–83
Cosgrove, Patrick, 77 n. 15
Crane, Hart, 38, 173–74
Creeley, Robert, 19, 44, 46, 96, 125 n. 18,

130, 151, 170–71, 172–93, 194, 196, 206, 220–23 nn. 225, 227, 238; "The Dishonest Mailmen," 178–80; "The Flower," 176–77; *For Love*, 173–81, 185; "For W C W," 183–84; "Hart Crane," 173–74; "I Know a Man," 174–75; "The Kid," 181; The Language," 185–86; "Joy," 185; "Nine," 189; *Pieces*, 186, 222–23 nn; "The Pool," 178; "The Rhyme," 175–76; "The Sign Board," 176; "The Snow," 180; "They," 192; *Words*, 181–86; "Zero," 190–91

de Man, Paul, 50 n. 6, 75 n. 4, 124 n. 11
Dembo, L. S., 169 n
Derrida, Jacques, 26 n. 8, 123 n. 1, 124 n. 11, 126 nn. 23 and 25, 169 n. 32, 215, 224 n. 27
Dickey, James, 124 n. 7
Dickey, William, 46, 52 n. 21
Dorn, Ed, 52 n. 18, 125 n. 18
Duddy, Thomas, 240 n. 1
Duncan, Robert, 19, 38–39, 45, 48, 51 n. 17, 128–30, 150–63, 164, 165, 167–69 nn, 170, 182, 227, 238, 242 n; *Bending the Bow*, 154, 168–69 n. 26; "The Dance," 157–58; "The Law," 153; *The Opening of the Field*, 158; "Passages," 151; "Roots and Branches," 154–55

Ehrenpreis, Irvin, 76 n. 8
Eliot, T. S., 15, 16, 17, 34, 38, 43, 47, 50 n. 3, 52 n. 22, 57, 60, 74, 108, 123 n. 1, 137, 194, 196, 204
Ellmann, Richard, 51 n. 8
Emerson, R. W., 35, 240–41 nn. 5 and 7
Eshelman, Clayton, 52 n. 18

Fenollosa, Ernst, 46, 136
Follain, Jean, 196, 199–200

PS325 A37
+Enlarging the te+Altieri, Charles

0 00 02 0198027 3
MIDDLEBURY COLLEGE